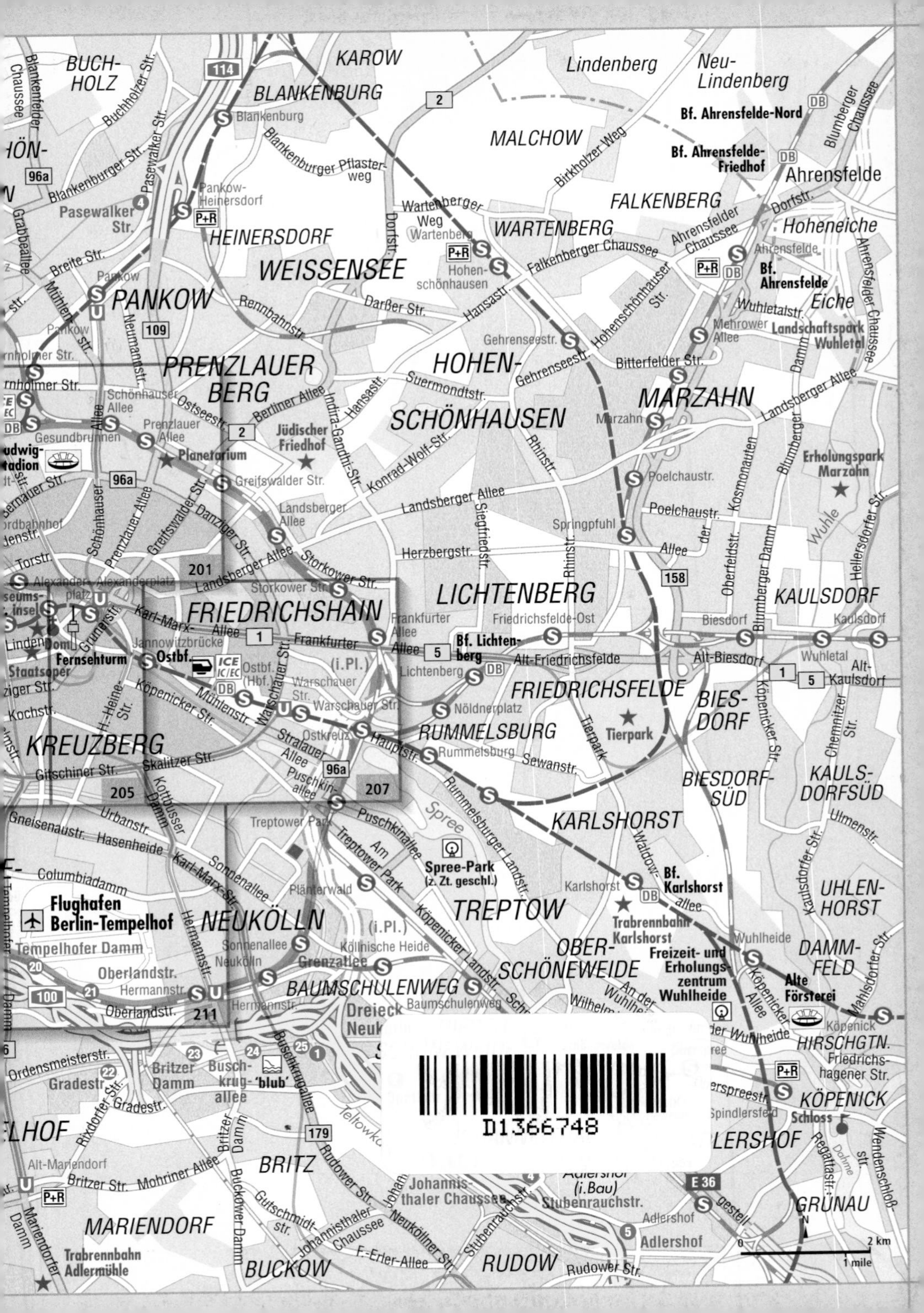
BUCHHOLZ
KAROW
BLANKENBURG
Lindenberg
Neu-Lindenberg
Bf. Ahrensfelde-Nord
MALCHOW
Bf. Ahrensfelde-Friedhof
Ahrensfelde
FALKENBERG
Hoheneiche
Pasewalker Str.
HEINERSDORF
WARTENBERG
WEISSENSEE
Bf. Ahrensfelde
Eiche
PANKOW
Landschaftspark Wuhletal
PRENZLAUER BERG
HOHENSCHÖNHAUSEN
MARZAHN
Jüdischer Friedhof
Planetarium
Erholungspark Marzahn
LICHTENBERG
KAULSDORF
FRIEDRICHSHAIN
Bf. Lichtenberg
Fernsehturm
Ostbf.
Staatsoper
FRIEDRICHSFELDE
BIESDORF
Tierpark
KREUZBERG
RUMMELSBURG
BIESDORF-SÜD
KAULSDORF-SÜD
KARLSHORST
Spree-Park (z. Zt. geschl.)
Bf. Karlshorst
UHLENHORST
Flughafen Berlin-Tempelhof
NEUKÖLLN
TREPTOW
Trabrennbahn Karlshorst
OBERSCHÖNEWEIDE
Freizeit- und Erholungszentrum Wuhlheide
DAMMFELD
BAUMSCHULENWEG
Alte Försterei
HIRSCHGTN.
KÖPENICK
Schloss
BRITZ
GRÜNAU
MARIENDORF
Adlershof
Trabrennbahn Adlermühle
BUCKOW
RUDOW
D1366748

Schloss Charlottenburg, Berlin's largest and most beautiful palace, was constructed in the Italian baroque style toward the end of the 17th century, for Princess Sophie Charlotte, who later became queen of Prussia.

Photo Guide

BERLIN

A reminder of the former close relationship between the Soviet Union and East Germany painted on one of the few remaining sections of the Wall that, until 1989, divided not just this city on the River Spree, but also the whole of the world.

ABOUT THIS BOOK

"For me, Berlin is a magical city. Magical because it's a mixture of dreams, desires, achievements, privations, joy, and despair, and because it conjures with success ... Berlin can bring reward and sorrow, Berlin sees life and death, but its atmosphere is always alive with yearning".

Hermine Körner, actor and director

Since it became the capital of a united Germany, millions of people now visit Berlin each year. Many are drawn as much by its reputation for cutting edge architecture – such as the spectacular glass dome of the Reichstag, Berlin's new landmark, or the sweeping tentlike atrium of the Sony Center in the strikingly revamped Potsdamer Platz – as by its historic buildings – such as the majestic Brandenburg Gate. Others come to experience its vibrant and cosmopolitan cultural lifestyle, to visit museums and galleries, or to stroll down Unter den Linden and enjoy the relaxed ambience of Kollwitzplatz and Kastanienallee in fashionable Prenzlauer Berg.

Since the fall of the Wall in 1989, the population of Berlin has been in a state of flux, with countless people migrating both to and from the city in an attempt to escape what at times must seem like an eternal building site. Yet today's Berlin welcomes young people from all over the world, giving them stimulation and the freedom to translate their ideas into action. History never stands still and everyone who lives in the city can play a part in its story. The words Walter Kiaulehn wrote in 1958 are just as true today: "You don't have to be born a Berliner – you can become one".

Berlin is one of a new and unique series. *Photo Guides* combine the lavishness of a coffee-table book with the practicality of a travel guide to create the perfect companion for your city visit. There are over 400 high-quality photographs and maps, together with comprehensive information about the essential highlights of the city and its festivals and lifestyle, district by district. Features about the city's history, gastronomy, and special cultural events are accompanied by a detailed timeline, guided walks with tips from the experts on shopping and eating, information on the major museums, and, of course, all the essential addresses. Each *Photo Guide* also includes a detailed city atlas to help you find your way about.

Note: To call Germany from abroad dial 00 49, followed by the local or zone code – 30 for Berlin – and then the relevant number, e.g. 00 49 30 123 45 67. When calling Berlin from within Germany, dial 030 + number, e.g. 030 123 45 67.
In the German language "ss" can also be written as "ß" – you will find examples of both in this book.

Resembling the tallest circus tent in the world, the sweeping roof over the atrium of the Sony Center, designed by architect Helmut Jahn, dominates Potsdamer Platz.

TIMELINE

THE HIGHLIGHTS

CONTENTS

This book consists of four parts. The Timeline provides detailed information about the city's history. The Highlights section uncovers Berlin's treasures, with stunning photographs, maps, ideas for places to eat, and special features. The City Explorer offers tips from the experts, district by district, on culture, sport and leisure activities, shopping, eating and drinking, accommodation, and seasonal events; it also presents the top museums and suggests guided walks. And, finally, the City Atlas will ensure you never get lost.

TIMELINE

Berlin's history is comparatively short, but eventful. The city was first documented in the 13th century. Within just 200 years, it had become the capital, and developed quickly with the rapid rise of its rulers – from Brandenburg (an independent state in north-east Germany) electors and Prussian kings, to finally German emperors. Berlin has long been a focal point for art and culture – except during the Nazi dictatorship. Germany's capital has recovered well from its 28 years divided into East and West sectors. It is now a creative and thriving metropolis, with an economy based firmly in the service sector, and serves as an important transport hub within continental Europe.

TIMELINE: THE AGES OF BERLIN

From 1415 onward, the Hohenzollern dynasty provided Brandenburg's electors – and Berlin was their capital city. The images show (from left) the rulers Frederick II (1440–70); Albrecht III Achilles (1470–86); Johann Cicero (1486–99); Joachim I Nestor (1499–1535); Joachim II Hector (1535–71); Johann Georg (1571–98); Joachim Frederick (1598–1608); and Johann Sigismund (1608–19).

1232, 1237, 1244
Spandau, Cölln, and Berlin are mentioned for the first time in documents.

1307
The twin cities of Berlin and Cölln join to form a union.

July 1320
Henry II, the last Ascanian margrave, dies.

1348
Plague destroys part of the population of Berlin and Cölln.

1359
After their 50-year union, Berlin and Cölln join the Hanseatic League.

1415
Frederick von Hohenzollern becomes Margrave of Brandenburg.

1451
Berlin-Cölln becomes the electors' capital.

1539
Elector Joachim II of Brandenburg converts to the Protestant faith.

1631, 1635
Berlin-Cölln is besieged twice by Swedish troops.

8 November 1685
Under the Edict of Potsdam, Brandenburg offers sanctuary to Huguenots persecuted in France.

9 May 1688
The Great Elector dies in Potsdam.

The first in a long line of prince-electors: the investiture of Frederick von Hohenzollern in 1415.

The medieval twin city

Today, Berlin is made up of a number of component towns and villages, most of which were founded in the 13th century. The towns of Berlin and Cölln form the historical heart that – separated only by the Spree – developed around the Nikolaiviertel (Berlin) and on the Spree island lying opposite (Cölln). Cölln was first mentioned in a document in 1237, and Berlin in 1244. Archeological finds, however, indicate that both towns had been around for significantly longer, having originally been settlements established by German traders and artisans.

The location of Berlin-Cölln was extremely convenient. It was at a crossroads of the trade routes from Leipzig to Stettin and from Magdeburg to Breslau. In addition, there was a navigable route from Berlin to Hamburg. Berlin and Cölln quickly developed into flourishing trading locations and became a hub for long-distance commerce. In the 14th century, the towns joined the Hanseatic League, but they never became as important as Cologne, Hamburg, or Antwerp.

Back in 1307, Berlin and Cölln had joined to form a union. A municipal authority, made up of 12 councillors from Berlin and six from Cölln, determined the fortunes of the city. City walls common to Berlin and Cölln probably surrounded the city from the last quarter of the 13th century, and were documented for the first time in 1319. Remains of the wall can still be seen today near Klosterstrasse.

The mid-14th century brought difficult times. As in many other parts of Europe and Asia, the plague of 1348 destroyed a significant proportion of the population. In 1376 and 1380, fires caused serious damage. In addition, there was political turbulence: after Henry II, the last Ascanian margrave (a hereditary title), died in 1320, Brandenburg was in danger of falling into chaos and anarchy. There were frequent changes of ruler and the Brandenburg Marches were bitterly disputed. Only after 1415, when the office of margrave was bestowed on the Nürnberg burgrave Frederick von Hohenzollern, did conditions

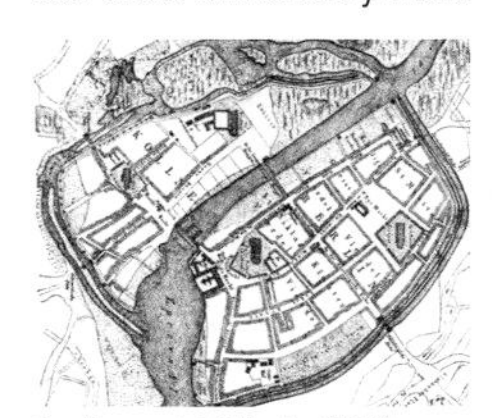

Berlin and Cölln in 1250.

The nucleus of Brandenburg power

gradually become more stable. The Hohenzollerns ruled in Brandenburg for 500 years.

Berlin, the electoral residence

Under its new rulers, Berlin lost a great deal of its municipal independence. In 1432, the elector (a member of the Holy Roman Empire's electoral college, responsible for electing the Holy Roman Emperor) separated the joint city administration of Berlin and Cölln, and decreed that in future both cities would form their own councils, whose members had to be approved by the ruler. In 1442, the city of Cölln had to provide land for the building of a castle for the elector. Construction was finished in 1451 – and Berlin-Cölln became the electoral capital. The citizens resented the castle, built on the Werder island in the Spree, as its purpose was less to ward off future attacks from foreign enemies and more to protect against possible uprisings in the city itself. Accordingly, the people called the castle "the Cölln oppressor".
Berlin and Cölln survived the Reformation in the first half of the 16th century without bloodshed. Many citizens were drawn to the new faith. The elector Joachim II converted to Protestantism in 1539. His period of rule, lasting over three decades from 1535 until 1571, was characterized by intensive building work. In addition to the electoral castle, a series of prestigious country houses were built in Köpenick to the east of Berlin, and in Potsdam further to the west; the Jagdschloss Grunewald (hunting lodge) was constructed in around 1540.
The Marches of Brandenburg did not have a powerful army of their own, and during the Thirty Years War (1618–48) foreign troops continually moved through the country, leaving a trail of devastation. Berlin and Cölln escaped final military conquest, but were besieged several times by Swedish troops, who demanded high levels of protection money. Plague epidemics struck the city five times. The population is thought to have shrunk from about 12,000 to 6,000 people, and the economic backbone of trade and industry was almost destroyed.
The reconstruction of the city after the war under the young and successful commander Frederick William – known as the Great Elector – gave Berlin-Cölln a huge economic boost. The elector enlisted numerous settlers, mainly from Holland. Under the Edict of Potsdam (1685) he guaranteed religious freedom, and about 5,000 persecuted Huguenots arrived in Berlin from France. They settled mainly in Dorotheenstadt, one of three baroque suburbs – along with Friedrichstadt and Friedrichswerder – which were built during the reign of the Great Elector, which lasted almost 50 years, from 1640 until his death in 1688. When he died, the number of inhabitants had risen to 18,000 – three times as many as at the start of his reign.

The Great Elector brought Huguenots to Berlin – hardworking new citizens, who helped Brandenburg and Berlin to progress.

From left: Frederick I became the first "King in Prussia" in 1701; his son, Frederick William I, the "Soldier King", built up a powerful army without ever deploying it himself; his son and heir, Frederick II, was the legendary "Frederick the Great" or "Alte Fritz". He introduced influential and progressive reforms in Prussia, but also a militaristic attitude, which became proverbial.

18 January 1701
Elector Frederick III crowns himself King Frederick I of Prussia.

17 January 1709
Berlin, Cölln, and three suburbs unite to become the capital city and royal seat of Berlin.

25 February 1713
Frederick William I, the Soldier King, takes the throne and starts to build up an army.

31 May 1740
Frederick II becomes king.

from 1740
Berlin gains a prestigious heart in the "Forum Fridericianum".

December 1740
Frederick II and his troops invade Silesia.

1744–45
In the Second Silesian War, Frederick's army defeats the Austrians.

1747–53
Frederick II surrounds himself with leading European intellectuals and introduces Enlightenment ideas to Prussia.

1756–63
The Seven Years' War leads to an economic crisis. Berlin is occupied at different times by Austrians and Russians.

17 August 1786
Frederick II dies, leaving Prussia as one of the great European powers. Frederick William II succeeds him.

From the parade ground to the court

The expansion of Berlin was pushed forward under the son and successor of the Great Elector. The city had become a royal seat in 1701, after Frederick had obtained the right from the Holy Roman Emperor Leopold I to exchange his electoral position as "King in Prussia" for a royal crown. Frederick I wanted Berlin's architecture to strengthen its newly formulated claim to be a capital city of European rank – such as Paris or London. The first magnificent baroque buildings were constructed along the avenue named Unter den Linden, including the Zeughaus, completed in 1706. Before his coronation, Frederick had his own city castle converted by the architect and sculptor Andreas Schlüter to conform to the tastes of the time. For his wife, Sophie Charlotte, the king had Schloss Lietzenburg built close to the village of Lietzow to the west of the city; the castle and the surrounding village were renamed Charlottenburg on the death of the queen in 1705.

In 1709, the adjacent towns of Berlin, Cölln, Friedrichswerder, Dorotheenstadt, and Friedrichstadt were united to form one city, the capital city and royal seat of Berlin. At this time, the number of inhabitants had risen to 55,000 – and continued to grow: according to the first census in 1719, 64,000 people lived in Berlin. One in every five people was a member of the Huguenot community, which had migrated to Berlin from France after 1685.

On the "Soldier King" Frederick William I's accession in 1713, public life in Berlin gained a militaristic character. The new ruler was less interested in prestigious buildings and much more in expanding the Prussian army. Parade grounds were constructed in many locations in the city, such as in the current Pariser Platz. Primarily because of the need for uniforms for the growing army, Berlin became a city with an important textile industry. The "Royal Warehouse" in Klosterstrasse alone employed 4,000 workers and at that time was the largest cloth manufacturer in Europe. Silk manufacturing also made a considerable contribution to the economic upswing of the city.

Although uniforms were still regularly seen on the streets of the city, the intellectual climate changed suddenly on the death of the Soldier King in 1740. The new king, Frederick II, wanted to make Berlin the heart of the Enlightenment in Europe. Science and culture flourished and a group of academics, musicians, and intellectuals gathered around the Jewish philosopher Moses Mendelssohn and the publisher Friedrich Nicolai, who eagerly discussed a range of philosophic, scientific, and political questions in the many new clubs and societies.

Immediately on succession to the throne, Frederick set about founding a new, prestigious heart to the city around the square called the Forum Fridericianum (now Bebelplatz) and the street that would later become the magnificent Unter den Linden. This included the Opera House, completed in 1743, the church of St Hedwig, the Royal Library, and the Prinz Heinrich palace, today home to the Humboldt University.

When Frederick II died in 1786, Berlin, with around 150,000 inhabitants, was one of the largest cities in Europe. The Prussian capital was, however, still some way

The Soldier King formed a regiment of very tall guards: they were nicknamed the "*Lange Kerls*", or "long guys".

from becoming a metropolis. Away from the showpiece streets that lay at the heart of the city, there was little for visitors to Berlin to admire. A few contemporary reports speak of dirty, dark, unpaved streets, a shortage of homes, and fast-growing levels of prostitution. Large sections of the lower classes, who had settled mainly in the northern and eastern suburbs of the city, lived in harsh poverty. During difficult years such as 1761, at the height of the Seven Years' War, one-third of the population of Berlin relied on the distribution of charity and food donations from the city.

Frederick II as army commander

Today, Frederick II, called "the Great", is primarily viewed as a philosopher of the Enlightenment, a modernizer, and a promoter of art and science. In his attempts to procure a place for Prussia among the great European powers, however, he also waged three wars of aggression – which would today be considered controversial under international law.

In December 1740, six months after ascending the throne, the monarch and his army attacked Silesia, which then belonged to Austria. The First Silesian War lasted until summer 1742 and ended in Prussia conquering this region. Frederick also won the Second Silesian War against Austria (1744–45).

Frederick the Great leading his troops.

In the so-called Seven Years' War (1756–63) against a coalition of Russia, Austria, France, Sweden, and Saxony, and in spite of an alliance with Great Britain, Prussia was several times on the brink of defeat. The royal seat of Berlin was directly affected by the war: in 1757 and 1760, enemy troops occupied the city and did not withdraw until a large amount of money had been paid.

The history of the 19th century has drawn an idealized image of Frederick II as an ingenious commander, and for many years the idea of invincibility through discipline and iron will was eagerly incorporated in the German consciousness. This myth has essentially continued. What is certain is that Frederick II – unlike other leaders of his time – took part in all of his wars. He personally led his troops into the field. Apparently, he had little concern for his own life and flung himself into the tumult of battle, sometimes to the displeasure of his generals. On a number of occasions, Frederick II's horse was killed under him, and he narrowly escaped being shot by the enemy.

Many tributes have been paid to Frederick, including naming the World War I battleship SMS *Friedrich der Grosse* after him, and an equestrian statue of the Prussian king has pride of place on Unter den Linden.

Alte Fritz – shown here with the Order of the Black Eagle – shaped his country as no other leader had done.

In the early 19th century, Berlin was characterized by men of letters, philosophers, and researchers (from left): August Wilhelm von Schlegel (1767–1845); Friedrich von Schlegel (1772–1829); Wilhelm von Humboldt (1767–1835); Clemens Brentano (1778–1842); Heinrich von Kleist (1777–1811); Adelbert von Chamisso (1781–1838); Alexander von Humboldt (1769–1859); and Jacob and Wilhelm Grimm (1785–1863).

1791
Carl Gotthard Langhans completes the Brandenburg Gate.

16 November 1797
Frederick William II dies; his son succeeds him as Frederick William III.

14 October 1806
At Jena and Auerstedt, Prussia is defeated by the armies of Napoleon I. The French occupy Berlin – and again in 1808.

19 October 1807
Prussia abolishes the feudal status of serfdom.

April 1809
Free and secret voting for a city parliament in Berlin for the first time.

19 July 1810
Queen Louise of Prussia dies, aged 34.

1813
After the French occupation of Berlin in 1812, they are defeated at Leipzig.

1818
Karl Friedrich Schinkel builds the Neue Wache.

14 July 1819
During the Restoration, the father of gymnastics Friedrich Ludwig Jahn is arrested.

1825–41
Berlin triples in size by incorporating the surrounding communities.

1838
The railway age in Berlin begins with the opening of the line to Potsdam.

Unter den Linden in 1830: the large-scale road layout of an ambitious capital city.

New ideas, action, and reaction

Unlike Frederick the Great, his successor Frederick William II had less interest in and respect for the ideas of the Enlightenment, and he increased censorship. Yet Berlin in around 1800 had developed into a hub of intellectual life: poets and thinkers such as Friedrich von Schlegel, Wilhelm and Alexander von Humboldt, Johann Gottlieb Fichte, and Ludwig Tieck met – sometimes in the upper-class Jewish salons of Henriette Hertz or Rahel Varnhagen – and debated about philosophy, art, and literature. Most of these intellectuals were strongly influenced by the fashion for Romanticism, with its tendency toward inspired, effusive, unpolitical thought.

After the destructive military defeat of Prussia at Jena and Auerstedt, Napoleon's troops marched into Berlin toward the end of 1806. The two-year occupation by the French seriously burdened the people of Berlin, as the city, now home to 170,000 inhabitants, had to bear all the costs for the enemy army stationed there. It was particularly humiliating for the inhabitants when Napoleon removed the four-horsed chariot from the Brandenburg Gate, completed in 1791, and had it transported back to France.

After the French withdrawal, the Prussian court returned from Königsberg in 1809, where it had fled after defeat by the French. Extensive reforms were set in place to adapt the Prussian state to modern requirements. The measures linked to the names of Stein and Hardenberg – the far-sighted initiators of the movement – would fundamentally change the country. Serfdom had been abolished in 1807, and there were military and administrative reforms and changes to education, leading to the foundation of the University of Berlin in 1809. In the same year, the people of Berlin elected an assembly of city councillors for the first time.

In 1812, the French army marched into Berlin again, but it was finally beaten in the wars of liberation between 1813 and 1815. Subsequently, the short phase of civil reforms in Prussia came to an end, and the power of the nobles and king was restored. In 1819, a wave of arrests in Berlin affected everyone who was liberally or democratically minded. This meant the end of liberal intellectual culture in Berlin for decades.

Less politically ambitious: King Frederick William II.

A regent in restless times: King Frederick William III.

BERLIN 1786–1838

Reform, action, and reaction

The master builder of classical Berlin

The architect, painter, and set designer Karl Friedrich Schinkel left his mark on the cityscape of Berlin in the 19th century like no other. He completed more than 50 building projects in the Prussian capital alone, including Schloss Tegel, the Friedrichswerder Church, and the Bauakademie (Academy of Architecture), which was badly damaged by bombs in 1945 and demolished in 1962.

Karl Friedrich Schinkel was born on 13 March 1781 in the small Brandenburg town of Neuruppin, the son of a priest. After the early death of his father, the family moved to Berlin in 1794, where Schinkel attended the Gymnasium school. The multitalented student showed promise as an artist but later decided to embark on a career as an architect.

Schinkel's architectural ideals were formed by the buildings of classical antiquity, which he saw on a study visit to Italy between 1803 and 1805. He became the most important protagonist of the specifically Prussian expression of the classical style that was popular at that time. At first, he earned his living as a painter and set designer, but in 1810 he became a building assessor, thanks to a recommendation from Wilhelm von Humboldt, and five years later he was appointed chief building officer.

Schinkel was responsible for converting the unprepossessing Berlin into a prestigious capital to match the city's ambitions. His first large-scale building in the capital was the Neue Wache (New Guard House), completed in 1818 in Unter den Linden, which alone would justify Schinkel's fame. The Schauspielhaus in the Gendarmenmarkt, the Schlossbrücke, and the Altes Museum (Old Museum) followed a few years later.

In 1830, Schinkel became director of building and five years later the state director of building – an office that he only held for a few years. A stroke in September 1840 left Prussia's great master builder paralyzed down one side. Karl Friedrich Schinkel died in Berlin on 9 October 1841 aged 60.

The Neue Wache (New Guard House), Altes Museum (Old Museum), and the Schauspielhaus (Berlin Theater) (from top to bottom): Karl Friedrich Schinkel's ideas were based on classical forms.

Artist and architect Schinkel shaped Berlin.

The railway, symbol of industrialization. From left: The Borsig locomotive led the way in Germany in 1841; it was followed three years later by the "Beuth" model. This was an age of dynamism – politically, socially, and economically. The great locomotive of 1875 was a major advance in the development of the railways – and Berlin experienced a similar advance when it became the capital city of the German empire in 1871.

1839
Horse-drawn taxis are used in Berlin for the first time.

1840
Frederick William IV becomes king of Prussia.

1847
The telegraph construction company Siemens and Halske is founded in Berlin – the nucleus of a future global concern.

18 March 1848
Revolution in Berlin. In 1849, Prussian king Frederick William IV refuses to become emperor of a German empire with a parliamentary constitution.

1850
First elections to the assembly of city councillors under the new three-class electoral system.

1861
William I becomes king of Prussia. The city area of Berlin is enlarged by about 70 percent through the incorporation of surrounding towns.

1862
A development plan determines the road layout in areas of new building. Otto von Bismarck becomes Prussian prime minister.

18 January 1871
King William I of Prussia is proclaimed German emperor; Bismarck is nominated imperial chancellor of the new German empire. Berlin is the new capital of the empire.

The Revolution of March 1848

In 1848, the whole of Europe was in ferment. Groups of civilians in many towns and cities made a wide variety of political demands, based on new ideas of nation, constitution, and civil liberty.
On 18 March 1848, unrest reached the Prussian capital. During a large demonstration in which many citizens gathered to press their demands, the military opened fire on the crowds. The situation escalated, barricades were erected, and the people armed themselves. After a bloody battle, with almost 300 casualties, King Frederick William IV gave way, withdrew the troops from Berlin, and agreed to a constituent assembly for Prussia, among other things. A civil liberal government was formed, but the democratic impulse was already dwindling and there was no real change in power.
When riots between demonstrators and the militia occurred in the autumn, the king sent troops into the city to restore order. By the end of 1848, Bismarck and the Prussian aristocrats had regained power once more in Berlin and the spirit of revolution was finally over.

From top: 1848 – street fights and barricades; Frederick William IV appears before the citizens; the Prussian king in 1849 with delegates of the Frankfurt National Assembly, offering him the imperial crown.

A steam-powered city

By the start of the 19th century, apart from being the Prussian capital, Berlin was also a military and manufacturing city with almost 170,000 inhabitants. Technical innovations from England in the 18th century – including the development

A romantic on the throne: Frederick William IV.

of steam engines and spinning machines, as well as the railway – had roused Berlin from its torpor. A major impetus came from the changed economic and political conditions in Germany. There was freedom of trade from 1810, and customs barriers were removed in 1834 – creating a very large single market. Against this background, Berlin began its transformation into an industrial city in the mid-1830s. The construction of the first railway routes in the 1840s revolutionized traffic and transport. Berlin, with its long commercial tradition and function as a

BERLIN 1838–1871
The advance of an industrial city

capital city, became a very attractive location. Ever-larger influxes of people from the surrounding countryside and abroad moved to the city in search of work. Berlin was also successful in its policy of industrial espionage, whose promoters included Johann Friedrich Dannenberger, the owner of a calico printing works. In 5,000 workers. Industrial pioneers such as Borsig and Siemens set the course for a dynamic future. Both the companies they founded are still trading today – Borsig as part of an engineering group and Siemens is a household name across Europe.

The boom and industrial growth had a great effect on the city structure, both spa- ings accessible only through the courtyard. Investors had a pretty free hand. Following the order issued by the building control department in 1853, developers simply had to make sure that the inner courtyards were 5.34 x 5.34 m (17.5 x 17.5 feet), in order to facilitate the use of fire hoses and a jumping sheet in case of fire. The living conditions

Industrialization changed the cityscape: Borsig's mechanical engineering works (1847).

Adolph von Menzel's *Eisenwalzwerk* (*Iron Rolling Mill*, 1875) simultaneously shows the hardships of working life, and fascinating technology.

Industrialists: August Borsig and Werner von Siemens.

addition to textiles, mechanical engineering and metalworking developed into leading industries by the 1870s. At the start of the century, there had only been one engineering works in the city. In the following 60 years, this number grew to 67, employing more than

tially and socially. By the middle of the century, the population had more than doubled to almost 400,000, and by the time of the foundation of the empire in 1871 had again grown by more than 370,000 people. This brought an increasing demand for accommodation, of which there was a great shortage.

The Wilhelminische tenement belt grew up around the old heart of the city by the former 18th-century customs wall. This enclosed development was dominated by four- to six-floor apartment blocks with wings and rear build-

in these small, gloomy, two- to three-roomed apartments were poor, and high levels of occupation made life almost unendurable. The death rate in these working-class areas in 1869 was twice as high as in middle-class areas. The population also grew rapidly in the suburbs: Charlottenburg and Spandau in 1871 were home to 19,587 and 20,451 people respectively; what would later become Neukölln had 8,125 inhabitants, and Köpenick had 5,265. Even semi-rural areas such as Pankow and Lichtenberg soon had more than 3,000 inhabitants.

Zille, the artist

No artist recorded the social conditions in Berlin's working-class areas as strikingly as Heinrich Zille (1858–1929). The narrow rear courtyards of the rented apartments and the streets around them were his subjects, known as "Zille sein Milljöh" (Zille's milieu). He observed the everyday life

A rear courtyard as seen by the camera – and by Zille.

of the workers and petty bourgeois of the city, and put his discoveries on paper with wit and irony. Zille's work reflected his criticisms of the social conditions that prevailed during the industrialization of Berlin.

On 18 January 1871, Prussian king William I (second right) was proclaimed German emperor in Versailles – but in reality only one person was calling the political shots in the new empire: Chancellor Otto von Bismarck (first right, in white uniform). Emperor Frederick III (third right) ruled for just 99 days in 1888; his son and successor William II (far right) dismissed Bismarck and made his mark in the Wilhelminische period.

18 January 1871
After the end of the Franco-Prussian War, King William I of Prussia becomes the German emperor, and Bismarck the imperial chancellor.

1877
The population of Berlin exceeds one million.

14 June 1888
After the short-lived reign of Frederick III (just 99 days), Emperor William II ascends the throne.

20 March 1890
Bismarck dismissed.

15 February 1902
Berlin's underground railway opens.

1905
Berlin has over two million inhabitants.

1907
The vast Kaufhaus des Westens (KaDeWe) department store opens its doors.

1913
In Berlin, work starts on the AVUS, the world's first motorway.

August 1914
News of the outbreak of World War I is greeted with great enthusiasm.

from 1917
Strikes and mass demonstrations in Berlin against hunger and war.

9 November 1918
William II abdicates as emperor. Germany's cities are caught up in strikes and revolution.

Berlin, the imperial capital

By 1871, everything was beginning to change: Prussia was the most important country in the new German empire, its king was the emperor of all the Germans – and the most powerful man in the country was previously the most powerful Prussian, now the imperial chancellor, Prince Otto von Bismarck. The capital of the new state was, naturally, Berlin, the largest city on German soil – whose dynamic development accelerated even faster as the capital of such a powerful and ambitious state.
Berlin's population positively exploded: in 1877 it reached the million mark, and less than 30 years later there were two million inhabitants in the metropolis. There was a correspondingly huge shortage of housing, and soon there was no more room to expand within the city area. Growth then focused on the surrounding areas. The current district of Schöneberg, for example, which had just 4,500 inhabitants in 1871, grew by 1910 into a town of at least 200,000 people. The population of the "boom town" of Charlottenburg rose in the same period from 200,000 to over 300,000. A second heart to the city grew up here – next to the old central city around Friedrichsstrasse – around

The emperor and his chancellor: William I receives Prince Otto von Bismarck in the historic corner room of the royal palace.

BERLIN 1871–1918
A glittering imperial stage

From top: A boom time. A tranquil scene: Unter den Linden in 1905 with the equestrian statue of Frederick the Great; life was clearly more dynamic ten years later at the Friedrichstrasse station; built between 1884 and 1894, the imposing building of the Reichstag resembles a castle (image from 1898); a Wilhelminische building in a grandiose setting: Berlin Cathedral in 1905.

the Kurfürstendamm, with chic shopping arcades and large department stores. Best-known was the Kaufhaus des Westens (KaDeWe) (department store of the West) on Wittenbergplatz, which opened in 1907, and 100 years later is still the largest temple to shopping of its kind in the whole of Europe.

By 1890, Berlin had a central water supply. The expansion of the sewerage system improved sanitation in the city. Public transport, too, took shape. In 1902, the first Berlin underground railway began operation – as an elevated railway on the stretch of the current U1 and U2 underground lines, it connected the Warschauer Brücke with the zoo. Finally, the world's first freeway was built in Berlin between 1913 and 1921: the AVUS (Automobil-Verkehrs- und Übungs-Strasse) (automobile traffic and practice road).

The new age also saw the introduction of a new style of architecture: instead of the classicism of the Schinkel era, there was historicism and, around the turn of the century, "Wilhelminische baroque", as embodied in Berlin Cathedral. This grandiose style is so called because of its links with the aesthetic tastes of Emperor William II (1888–1918). This brash monarch also made his mark politically. With his aggressive power politics, he seized a position of supremacy for the German empire in Europe and – although he was not solely responsible – led it just a few years later into the devastation of World War I.

World War I

In August 1914, the population of Berlin, like that of other German cities, was gripped by a tremendous fervour for the war. Even people living in the poor tenement housing hung out patriotic flags every time a victory was reported. As the war progressed, and food and

Top: Parade in 1914.
Above: Return in 1918.

other essential supplies were stretched beyond their limits, the population's enthusiasm for the war increasingly declined and finally turned to opposition: from 1917 onward, there were mass anti-war demonstrations and strikes that, following the defeat of the German empire, led to the November Revolution of 1918.

In the 1920s, Berlin's flourishing cultural scene was world renowned. From left: Bertolt Brecht (1898–1956) revolutionized drama with plays criticizing society; Alfred Döblin (1878–1957) wrote what is still the most important novel about Berlin, *Berlin Alexanderplatz*; the novelist Heinrich Mann (1871–1950) wrote scathing attacks on German society; and Kurt Tucholsky (1890–1935) was a witty critic of the times.

9 November 1918
Emperor William II abdicates. Both the SPD and radical left-wing socialists call for a republic.

December 1918
Councils of workers and soldiers decide on votes for the National Assembly.

1919
January: Murders of the left-wing socialists Rosa Luxemburg and Karl Liebknecht. March: 1,200 people are killed in the suppression of a general.

1920
March: The Kapp Putsch, an attempted right-wing coup, is averted by the general strike. October: Through incorporations, Greater Berlin's population reaches 4 million.

1923
Hyperinflation: Unemployment for 235,000 Berliners. October: German radio starts with Radiostunde AG, Berlin.

1924
October: Berlin's first airport is opened at Tempelhof. December: First radio and television exhibition.

1926
September: Berlin's radio tower goes into operation. November: Goebbels becomes NSDAP Gauleiter of Berlin-Brandenburg.

20 July 1932
Imperial Chancellor von Papen dismisses Prussia's SPD-led government – one step forward in Hitler's march to power.

Revolution, uprisings, strikes ...

A crisis in domestic politics culminated in Germany in the November Revolution of 1918. After Imperial Chancellor Max von Baden announced the abdication of the emperor, both the social democrat Philipp Scheidemann and the communist Karl Liebknecht called for a republic in Berlin on 9 November. There followed intense, initially verbal, debates on the future structure of the republic, which peaked in January and March 1919 in uprisings by the Spartacus league. These were both violently suppressed.

Scenes from 1919 (from top): machine gun emplacement; soldiers on the Brandenburg Gate; battle in Bülowplatz.

Golden times for art and cabaret

As the political situation in Germany stabilized after 1923, the economy also gradually recovered from the consequences of World War I. With a slowly improving standard of living and influenced by the rapid development of the mass media of radio and film, people felt freed from the traumas of the previous ten years. Berlin developed into a city of the avant-garde, where there was lively interest in the new art of expressionism, and the worlds of film and drama, cabaret and revues. After the construction of the large Capitol and Ufa-Palast cinemas, the Kurfürstendamm became a meeting point for young film fans. In the new ballrooms that sprang up like mushrooms, people danced to the hot sounds of jazz and the Charleston. International performers celebrated triumphs in Berlin: Duke Ellington spent 1924 in the city with his "Chocolate Kiddies", and Josephine Baker caused a furore in 1927 with her minimal costumes. As theater censorship ended

Hats off to film: Hans Albers, Emil Jannings, and Gustaf Gründgens were early heroes of a new medium.

Seductive: Tilla Durieux. Glamorous Ufa divas: Marlene Dietrich and Greta Garbo went on to conquer Hollywood.

after World War I, cabaret blossomed on numerous small stages. Revues and vaudeville provided contemporary entertainment to the apparently tireless audience – and in the Berlin Wintergarten, the public enthused over the witty and cryptic couplets of Claire Waldoff and Otto Reutter. The new openness and the air of *savoir-vivre* in the city became famous and attracted artists from all over the world. The avant-garde drew large audiences. Art exhibitions showed works by expressionists and surrealists. Politics penetrated culture, as was reflected in works by Carl Zuckmayer and Bertolt Brecht, among others. Plays such as *Der Hauptmann von Köpenick* (*The Captain of Kopenick*) and *The Threepenny Opera* started out from Berlin on their march to fame.

These cultural golden times came to a sudden end when the New York stock exchange crashed on 25 October 1929. After Black Friday, the global economy was in serious trouble. Mass unemployment and the impoverishment of ordinary people had serious consequences for a glittering metropolis such as Berlin. The city's intoxicating, fashionable, tolerant ways contrasted with the conservative or even reactionary attitudes all around, and impoverished people were increasingly open to simple solutions to their problems from both the political Left and Right. When the National Socialists took control of the country in 1933 it was the end – for the time being – of multicultural life in the city of Berlin.

Berlin, movie metropolis

The origins of Berlin as a film city can be traced back to 1911, when the first large film studio in the world opened in nearby Babelsberg. In 1917, the Universum-Film AG (Ufa)

Films such as *The Blue Angel* and *Metropolis* became world famous.

studio was founded – an institution that quickly became a synonym for German film. In the postwar years period films such as *Fridericus Rex* (1922) were popular. However, expressionist films such as *Das Cabinet des Dr Caligari* (*The Cabinet of Dr Caligari*) (1920), *Dr Mabuse* and *Nosferatu* (both 1922) gained worldwide fame. One of the best-known Babelsberg films is Fritz Lang's *Metropolis* (1926), which was placed on the Memory of the World International Register by UNESCO in 2001. Lang, one of the most influential silent film directors, emigrated to the USA, like many other Ufa stars, in 1933.

Because of (West) Berlin's unusual situation, its ruling mayor was often in the public eye (from left): Ernst Reuter (1948–53) was a legend in the menacing postwar period; Willy Brandt (1957–66) showed courage during the early days of the Wall; Heinrich Albertz (1966–7) stepped down during the period of student unrest; under Richard von Weizsäcker (1981–4), the divided city was able to breathe easily.

1945
Berlin, under Allied control, is divided into four sectors.

1946
October: The first (and last) free elections for councillors for the whole of Berlin. In winter, hundreds die of hunger in the city.

June 1948
Blockade of the Western sectors by the Soviets. The Western Allies supply the city by airlift.

27 November 1958
The Berlin Ultimatum: The Soviet Union threatens to have access routes to West Berlin controlled by the DDR.

August 1961
The Wall crisis: Mayor Brandt asks the USA for help, which US Vice President Johnson sends.

26 June 1963
US President Kennedy coins the phrase: "Ich bin ein Berliner".

1963–66
Relatives can visit East Berlin with a pass.

11 April 1968
Student leader Rudi Dutschke is shot in an assassination attempt.

3 September 1971
A four-power agreement controls free access to West Berlin from the Federal area.

9 November 1989
Thousands celebrate the fall of the Wall.

Rescue from the sky

On 23 June 1948, the Western military governors of Berlin announced the introduction of the Deutschmark in the Western sectors of the city. One day later, the Soviet military administration blocked all connecting routes to West Berlin. The Western Allies responded with an airlift: 380 aircraft – known as *Rosinenbomber* ("raisin bombers") by the Berliners – made a series of continuous flights, supplying the divided city with food, medicines, and other items. There was a flight every 90 seconds during the blockade, which lasted almost one year, and almost 1.8 million tonnes (2 million US tons) of material was transported in over 200,000 flights. To relieve Tempelhof, in 1948 a second airport was built within 62 days. Since the days of the airlift, West Berlin has felt a close attachment to the free West.

A low-flying *Rosinenbomber*: during the blockade Berliners were kept alive by supplies dropped by air freight.

Frontier town and showcase

At the end of the war in 1945, Berlin was a field of rubble. In the years that followed, supplies remained extremely scarce, particularly as thousands of refugees from the former Eastern areas flooded into the city each month.
For administrative purposes, Berlin was divided into four sectors and placed under quadripartite power. However, the increasing differences between the three Western Allies and the Soviet Union soon led to increasing divisions in the city. In the eyes of many, West Berlin became a symbol of the free world, worth protecting from the Soviet Union. The dramatic speech by West Berlin's mayor Ernst Reuter on 9 September – "People of the world, look at this city!" – during the blockade appealed for international support for the encircled city.
As so many companies had deserted the city, West Berlin was unable to support itself economically and had to be aided by massive subsidies for decades. Companies received tax breaks; workers got a Berlin bonus. A new central area developed around the Kurfürstendamm, along with the Kulturforum near the Wall, home to the Philharmonie, the Neuer Nationalgalerie, and Staatsbibliothek (State Library).
In the late 1960s, West Berlin started to recruit numbers of *Gastarbeitern* (guest workers), primarily from Turkey, who made their mark on the areas of Kreuzberg, Neukölln, and Wedding. West Berlin was always attractive to artists, conscientious objectors, and, last but not least, students. This is where the social and political protest movement of the 1960s started, and later the squatter scene, when, enraged by the number of buildings being left vacant in a time of severe housing crisis, young squatters moved in. Under these various influences, Berlin is still a focus for alternative lifestyles.

Modern architecture (clockwise from top right): Gedächtniskirche; ICC Kongresszentrum; Kongresshalle; Philharmonie.

BERLIN 1945–1990

The West: an island in a turbulent sea

Willy Brandt

One of the most important political figures in Berlin's postwar world, along with Ernst Reuter and Richard von Weizsäcker, was Chancellor Willy Brandt, the former leader of the SPD (Social Democratic Party). He was the mayor of Berlin (West) between 1957 and 1966.
He was born Herbert Frahm, in Lübeck on 18 December 1913, the illegitimate son of a sales assistant, Martha Frahm. Brandt was a talented boy and attended the Gymnasium school; as a teenager he was involved in the "Socialist Youth". After the National Socialists came to power he emigrated to Norway, where he worked as a journalist and took the name under which he later became famous: Willy Brandt.
At the end of the war, Brandt went to Berlin in 1945 as a correspondent for a number of Scandinavian newspapers. In 1949, he became a member of the German parliament for the SPD, and the next year, in 1950, he became a member of the Berlin House of Representatives.
He was elected mayor of Berlin as a successor to Otto Suhrs in 1957. His determined and intransigent attitude in conflicts with the Soviet Union and the DDR, particularly during the construction of the Wall in 1961, made Willy Brandt enormously popular with the people of Berlin.
Leader of the SPD since 1964, Brandt moved to Bonn in 1966 to become foreign minister, and in 1969 he entered office as chancellor of the Federal Republic of Germany. A new Ostpolitik was introduced during his era, which aimed at a reduction in tension towards the Eastern bloc states of the Soviet Union, Poland, and Czechoslovakia, as well as between the two German states. Brandt was widely criticized for this policy, which earned him the Nobel Peace Prize in 1971. When one of his closest colleagues was exposed as a spy for the DDR in 1974, Brandt resigned as chancellor. Willy Brandt could never accept the division of Germany. Immediately after the fall of the Berlin Wall in 1989, he said "now what belongs together, grows together". Willy Brandt only survived reunification by a few years. He died on 8 October 1992 in Bonn.

A memorial to a died-in-the-wool politician: made of solid bronze and 3.40 m (11 feet) high, Willy Brandt stands in Willy-Brandt-Haus, the SPD's headquarters, opened in 1996.

Popular acclaim: Brandt and John F. Kennedy in West Berlin.

As the capital, the Eastern section of Berlin was comparatively privileged: the interests of the state took a central position. From left: The Politburo of the Central Committee of the SED, was the seat of power of the DDR. Its leadership projected a rigid and authoritarian image, particularly Walter Ulbricht (1893–1973) as party leader and later head of state. His successor Erich Honecker (1912–1994) had to concede power in 1989.

7 October 1949
East Berlin becomes the capital of the DDR: the division of Germany is complete.

17 June 1953
The people's uprising in East Berlin is suppressed by the Soviets.

13 August 1956
Death of Bertolt Brecht, whose "Berliner Ensemble" made East Berlin famous in theatrical circles.

13 August 1961
The DDR army and police start to build the Wall.

3 October 1969
The Television Tower in Alexanderplatz is opened.

3 May 1971
Resignation of Walter Ulbricht; Erich Honecker succeeds him as DDR head of state.

28 August 1973
The World Youth and Student Games takes place.

17 October 1976
The DDR expatriates singer-songwriter Wolf Biermann, who is critical of the state.

1986
The Umweltbibliothek (Environmental Library) emerges as a future focal point of DDR opposition.

1989
5 February: Chris Gueffroy is the last DDR refugee to be shot by border guards.
9 October: The opening of the Wall is announced by Günter Schabowski.

The socialist city in action

When Berlin was divided into sectors, the Soviet occupying powers were granted the city areas of Mitte, Prenzlauer Berg, Pankow, Friedrichshain, Treptow, Köpenick, Weissensee, and Lichtenberg. From 1949, they were jointly known as "Berlin, capital city of the DDR".

Compared to the Western sectors, economic progress was much slower in the Eastern sector of the city, partly because the Soviet Union did not allow its occupied areas to take part in the Marshall Plan for the rebuilding of Europe. However, to achieve a noticeable economic upswing, the DDR government, based in Pankow under Walter Ulbricht, announced higher average work rates in 1952. Because the supply of goods was worsening at the same time, there was worker unrest in June 1953. On 17 June, Soviet tanks bloodily suppressed the resulting disorder and uprising.

By 1950, socialist principles of urban development came into effect. Under these, East Berlin was to have a central axis running from the Brandenburg Gate, across Alexanderplatz to Stalinallee (today Karl-Marx-Allee). From the end of the 1950s, prefabricated buildings were erected in the inner city, and the large residential towns of Marzahn, Hohenschönhausen, and Hellersdorf grew up in the 1970s.

Socialist ancestors: the Marx-Engels Monument and East Berlin's Fernsehturm.

BERLIN 1945–1990

East Berlin steers the region

In 1969, the second-tallest building in Europe was constructed in the middle of the Alexanderplatz, the 365-m (1,197-foot) high Fernsehturm (Television Tower). In 1976, the Palast der Republik (Palace of the Republic) was

A disillusioned end (from top): the Palast der Republik from outside (1999); the interior in 1985; and demolition in 2006.

built in the square of the former Berlin Stadtschloss; the DDR parliament met here, and it was also used for cultural events. Because of its many lights, people soon began calling it "Erich's lamp shop".

The DDR underwent a period of consolidation in the 1960s and 1970s, but from the mid-1980s East Berlin and Leipzig emerged as focal points of the civil rights movement. Activities in these cities, along with the mass exodus via the Hungarian border to Austria in the summer of 1989, led to the opening of the Berlin Wall on 9 November 1989, and finally to the dissolution of the DDR. As witnesses to the former division, many institutions are duplicated in Berlin, such as the opera houses.

An image that moved the world: young Berliner Peter Fechter was shot on 17 August 1962 and simply left to die.

The Berlin Wall

Around three million people left the Soviet-controlled area of Germany between 1949 and 1961. Most of these were young, well-educated people who had high hopes of a better future in the West. When this flight from the DDR threatened to bleed the country dry economically, units of the National People's Army and the People's Police began to seal off the sector's border between East and West Berlin in the early hours of 13 August 1961.

Subsequently, a 155-km (96-mile) long and almost 4-m (13-foot) high concrete wall was erected around West Berlin to prevent further waves of people leaving. A second fence was erected parallel to the Wall, around 100 meters into the East German territory. The houses between the Wall and the fence were demolished to create the empty space that became known as No Man's Land. Those who attempted to leave often paid with their lives. On 24 August 1961, the order to shoot was given for the first time, with fatal consequences. The last victim on the border was 20-year-old Chris Gueffroy in February 1989. It is still unclear how many people died at the Wall between 1961 and 1989. Estimates vary widely; numbers between 80 and 230 have been suggested.

Soon after the opening of the German-German border, the DDR authorities began to dismantle the Wall. Just a few sections remain and have been protected as historical monuments, for example along Bernauer Strasse in the Mitte area of Berlin. Where the Wall was removed in significant locations, a line on the ground indicates its former course. This is particularly striking below the modern buildings in Potsdamer Platz.

Dramatic scenes when the Wall was built.

After the reunification of Germany and the decision to make Berlin the capital, there was a unique opportunity to set up a new government district. At the heart of this project is the redeveloped Reichstag (right), designed by top British architect Sir Norman Foster. The nearby Bundeskanzleramt (Federal Chancellor's Office) (far right) was designed by Axel Schultes and Charlotte Frank.

1990
18 March: The CDU party wins the first free parliamentary elections. 3 October: The DDR joins the Federal Republic. December: After 44 years, the whole of Berlin elects its city parliament. Again, the victors are the CDU (under Eberhard Diepgen).

20 June 1991
Berlin is chosen as the German seat of government by the German Bundestag (parliament).

1 January 1992
The local transport companies BVG (West) and BVB (East) merge.

1993
Berlin becomes the official residence of the Federal president.

1999
The Bundestag and government move to Berlin.

1 January 2001
The 23 city regions are cut to 12 larger regions.

21 May 2003
The broadcasters SFB and ORB amalgamate to form RBB (Rundfunk Berlin-Brandenburg).

12 May 2005
Official opening of the Memorial to the Murdered Jews of Europe.

2006
May: The new Hauptbahnhof (main station) opens. September: Klaus Wowereit's SPD party – in coalition with the Left since 2002 – wins the elections.

Reunification

After the fall of the Berlin Wall on 9 November 1989, demands for the reunification of Germany were heard in East and West. On 28 November, the Federal Chancellor Helmut Kohl (leader of the Christian Democratic Union

From top: Fireworks at the Brandenburg Gate celebrate the fall of the Wall; part of the Wall near the Reichstag.

party, CDU) presented a ten-point plan in the Bonn Bundestag, which aimed at a confederacy. Soon after the DDR parliamentary election in March 1990, the Federal government started negotiations with the new DDR government under Lothar de Maizière (CDU) on economic, monetary, and social union, which came about on 1 July 1990. After the four powers (France, the UK, US, and the Soviet Union) agreed in the Two-Plus-Four agreement, the way was smoothed for German unity. On 31 August 1990, representatives of the two German states signed a unification treaty, and on 3 October 1990, hundreds of thousands of people celebrated the Day of German Unity, which has since then become a public holiday.

The new old capital

The unification treaty between the DDR and the Federal Republic designated Berlin as the capital of a reunited Germany. Whether the city wanted to be the seat of government was disputed. The number of supporters of Berlin on the one hand and Bonn on the other was about level in general, across all parties. Finally, after an emotional debate on 20 June 1991, the German Bundestag voted by a tiny majority (338 to 320 votes) to move the government to the city on the Spree. In September 1999, the German Bundestag started work in Berlin, and one year later the Bundesrat (upper house of parliament) took their seats in the Prussian upper chamber in Leipziger Strasse near Potsdamer Platz.
Berlin's politicians were also relocated after reunification: the mayor of Berlin and the Senate moved from Schöneberger into the Rotes Rathaus on Alexanderplatz, and the House of Representatives moved into the former Prussian Landtag building, which was located on Stresemannstrasse.
In the euphoria of the first few years after reunification, many experts forecast a gigantic economic boom for the new capital. However, little can be witnessed of that yet: neither the West Berlin economy, highly subsidized up until 1990, nor East Berlin's planned economy, managed the transfer to the free market unscathed. Almost half of all industrial jobs in Berlin were lost in the 1990s.

BERLIN SINCE 1990
Capital of the Federal Republic of Germany

Today, it is essentially the service sector that drives the city's economy. Tourism has developed: with ever increasing visitor numbers – and a record figure of seven million visitors in 2006 – Berlin is an established bastion of city tourism, alongside Paris and London. Berlin has also become an important location for science and the media in recent years.
The rate of unemployment is still well above the national average. In city areas such as Wedding, Neukölln, and Kreuzberg in particular, with their high numbers of immigrants, social problems are increasing. Political countermeasures are unlikely to be able to help, in view of a mountain of debt of 63.5 billion Euros (2006). In 2002, the Berlin Senate had recognized the budgetary disaster and sued the Federal government and other Federal states for help with its debt. The action was, however, dismissed by the Federal Constitutional Court in October 2006.
In spite of this, there is no reason to be pessimistic, because the reunited Berlin, with its rich musical, theatrical, and art scene, continues to flourish. Having already embraced electronic music, in the 1990s the city was partly responsible for the birth of techno music and clubs and raves sprang up everywhere. Today, Berlin still attracts young, creative people from all over Europe.

Under the dome of the Sony Center in Potsdamer Platz are numerous restaurants, eight cinema screens, and a fountain.

Berlin – the largest building site in Europe

Reunification had far-reaching consequences for Berlin's skyline – in the 1990s, the city became the largest building site in Europe. The area between Potsdamer Platz, the Reichstag, and the former Platz and the Brandenburg Gate, the Memorial to the Murdered Jews of Europe (usually known as the Holocaust Memorial) is a powerfully symbolic field of concrete slabs, or stelae, designed by American architect Peter Eisenman and erected between 2003 and 2005. The

Deutsches Historisches Museum (top); Hauptbahnhof (above).

Lehrter station, which lay empty until the 1990s, has been given a whole new look. A glittering heart to the city was created in Potsdamer Platz between 1991 and 2000, to designs by Renzo Piano, Christoph Kohlbecker, and other top architects. Particularly spectacular is the Sony Center designed by Helmut Jahn, a steel and glass construction of seven buildings, with a roofed forum in the middle. Between Potsdamer relocation of parliament and government from Bonn to Berlin resulted in more construction: a new government district was built around the Reichstag, including the Bundeskanzleramt (Chancellor's Office) and office blocks; an extensive residential complex is planned at Spreebogen.
The most recent new building is the multilevel Hauptbahnhof (main station) on the site of the former Lehrter station, completed in 2006.

THE HIGHLIGHTS

BERLIN'S HISTORICAL HEART

When the Berlin Wall was opened on 9 November 1989, the city regained its historical heart. Much of Berlin had been destroyed during the Allied bombing raids of World War II, and while some of the city had been reconstructed during the DDR era, a substantial part was in need of extensive renovation. The famous boulevard Unter den Linden, which has seen the city's fortunes change over the centuries, continues to be a big draw, while the Nikolaiviertel district, dating from around 1200, is Berlin's new "old city", and the Museumsinsel, a UNESCO World Heritage Site, which is currently undergoing restoration, will be a reminder of Berlin's former glory.

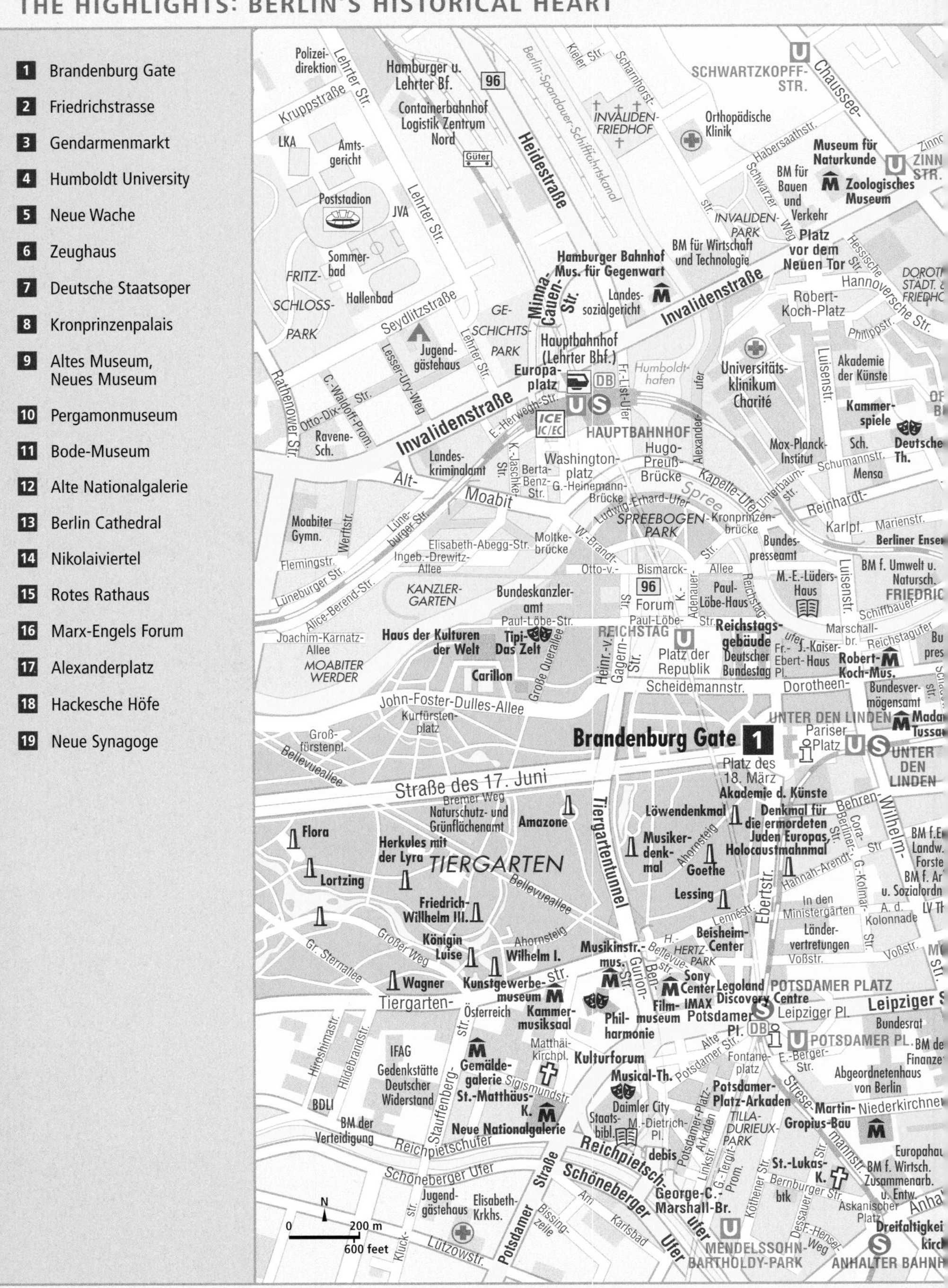
1 Brandenburg Gate
2 Friedrichstrasse
3 Gendarmenmarkt
4 Humboldt University
5 Neue Wache
6 Zeughaus
7 Deutsche Staatsoper
8 Kronprinzenpalais
9 Altes Museum, Neues Museum
10 Pergamonmuseum
11 Bode-Museum
12 Alte Nationalgalerie
13 Berlin Cathedral
14 Nikolaiviertel
15 Rotes Rathaus
16 Marx-Engels Forum
17 Alexanderplatz
18 Hackesche Höfe
19 Neue Synagoge
Brandenburg Gate
Hamburger u. Lehrter Bf.
Containerbahnhof Logistik Zentrum Nord
Heidestraße
INVALIDEN-FRIEDHOF
SCHWARTZKOPFF-STR.
Chaussee-
Orthopädische Klinik
Museum für Naturkunde
Zoologisches Museum
Hamburger Bahnhof Mus. für Gegenwart
Invalidenstraße
Platz vor dem Neuen Tor
Robert-Koch-Platz
Hauptbahnhof (Lehrter Bhf.)
HAUPTBAHNHOF
Universitätsklinikum Charité
Akademie der Künste
Kammerspiele
Deutsches Th.
Alt-Moabit
Washingtonplatz
SPREEBOGEN-PARK
KANZLER-GARTEN
Bundeskanzleramt
Haus der Kulturen der Welt
Tipi-Das Zelt
REICHSTAG
Reichstagsgebäude Deutscher Bundestag
Platz der Republik
Scheidemannstr.
Dorotheen-
John-Foster-Dulles-Allee
Carillon
UNTER DEN LINDEN
Pariser Platz
Platz des 18. März
Straße des 17. Juni
TIERGARTEN
Tiergartentunnel
Amazone
Flora
Lortzing
Herkules mit der Lyra
Friedrich-Wilhelm III.
Königin Luise
Wilhelm I.
Wagner
Löwendenkmal
Denkmal für die ermordeten Juden Europas, Holocaustmahnmal
Goethe
Lessing
Musiker-denk-mal
Beisheim-Center
Sony Center
Legoland Discovery Centre
POTSDAMER PLATZ
Leipziger Pl.
Leipziger
Musikinstr.-mus.
Kunstgewerbe-museum
Kammer-musiksaal
Phil-harmonie
Film-museum
Kulturforum
Gemälde-galerie
St.-Matthäus-K.
Neue Nationalgalerie
Gedenkstätte Deutscher Widerstand
Musical-Th.
Daimler City
Staats-bibl.
Potsdamer-Platz-Arkaden
Martin-Gropius-Bau
Abgeordnetenhaus von Berlin
Bundesrat
Niederkirchner
Reichpietschufer
Schöneberger Ufer
Potsdamer Straße
Lützowstr.
George-C.-Marshall-Br.
MENDELSSOHN-BARTHOLDY-PARK
ANHALTER BAHNHOF
St.-Lukas-K.
Dreifaltigkeitskirche
0 200 m
600 feet
N

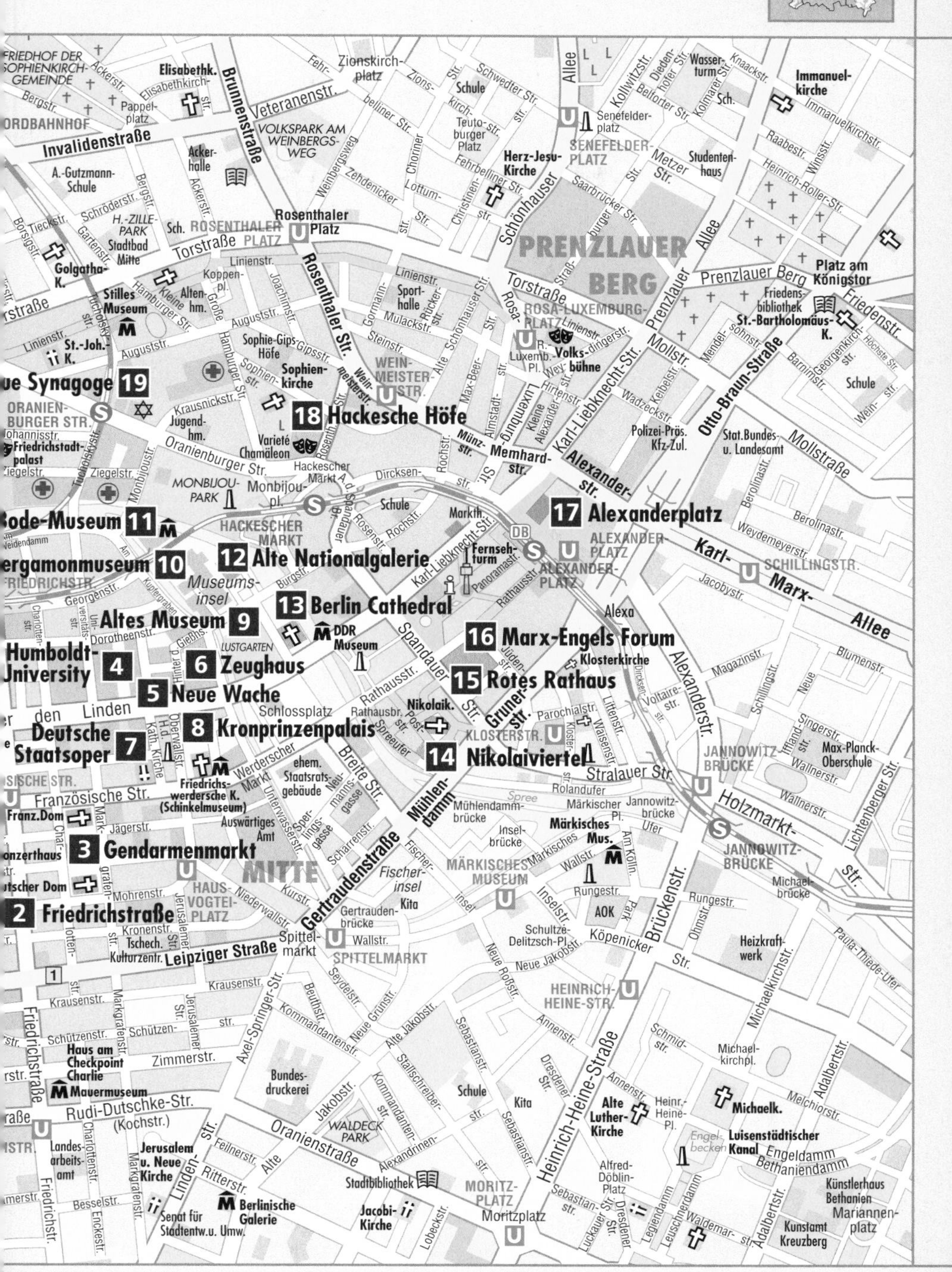

FRIEDHOF DER SOPHIENKIRCH-GEMEINDE
Elisabethk.
Brunnenstraße
Zionskirch-platz
Schule
Immanuel-kirche
Invalidenstraße
Veteranenstr.
VOLKSPARK AM WEINBERGSWEG
Senefelder-platz
SENEFELDER-PLATZ
Acker-halle
A.-Gutzmann-Schule
Herz-Jesu-Kirche
Studenten-haus
Rosenthaler Platz
ROSENTHALER PLATZ
H.-ZILLE-PARK
Stadtbad Mitte
Torstraße
PRENZLAUER BERG
Golgatha-K.
Stilles Museum
Sport-halle
Platz am Königstor
Friedens-bibliothek
St.-Bartholomäus-K.
Rosenthaler Str.
ROSA-LUXEMBURG-PLATZ
Volks-bühne
Prenzlauer Allee
Mollstr.
St.-Joh.-K.
Sophie-Gips-Höfe
Sophien-kirche
WEIN-MEISTER-STR.
Schule
Neue Synagoge 19
ORANIEN-BURGER STR.
18 Hackesche Höfe
Karl-Liebknecht-Str.
Otto-Braun-Straße
Varieté Chamäleon
Friedrichstadt-palast
Memhard-str.
Polizei-Präs. Kfz-Zul.
Stat.Bundes- u. Landesamt
Mollstraße
Oranienburger Str.
Hackescher Markt
MONBIJOU-PARK
Monbijou-pl.
Bode-Museum 11
HACKESCHER MARKT
17 Alexanderplatz
Alexander-str.
Pergamonmuseum 10
12 Alte Nationalgalerie
Fernseh-turm
ALEXANDER-PLATZ
Karl-Marx-Allee
SCHILLINGSTR.
Museums-insel
13 Berlin Cathedral
Altes Museum 9
DDR Museum
16 Marx-Engels Forum
Alexa
Humboldt-University 4
6 Zeughaus
LUSTGARTEN
15 Rotes Rathaus
Klosterkirche
5 Neue Wache
Unter den Linden
Schlossplatz
Nikolaik.
Deutsche Staatsoper 7
8 Kronprinzenpalais
KLOSTERSTR.
14 Nikolaiviertel
JANNOWITZ-BRÜCKE
Max-Planck-Oberschule
Friedrichs-werdersche K. (Schinkelmuseum)
ehem. Staatsrats-gebäude
Stralauer Str.
Französische Str.
Franz.Dom
Spree
Mühlendamm
Mühlendamm-brücke
Märkischer Pl.
Jannowitz-brücke
Holzmarkt-str.
Auswärtiges Amt
Märkisches Mus.
3 Gendarmenmarkt
MITTE
MÄRKISCHES MUSEUM
JANNOWITZ-BRÜCKE
Michael-brücke
Deutscher Dom
HAUS-VOGTEI-PLATZ
Gertraudenstraße
Fischer-insel
2 Friedrichstraße
Gertrauden-brücke
Spittel-markt
SPITTELMARKT
AOK
Brückenstr.
Köpenicker Str.
Heizkraft-werk
Leipziger Straße
HEINRICH-HEINE-STR.
Friedrichstraße
Haus am Checkpoint Charlie
Mauermuseum
Zimmerstr.
Axel-Springer-Str.
Bundes-druckerei
Schule
Kita
Heinrich-Heine-Straße
Michael-kirchpl.
Michaelk.
Alte Luther-Kirche
Rudi-Dutschke-Str. (Kochstr.)
Oranienstraße
WALDECK PARK
Luisenstädtischer Kanal
Engeldamm
Bethaniendamm
Landes-arbeits-amt
Jerusalem u. Neue Kirche
Lindenstr.
Ritterstr.
Berlinische Galerie
Senat für Stadtentw.u. Umw.
Stadtbibliothek
MORITZ-PLATZ
Moritzplatz
Jacobi-Kirche
Alfred-Döblin-Platz
Künstlerhaus Bethanien
Mariannen-platz
Kunstamt Kreuzberg

THE HIGHLIGHTS: BERLIN'S HISTORICAL HEART

A brief timeline of the Brandenburg Gate. Below left, from top: Emperor William II in around 1910, looking dashing on a white horse; during World War II the structure was seriously damaged and the four-horsed chariot practically destroyed; after 13 August 1961, a lonely Gate and sections of Wall. Below and right: Restored to glory, with chariot intact.

TIP Theodor Tucher

A charming and cozy mixture of café, literary salon, cabaret, music venue, bookshop, and high-quality restaurant.

Pariser Platz 6 a; Tel (030) 22 48 94 64; 9.00–1.00, daily; S-Bahn Unter den Linden.

The Brandenburg Gate (Brandenburger Tor) is a triumphant finale to the magnificent street of Unter den Linden. Created between 1788 and 1791 by Carl Gotthard Langhans, this massive, 26-m (85-foot) high, 65-m (218-foot) wide, sandstone construction is much more than just a gate to the city: it symbolized the strength of Prussia, and was inspired by the Propylaea (monumental gates) of the Acropolis in Athens. Twelve Doric columns divide the double portico into five passageways. The central one, 5.5 m (18 feet) wide, was reserved for royal equipages, and the rank and file used the narrower side passageways. The relief on the roof parapet shows the entry of the gods of peace into the city; the ornamentation in the passageway illustrates the legend of Hercules, with Mars and Minerva in the side halls. The magnificent Quadriga (four-horsed chariot) crowning the Gate was designed by Johann Gottfried Schadow and completed in 1791.

Insets below, from left: A uniformed bellboy welcomes guests just as his predecessor might have done a century ago; guests meet around the fountain in the foyer for coffee or tea; when the weather permits, you can sit on the terrace and enjoy the view of the Brandenburg Gate.

THE ADLON: FIVE-STAR TRADITION

There is certainly no shortage of five-star hotels in Berlin. New ones continually spring up – but Hotel Adlon remains special. Emperor William II called it a "temple of pleasure" and insisted on being the first to cross the threshold when it opened in 1907. The foyer was aglow with magical lights and there was a distinct hint of raciness if not decadence in the air, along with the clinking of big money. It boasted luxurious bathrooms and fripperies such as bell-pulls with tassels for service. Berlin's most famous hotel was founded by builder and property developer Lorenz Adlon, who already owned several other hotels and restaurants. The magnificent Adlon hotel managed to survive the destruction of World War II only to fall victim, in May 1945, to a match dropped carelessly in the wine cellar. The resulting blaze almost destroyed the building entirely. Before its demise, in its heyday, many of the world's rich and famous passed through the doors of the Adlon, including European royalty and Hollywood stars such as Charlie Chaplin. After the collapse of the communist system, a fund was set up to restore the hotel, and in 1996 the Adlon was the first new building on Pariser Platz. It should prove to be a valuable source of income not just for the city, but also for its 3,500 investors. Some critics describe its architecture as rather "Monarch of the Glen" in style, but the design also has many fans. The light-green copper roof is a landmark for visitors to Berlin.

THE HIGHLIGHTS: BERLIN'S HISTORICAL HEART

A blaze of light: one of the most famous and busy streets in Berlin, until much of it was destroyed during bombing in World War II, Friedrichstrasse has come alive once more. Inset, below: Quartier 206, an upmarket store that is shopping heaven; instantly recognizable from its striking exterior, inside all is luxury and high-end design.

TIP Mauermuseum Haus am Checkpoint Charlie

A small museum that documents the history of the Wall and the courageous attempts to flee from East Berlin and the DDR, through often chilling images and exhibits.

Friedrichstr. 43–45; Tel (030) 2 53 72 50; 9.00–22.00, daily; U-Bahn Kochstrasse.

FRIEDRICHSTRASSE 2

At the start of the 20th century the writer Franz Hessel came up with an evocative description of Friedrichstrasse: "the narrow pavement covered with a carpet of light ... on which dangerous young women moved as though on silk". He was referring to the central section of the street, extending from Unter den Linden to Leipziger Strasse, with its luxury restaurants, cafes, bars, and gambling dens. Having suffered a long decline, Friedrichstrasse is bustling once more – along with its fine new restaurants and expensive shops, the eagerly-awaited emergence of a new golden age seems to be under way. But this is just a small section of the street: Friedrichstrasse extends for over 3 km (1.8 miles), from Oranienburger Tor in the north to Mehringplatz in the south. The new office blocks near Checkpoint Charlie stand empty. To the north, behind the Friedrichstrasse station, more new buildings are starting to appear.

French architect Jean Nouvel designed the floors of the Galeries Lafayette around two spectacular glass spheres; shoppers pause for a while to admire his innovative work. A number of international designers are represented within the store (inset and right).

SHOPPING IN CENTRAL BERLIN

Sunglasses displayed like jewels; exquisite shoes on show as if exhibits in an art gallery; innovative décor with mirrors as tall as a house, exotic plants, and gleaming, polished stonework lure curious shoppers inside for a closer look. Shopping in central Berlin is all about presentation, drama, entertainment, and not forgetting pleasure, even for window shoppers – while for shopping connoisseurs it is a truly aesthetic experience. The large, prewar department stores in the heart of the city around Alexanderplatz have disappeared, to be superseded by modern shopping malls, like the one in Potsdamer Platz. Many of the shops in the historical heart of the city are small, meticulously designed retail emporia in minimalist style, with upmarket and quirky goods designed to attract the interest of passers-by. And if shoppers find there is not enough to look at, they can listen to the DJs at mixing desks, providing background music for shoppers working out what to buy or trying on outfits. In some shops, customers are invited to watch goods being made, or even take part in their preparation. Concept stores, which first appeared in the 1990s in various European cities, offer a complete "lifestyle concept". Their exclusive and expensive goods are aimed at sophisticated consumers, and are often displayed with accessories or on items of furniture that are also for sale.

THE HIGHLIGHTS: BERLIN'S HISTORICAL HEART

Along with the Konzerthaus, Französischer Dom (below right), and Schiller statue (below), the Gendarmenmarkt has chic bars and restaurants, such as the Newton Bar, Borchardt (popular with politicians and media types), and Lutter & Wegner (right).

TIP Lutter & Wegner

A traditional restaurant (founded in 1811) with Austrian-inspired cuisine; there is also a cozy wine bar and wine shop.

Charlottenstr. 56; Tel (030) 2 02 95 40; 11.00–2.00, daily; U- Bahn Französische Strasse.

GENDARMENMARKT 3

The Gendarmenmarkt is considered to be one of the most beautiful squares in Berlin, a perfect example of Romantic Classicism, with the Schauspielhaus (known today as the Konzerthaus), Deutscher Dom and Französischer Dom (German and French cathedrals), and the marble statue of Schiller. The square is named after the Gens d'Armes, a regiment of cuirassiers who were based here until the mid-18th century. The two churches were not originally "identical twins", but were altered and given their domed towers by Carl von Gontard at the behest of Frederick the Great. Reinhold Begas' statue of Schiller is some 6 m (19 feet) tall and is surrounded by the symbolic figures of lyricism, drama, philosophy, and history. It was removed from here in 1935 but was returned to its original place in 1987; in its later years, the DDR placed increasing value on its national heritage.

THE HIGHLIGHTS: BERLIN'S HISTORICAL HEART

Humboldt University has always adapted itself to the times. The Marx quote in the entrance hall (below) says: "Philosophers have interpreted the world in various ways; the point is to change it". An unlikely setting: computers in a room designed by Knobelsdorff (below right). Naturalist Alexander von Humboldt (right) would not have complained.

TIP Book market

Good-value reading material – satirical and standard works, scientific texts and literature – can all be found in the bookstands at the entrance to Humboldt University.

Unter den Linden 6; from about 9.00, daily; S-Bahn Unter den Linden.

HUMBOLDT UNIVERSITY 4

Among its former students, Humboldt University (known as Friedrich Wilhelm University until 1946) can boast 29 Nobel Prize winners, including Albert Einstein (physics), Otto Hahn (chemistry), Robert Koch (medicine), and Theodor Mommsen (literature). Statutes of the great natural scientist Alexander von Humboldt and his brother Wilhelm, of equal academic renown, watch over the entrance, with its well-stocked bookstands and browsing readers. The building, constructed between 1748 and 1765 to plans by Knobelsdorff, architect to Frederick the Great, was intended for Frederick's brother Prince Henry, but then became home to Berlin University, jointly founded by Wilhelm von Humboldt. The first vice chancellor in 1810 was Johann Gottlieb Fichte. Many great names have taught here, including Hegel, Schleiermacher, the brothers Grimm, Planck, Virchow, and Sauerbruch – a true *Who's Who* of European scientific history.

THE HIGHLIGHTS: BERLIN'S HISTORICAL HEART

In the Neue Wache, the *Mother with her Dead Son*, a bronze pietà by Käthe Kollwitz, symbolizes the suffering of all victims of violence (below). Karl Friedrich Schinkel's neoclassical royal guard house, the Neue Wache, has a portico with Doric columns (right).

INFO Neue Wache

The former guardhouse of the royal troops is today the Central Memorial of the Federal Republic for the Victims of War and Tyranny.

Unter den Linden 4; 10.00–18.00, daily; S-Bahn Unter den Linden.

Designated a war memorial in 1931, in 1993 the Neue Wache (New Guard House) was rededicated the Central Memorial of the Federal Republic to the Victims of War and Tyranny (Zentrale Gedenkstätte der Bundesrepublik Deutschland für die Opfer des Krieges und der Gewaltherrschaft). The original building, a royal guard house designed by Karl Friedrich Schinkel in 1818, served as a memorial to victims of World War I. Destroyed in World War II, it was rebuilt between 1951 and 1957 and became a focal point for photographers from the early 1960s, when DDR guards changed at the "Memorial to the Victims of Fascism and Militarism" every Wednesday. The communist government altered the interior, and in 1969 added a crystal cube with an eternal flame, as well as the remains of the "Unknown Resistance Fighter", and two bronze slabs covering "blood-soaked earth from fascist concentration camps" and from battlefields.

THE HIGHLIGHTS: BERLIN'S HISTORICAL HEART

Since reunification, the Deutsches Historisches Museum (DHM) has been housed in the Berlin Zeughaus. In the summer, concerts are held in the covered courtyard (below). The enormous collection (insets, far right) is an absolute must for history fans.

INFO Deutsches Historisches Museum

Two thousand years of German history are documented in this permanent exhibition, with over 8,000 items on display; there are also special temporary exhibitions.

Unter den Linden 2; Tel (030) 20 30 40; 10.00–18.00, daily; S-Bahn Unter den Linden.

The Zeughaus on the boulevard Unter den Linden is one of the oldest buildings in Berlin, constructed between 1695 and 1706 as an arsenal by Johann Nering, Andreas Schlüter, and Jean de Bodt. Until 1876, the upper floor was stacked with rapiers and muskets, and heavy artillery weapons were stored on the ground floor. Schlüter's main contribution is the sculptural decoration – the carved heads of dying warriors above the windows in the interior courtyard are examples of some of his most accomplished work. At the end of the 19th century, the Zeughaus ceased to be a weapons store; from then on, the rooms were used for historical exhibitions. Today, with a striking new glass building by the American-Chinese architect Ieoh Ming Pei, the Zeughaus is home to the Deutsches Historisches Museum. The permanent exhibition covers 2,000 years of German history and includes some rare items, such as Frederick the Great's camp-bed.

THE HIGHLIGHTS: BERLIN'S HISTORICAL HEART

Enrico Caruso once sang at the Deutsche Staatsoper – and the brilliant prima ballerina Steffi Scherzer (below right) performed here. The last reconstruction of the Staatsoper (below) took place in 1955 – after being destroyed twice in World War II. The Kronprinzenpalais (right) was used by the DDR government as guest accommodation.

TIP Operncafé

A lavishly decorated café with a sophisticated atmosphere, offering a heavenly selection of temptingly delicious tarts and cakes.

Unter den Linden 5; Tel (030) 20 26 83; 8.00–24.00, daily, S-Bahn Unter den Linden.

DEUTSCHE STAATSOPER 7
KRONPRINZENPALAIS 8

These two buildings have varied and long histories. The Deutsche Staatsoper (German State Opera House) was the vision of the young King Frederick II. His Forum Fridericianum was intended to unite the sciences, arts, and monarchy of Prussia in an architectural ensemble: the first building was a "magical castle", an opera house. The architect Georg Wenzeslaus von Knobelsdorff started work in 1741, and the opera house was the first self-contained German theater, standing in what is today's Bebelplatz. In 1789, it was opened to the "ordinary" public. Only a fragment remains, however, of Frederick's large ensemble. The Kronprinzenpalais (Crown Prince's Palace) at Unter den Linden 3, constructed in 1663 and redesigned several times, was significant not only as the city address of princes, and later as a DDR guest house. On 31 August 1990, this is where the treaty was signed for the DDR to join the Federal Republic of Germany.

THE HIGHLIGHTS: BERLIN'S HISTORICAL HEART

Schinkel's masterpiece, bathed in light: 18 columns support the front of the Altes Museum (below). The statue of an Amazon fighting a lion by August Kiss (right) can be seen from outside the museum. Inside there are treasures from the Egyptian Museum (insets, below) including the famous head of Nefertiti.

INFO Altes Museum

Greek and Roman antiquities are displayed in the Altes Museum. The Neues Museum reopens in 2009 after restoration work.

Am Lustgarten; Tel (030) 20 90 55 77; 10.00–18.00, daily, Thurs 10.00– 22.00; U-/S-Bahn Friedrichstrasse.

ALTES MUSEUM, NEUES MUSEUM 9

In front of the Altes Museum (Old Museum) is a monumental granite dish carved by Christian Gottlieb Cantian in 1830. Known as "the largest soup bowl in Berlin", it certainly catches the eye – as does so much on the Museumsinsel (Museum Island), which is now a UNESCO World Heritage Site. The Altes Museum, one of Berlin's most important neoclassical buildings, was designed in 1823 by Karl Friedrich Schinkel in a Greek style, with 18 Ionic columns supporting the portico. The rooms display a collection of classical antiquities from ancient Greece and Rome. The upper floor has been home to the Egyptian Museum – but in 2009 this will return to its former location in the Neues Museum (New Museum, built between 1843 and 1855). The world-famous bust of Nefertiti alone makes a visit worthwhile. Exhibits from the Charlottenburg Museums of Pre- and Early History will also be displayed in the Neues Museum.

THE HIGHLIGHTS: BERLIN'S HISTORICAL HEART

A must-see for visitors: the Pergamon Altar (below), the Ishtar Gate (far right, top) with the Processional Way of Babylon (far right, below), and the Market Gate of Miletus (inset, middle). Inset below, left: The Athena propylon. There are also sculptures from Miletus, Samos, and Naxos (right).

INFO Pergamonmuseum

This is the most visited museum in Berlin; the architectural objects on display are outstanding. It's worth getting an audioguide.

Am Kupfergraben; Tel (030) 20 90 55 77; 10.00–18.00, daily, Thurs 10.00–22.00; U-/S-Bahn Friedrichstrasse.

One of Berlin's grandest staircases leads up 27 steps, past deities and heroes, to the Pergamon Altar, where sacrifices were made to the gods 2,000 years ago. This altar, built around 180–160 BC, was a gift of King Eumenes to Zeus and Athena, goddess of the city of Pergamon in Asia Minor (today Bergama in Turkey). It was excavated by Carl Humann and brought to Berlin in 1902. Due to its size, an exhibition space of generous proportions was required, hence the building of the world's first architectural museum, based on plans by Alfred Messel and Ludwig Hoffmann (1909 to 1930). Today it is still the most visited museum in Berlin and the heart of the Museumsinsel. The Museum of the Ancient Near East, part of the Pergamon Museum, has a collection of antiquities covering 4,000 years – the majority excavated by the German Oriental Society between 1898 and 1917 – as well as displays of oriental history and culture (see p. 178).

THE HIGHLIGHTS: BERLIN'S HISTORICAL HEART

Separated into two collections in 1939, the Sculpture Collection and the Museum of Byzantine Art, have been reunited in the Bode Museum. The museum's dome (right) is a fitting focal point for this already imposing building. Below: The small domed hall with a rococo staircase dating from the time of Frederick the Great.

INFO Bode-Museum

The historic Bode-Museum is a fitting exhibition space for the collections of Byzantine art and European sculptures from the 13th to 19th centuries.

Monbijoubrücke; Tel (030) 20 90 56 01; 10.00–18.00, daily, Thurs 10.00–22.00; U-/S-Bahn Friedrichstrasse.

From the Museumsinsel on Monbijoubrücke, the neobaroque Bode-Museum rises up over the Spree like a ship's bow. A rather overwhelming building, with a basilica, domed halls, statues of royalty, and Italian fireplaces, it was designed by Ernst von Ihne, and opened in 1904 as the Kaiser-Friedrich-Museum; it was renamed in 1956 after its director Wilhelm von Bode. General repairs were carried out before the new millennium, and the building regained its original charm: the ashlar divisions in the dome and vaulting have been reconstructed, the hall is now flooded with light, and the marble inlays of the basilica have been recreated. The Tiepolo Gallery and its frescoes can be enjoyed once more. The Coin Gallery, the Museum of Byzantine Art, and the Sculpture Collection, with 1,700 exhibits from late antiquity to the end of the 18th century, are also housed in the Bode-Museum.

Music alfresco: in the summer, open-air events take place in the garden of the Alte Nationalgalerie (below). Inside the gallery is a collection of stunning paintings and graceful sculptures (below right). Right: A bust by Christian Friedrich Tieck depicts the architect Karl Friedrich Schinkel.

INFO Alte Nationalgalerie

One of the best collections of 19th-century Romantic, classical, and Impressionist painting and sculpture in Germany, displayed in fine exhibition spaces.

Bodestr. 1–3; Tel (030) 20 90 58 01; Tues–Sun 10.00-18.00, Thurs 10.00–22.00; U-/S-Bahn Friedrichstrasse.

ALTE NATIONALGALERIE 12

The Alte Nationalgalerie (Old National Gallery) stands like a Corinthian temple on a massive base. Schinkel's pupil Friedrich August Stüler designed the building in 1865 to house the collection of 262 paintings bequeathed to the state by the consul Wagner in 1861. However, by the beginning of the 20th century, the gallery's directors had moved away from Wilhelminische taste in art and purchased Menzel, Manet and Monet. In 1939, this exhibition of "degenerate art" was closed by the Nazis. After the war, the building was the first to be rebuilt on the Museumsinsel; it was comprehensively restored in the late 1990s. Today it is home to the great art of the 19th century. Romantic painters such as Caspar David Friedrich and Adolph von Menzel are represented, as well as Impressionists – Liebermann, Manet, and Monet – and pioneers of the modern art movement such as Paul Cézanne (see p. 174).

THE HIGHLIGHTS: BERLIN'S HISTORICAL HEART

On the 100th anniversary of its official opening, the artist Matthias Zeckert put on a spectacular light display in the cathedral, which reached its high point in a heavenly blue (right and below right). The sumptuous organ, with its 113 stops and more than 7,200 pipes (below), is a showpiece of the cathedral.

INFO Berlin Cathedral

From the outer dome walkway, you get a fantastic view of the Museumsinsel on the Spree, a UNESCO World Heritage Site since 1999.

Am Lustgarten; Tel (030) 20 26 91 52; Mon–Sat 9.00–20.00, Sun/public holidays 12.00–20.00, Oct–Mar to 19.00; U-/S-Bahn Alexanderplatz.

The burial place of the powerful Hohenzollerns, Berlin Cathedral (Berliner Dom) was built between 1893 and 1905 at the request of Emperor William II, on the site of a former simple domed building by the River Spree. As the main church of Prussian Protestantism it was destined to be a lavish construction and intended to be the court church, rather than the main seat of the bishop. The new building was designed in the style of the Italian high Renaissance, laden with towers and cupolas, to a controversial plan by the master architect Julius Carl Raschdorff. Raschdorff consulted different architectural handbooks and dozens of documents on historic buildings, resulting in a cathedral that is in parts more reminiscent of a temple, or of buildings found in London or Rome, but the true treasures of this church lie in the crypt – with 94 tombs and sarcophagi of Germany's ruling dynasty dating back over four centuries.

THE HIGHLIGHTS: BERLIN'S HISTORICAL HEART

Like identical twins: the distinctive towers of the Nikolaikirche (below, right) penetrate the night sky in the heart of the Nikolaiviertel; a short distance away lies Alexanderplatz (known simply as the "Alex" by the locals) and the ever-conspicuous Fernsehturm (Television Tower).

TIP Mutter Hoppe

An atmospheric old Berlin restaurant in the Nikolaiviertel, with a beer garden and good, solid German food. 1920s- and 1930s-style live concerts on Fridays and Saturdays.

Rathausstr. 21; Tel (030) 241 56 25; from 11.30, daily; U-/S-Bahn Alexanderplatz.

A church whose precursor was built in the 12th century, a piece of medieval city wall next to the oldest restaurant in the city – the "Letzte Instanz" at Waisenstrasse 14 – and the ruins of a monastery are all reminders of the old Berlin. What was a originally a ford across the Spree some 800 years ago is today a busy main road, and the area of Nikolaiviertel is one of central Berlin's main tourist attractions. There was almost nothing left after World War II, but now you will find a little of historic Berlin here once more, with many original bars and restaurants, and souvenir outlets. The municipal authorities of East Berlin had this traditional, historic area rebuilt in 1987 on the city's 750th anniversary: authentic old houses were transported to the site to sit alongside replicas of old gabled buildings. The result is a charming and attractive district that is perfect for an evening stroll.

THE HIGHLIGHTS: BERLIN'S HISTORICAL HEART

Berlin's town hall gets its name from its red brick walls. The Fernsehturm (Television Tower) and the 94-m (308-foot) high town hall tower both soar skyward (right). The square in front of the town hall contains the Fountain of Neptune, created by Reinhold Begas in 1891 (inset below).

TIP Ephraim's

A restaurant dating from the 1870s with a particularly beautiful library and a large terrace on the banks of the Spree. It serves down-to-earth German food.

Spreeufer 1; Tel (030) 24 72 59 47; from 11.00, daily; U-/S-Bahn Alexanderplatz.

ROTES RATHAUS 15

Fifty-eight years after the autonomous government of Berlin was abolished, the Rotes Rathaus (red town hall) in the heart of the city was finally returned to its original function, when, in 1991, the administration for the newly unified city moved in. When first erected, this attractive red brick building was a symbol of the self-assurance of Berlin's citizens. William I was present at the laying of the foundation stone. Built between 1860 and 1869 by Hermann Friedrich Waesemann, in the style of the Italian high Renaissance, the façade is decorated with the "Stone Chronicle", a frieze made of 36 terracotta tablets, depicting the history of the city since its foundation in the 13th century. Allegorical figures in the stairway represent shipping, agriculture, fishing, and commerce. The arms of all the Berlin districts decorate the windows of the Wappensaal (the heraldic hall).

THE HIGHLIGHTS: BERLIN'S HISTORICAL HEART

Striking, even when seen from a distance, the Fernsehturm (Television Tower) is brought into focus through the model of the solar system atop the world time clock in Alexanderplatz (below, left). Marx and Engels enjoy a permanent view of it (below, right). The large square is skirted by Karl-Liebknecht-Strasse (right).

TIP Telecafé in the Fernsehturm

You can admire the Berlin panorama here over coffee, cakes, and snacks. The café takes half an hour to make a complete 360-degree rotation.

Panoramastr. 1a; Tel (030) 242 33 33; 9.00–24.00, daily; U-/S-Bahn Alexanderplatz.

MARX-ENGELS FORUM 16
ALEXANDERPLATZ 17

The historical heart of Berlin is a complex maze of streets, squares, and monuments – from the Tiergarten to the Fernsehturm. To the south-west the Marx-Engels Forum extends to the Spree; to the north-east is the adjoining Alexanderplatz. Since 1986, a larger-than-life Engels has been standing next to a seated Marx, surrounded by metal slabs documenting the history of the class struggle. Where there was once a maze of alleys surrounding the Marienkirche, founded in 1270, the 368-m (1207-foot) high Fernsehturm now soars proudly upward. You can be "beamed up" to the viewing platform in just 40 seconds. The former cattle market by the Oderberger Tor was renamed Alexanderplatz in 1805 after the Russian tsar Alexander I. Few of the original buildings were left standing after World War II, and the new buildings form an uneven perimeter. Plans for high-rise buildings have disappeared into the backs of drawers.

THE HIGHLIGHTS: BERLIN'S HISTORICAL HEART

The eye-catching façade of the Hackesche Höfe has been renovated and the area now attracts visitors day and night: architect and designer August Endell wanted to show "the beauty of the large city". The courtyards of the Hackesche Höfe are an ideal place in which to shop or to pause for coffee amid quirky surroundings.

TIP Ampelmann Laden

DDR traffic-light men are still cult figures, years after the collapse of communism. The droll red and green figures can be found on T-shirts, vases, lamps, bags and umbrellas.

Hackesche Höfe V; Tel (030) 44 04 88 01; Mon–Sat 10.00–22.00, Sun 11.00–19.00; S-Bahn Hackescher Markt.

There is little to see from the outside, but enter Rosenthaler Strasse 40/41 and you'll find yourself in a network of spectacular art nouveau courtyards known collectively as the Hackesche Höfe. Golden, blue, and green glazed tiles, fired in a historic kiln and arranged in dynamic patterns, tall windows, and sweeping rooflines attract people to the Höfe like a magnet. The avant-garde artist and architect August Endell, who designed the first courtyard in 1906, wanted to juxtapose the Wilhelminische style of the time with something new; he came up with an enchanting design that became an architectural sensation at the start of the 20th century. With these eight courtyards, the original architect Kurt Berndt created the largest linked residential and building complex in Europe. Berlin's economy was flourishing, land prices were increasing, and these residential and commercial courtyards made optimum use of space.

The foundation stone for rebuilding the destroyed synagogue was laid in 1988, and the Jewish community celebrated its official opening on 7 May 1995. From outside, the building looks just as it did in the 19th century, and the gilded dome again shines in the sun.

TIP Tacheles

The remains of a former department store arcade built between 1907 and 1909 have housed an artists' collective since 1990, with studios, exhibitions, and live performance art.

Oranienburger Str. 54–56; Tel (030) 282 61 85; U-Bahn Oranienburger Tor.

NEUE SYNAGOGE 19

Golden domes dominate the skyline above Berlin's heart. Eduard Knobloch started the construction of the synagogue, inspired by the Alhambra in Spain, in 1859, and the building was completed by Schinkel's pupil August Stüler. When it opened in 1866, the Neue Synagoge was a self-confident expression of an established Jewish citizenry: organ music, a mixed choir, and prayers in German were part of the process of reform within the community. In September 1930, Albert Einstein played concerts of Bach and Handel here. A brave policeman managed to protect this Moorish-style masterpiece from Hitler's storm troopers on 9 November 1938, but in 1943 British bombers reduced it to ruins. Today, the Jewish community welcomes people to its Centrum Judaicum. An exhibition allows visitors an insight into daily Jewish life before the war and delivers an impression of the former vibrancy of this district.

THE HIGHLIGHTS

NEW CENTRAL AREA, GOVERNMENT DISTRICT, TIERGARTEN, POTSDAMER PLATZ

Reduced to ruins in World War II, for many years. Potsdamer Platz, which had been so lively and bustling in the 1920s, was left to rot during the Cold War – a grey no man's land bisected by the Berlin Wall. When the Wall finally fell, investors arrived, and the square became busy once more, this time as construction site. Today, Potsdamer Platz has come back to life with a vengeance. A modern district full of architectural surprises has now arisen from the largest inner-city building site in the Western world. A short walk through the Tiergarten will bring you to the brand new parliamentary buildings. The area now attracts thousands of visitors throughout the year who come to see the striking Reichstag dome and the Holocaust Memorial, or to visit its restaurants, shops, and cinemas. Potsdamer Platz has become a vibrant symbol of the new Berlin.

The Reichstag is a monumental structure with a turbulent history (below and right). Insets below, from top: In 1888, the Reichstag was opened by the emperor; a photograph taken in 1894; on 2 May 1945, soldiers of the Red Army raised the Soviet flag over the Reichstag.

INFO The Reichstag dome

One of the biggest attractions in Berlin, so expect long waiting times. You can watch a plenary sitting of the Bundestag from the public gallery.

Platz der Republik; Tel (030) 22 73 21 52; 8.00–24.00, daily; S-Bahn Unter den Linden.

There's no shortage of signposts pointing to the Reichstag, the building where the Bundestag, the modern German parliament meets. Designed by architect Paul Wallot, and built between 1884 and 1894, it was supposed to symbolize the size and strength of parliament. Emperor William II considered it "the height of poor taste". The inscription *Dem deutschen Volke* (To the German people) was added in 1916. The Reichstag was set on fire in 1933 and further damaged in World War II; it was reconstructed in the early 1960s and used as a conference venue. In 1995, Christo and his wife Jeanne-Claude banished the ghosts of the past by wrapping the building in silver fabric before an environmentally and architecturally innovative parliamentary building designed by Sir Norman Foster was constructed behind the historic façade. Initially the most controversial feature was the glass dome – it's now a Berlin landmark.

From morning to midnight, almost every day, you can visit the roof and dome of the Reichstag building, but get here early if you don't want to wait in line. The British architect Sir Norman Foster has made an eyecatching addition to the skyline of Berlin with this ultra-modern dome on top of the old façade.

NORMAN FOSTER'S DOME

The large glass dome of the Reichstag building rises majestically 23.5 m (77 feet) above the roof, with a diameter of some 40 m (131 feet). Take one of the double-helix ramps, each 230 m (753 feet) long, up to the observation platform; you'll hardly notice the steady eight-degree gradient. At the base of the dome, you'll come across information about the building. The glass dome is crucial to both lighting and ventilation in the parliamentary chamber below. The giant central mirror-covered hub is the ventilation system: stale air is drawn upward, as if through a funnel, due to thermal lift, and escapes at the highest point of the dome. The 360 mirrors reflect daylight down into the chamber. An ingenious computer-controlled system ensures that the sun does not dazzle the representatives. The glass panes of the dome, 3,000 sq m (32,291 sq feet) in total, overlap each other like scales. They gradually become more opaque as dust and dirt build up, and when the window cleaners do their job, which takes a couple of days, you are not allowed onto the roof, although visitors can still use the roof terrace restaurant. From the roof terrace, you can see the new government buildings and the Kanzleramt (Chancellor's Office) in the bend of the Spree. The dome and its spectacular views attract thousands of visitors each year. The queues can be long, so be prepared to wait.

The dome optimizes daylight for the delegates (right). A glistening aluminium eagle dominates the chamber (inset, below). The main work of the delegates takes place in Paul-Löbe-Haus, beside the River Spree (below).

DEUTSCHER BUNDESTAG

On 20 June 1991, the German parliament voted to move the seat of the Bundestag – the lower house – to Berlin. It was a closely fought decision, but was passed with a majority of 18 votes. Eight years later, on 19 April 1999, the first sitting of the elected representatives for the whole of Germany took place in the Reichstag building. At the beginning of the 1990s the building was in a sorry state. The German government held an international competition for designs to rebuild the Reichstag, but it was renowned British architect Sir Norman Foster who impressed with his plans and environmental strategy, and he was commissioned to design a new building in the old shell. Workers removed some 45,000 tonnes (49,604 US tons) of rubble from the interior until just the external walls and a few supporting walls remained. Inscriptions by the Red Army from May 1945 were uncovered during the work and some were retained to add to the sense of history. The crowning glory of the building is Foster's 1,200-sq-m (12,916-sq-foot) glass dome, three floors high, which floods the building with natural light. A large sun shield tracks the movement of the sun electronically. The view from the dome out over Berlin is impressive, particularly at night. Twelve narrow, 22-m (72-foot) high columns support the dome. As in the original Reichstag, the delegates sit looking east.

THE HIGHLIGHTS: NEW CENTRAL AREA

The German Chancellery is large (some say too large), prestigious, and modern (below). Well-known artists created the gallery of portraits of former chancellors (insets below, from left): Konrad Adenauer; Ludwig Erhard; Kurt Georg Kiesinger; Willy Brandt; Helmut Schmidt; Helmut Kohl; and Gerhard Schröder.

TIP Habel Weinkultur

An elegant restaurant with a terrace, wine cellar, and wine shop. The food is a mix of German and Mediterranean cuisine. Top-class breakfast buffet and business lunches.

Luisenstr. 19; Tel (030) 28 09 84 84; 7.00–22.30, daily; S-Bahn Unter den Linden.

Critics call the Bundeskanzleramt (Chancellor's Office) the "washing machine": Axel Schulte's and Charlotte Frank's cube on the River Spree, the Bundeskanzleramt, is the office of the head of the German Federal government. Its 55-m (180-foot) long sides are flanked by five-floor wings containing 300 offices. The German Chancellery moved to its new premises at Willy-Brandt-Strasse 1 in 2001. It took three and a half years to build, and cost 465 million Deutschmarks – to the horror of many Berliners, some of whom can be seen watching the events from behind the fence when state guests are received. A substantial part of the foyer can be seen through the glass wall, and a broad stairway guarantees a grand entrance that makes a perfect photo opportunity. The Chancellor's Office itself occupies 145 sq m (1,560 sq feet) and is protected behind 8-cm (3-inch) thick bulletproof glass windows, and enjoys the finest views of Berlin.

THE HIGHLIGHTS: NEW CENTRAL AREA

The Lehrter Bahnhof – the terminus of the rail link between Berlin and Lehrte, near Hanover – opened here in 1871. Today, there is no trace of the old Wilhelminische-style station. The upper hall of Berlin's youngest architectural highlight is a dazzling composition of glass and light.

TIP Hopfingerbräu Berlin

Beer from the most northerly Weissbier (wheat beer) brewery in Germany. And if you like sausages with your beer, you can try Berlin Currywurst and Munich Weisswurst here.

In the Hauptbahnhof; Tel (030) 20 62 46 24; April–Oct 9.00–22.30, daily; Nov–March 11.00–22.30, daily; S-Bahn Hauptbahnhof.

HAUPTBAHNHOF (LEHRTER BAHNHOF) 22

This breathtaking station opened on 28 May 2006: it is the largest rail junction in Europe and has Europe's largest photovoltaic system integrated into its roof, comprising 78,000 solar cells. Designed by architect Meinhard von Gerkan, the station can also boast 1,200 loudspeakers, 203 video cameras, six panoramic elevators, 43 conventional elevators, and 54 escalators. The Hauptbahnhof covers several levels, with the S-Bahn at level 2 rising 25 m (82 feet) above the platform for departures to Munich on level -2. The curved roof of the upper hall is made of 8,000 panes of glass. More than 85 km (52 miles) of steel cable provide stability. The construction teams faced many technical challenges, and the total cost is said to have been around 700 million Euros. Opened on 26 May 2006 by German Chancellor Angela Merkel, Berlin finally has an impressive connection for its east–west and north–south rail lines.

THE HIGHLIGHTS: NEW CENTRAL AREA

Every day, as many as 10,000 people come to walk among the thousands of stone slabs that make up the Holocaust Memorial. They vary in height, from 20 cm (8 inches) to almost 5 m (16 feet). In the information area, visitors come face to face with some of the millions of victims (inset, below).

INFO Information Point

The memorial itself is always open. The underground information area contains photos and personal documents of the victims.

Cora-Berliner-Str. 1; Tel (030) 200 76 60; Tues–Sun 10.00–20.00, Oct–Mar to 19.00; S-Bahn Unter den Linden.

HOLOCAUST MEMORIAL 23

Still a subject of controversy, the Holocaust Memorial (Holocaust-Mahnmal) consists of a field of 2,711 concrete slabs of various heights, laid out in a grid pattern, open day and night. Visitors to the Memorial to the Murdered Jews of Europe (the memorial's official name) have to find their own way in and out, examining their thoughts and feelings in the unsettling atmosphere of this field of stones. There are no names or dates on architect Peter Eisenman's memorial. In the underground information area, you can learn more about the Holocaust victims, and the concentration and extermination camps where they died. Visitors are confronted with the faces and life stories of Jewish men and women during the period of persecution. In the Family Room, you can find out about the different ways of life of European Jews before the Holocaust, and in the Room of Names, the names and brief biographies of murdered Jews are read out.

THE HIGHLIGHTS: NEW CENTRAL AREA

The Strasse des 17 Juni and the Siegessäule are the focus of Berlin's Love Parade music festival (below) and New Year's Eve celebrations. However, the Tiergarten is primarily a place of relaxation, with statues, bridges, and quiet corners. Friedrich Drake's "Goldelse" (the Berliners' name for the statue of Victory) crowns the Victory Column (right).

TIP Café am Neuen See

This café serves Weissbier (wheat beer) that will quench any thirst and tasty pretzels under the chestnut trees. It has a great view of the lake, where you can hire boats.

Lichtensteinallee 2; Tel (030) 254 49 30; from 10.00, daily (Sat/Sun only in winter); U-Bahn Zoologischer Garten.

TIERGARTEN 24
VICTORY COLUMN, STRASSE DES 17 JUNI 25

The Tiergarten park, 3 km wide and 1 km long (1.8 x 0.6 miles), starts at the Brandenburg Gate. It provides some welcome greenery in the city, and includes a lake, the Neuer See. In 2006 it gained an additional 45,000 sq m (484,375 sq feet) after the north–south relief road was replaced by the Tiergartentunnel. Until the 16th century, the area was an hunting ground for the prince-electors. In the 18th century, Frederick the Great had it laid out as a pleasure garden, with walks, statues, and mazes. The Strasse des 17 Juni is a major road through the park, running east from the Brandenburg Gate. It is interrupted by a traffic circle called the Grosse Stern (Big Star), in the middle of which is the Siegessäule, or Victory Column. The 8-m (26-foot) high Victoria on top of the column, nicknamed "Goldelse", commemorates Prussian victories in the 19th century. A spiral staircase inside the column takes you up to a viewing platform just below the statue.

THE HIGHLIGHTS: NEW CENTRAL AREA

Situated in the Schlosspark Bellevue, in the northern part of the Tiergarten, close to the river, the German president hosts state receptions at the Schloss Bellevue. Inside, the furnishings are surprisingly modern, complemented by abstract art (right).

INFO Schloss Bellevue

No longer a royal castle, but still a fitting palace for the ruler of Germany; the raised flag indicates when the president is in residence.

Spreeweg 1; not open to the public; S-Bahn Bellevue.

SCHLOSS BELLEVUE 26

This gleaming white castle was the first neoclassical structure in Prussia, built in 1785–86. It has had a varied history; since 1994 it has been the official residence of the German president. It was designed by Michael Philipp Daniel Bouman as a summer residence for Prince August Ferdinand of Prussia, the youngest brother of Frederick the Great. Emperor William II used it for consultations with his Supreme Command. In 1928, Bellevue became state property and in 1935 it was converted into a German folklore museum. It underwent further changes in 1938 when it was used as guest accommodation for the government of the Third Reich. When Bonn became the Federal capital in 1949, the castle was refurbished and became the residence of the Federal president; the fittings of that time were ridiculed and described as "Empire 1959". The most recent 2004–05 refurbishment is in better taste – to the delight of its VIP guests.

Not just pieces of modern art, but shafts that allow daylight to penetrate down into Potsdamer Platz station from the street above. Inset, below: In the foreground, the Beisheim Center with the Ritz-Carlton Hotel; on the left is the red Kollhoff-Haus and on the right the curving Sony Center.

TIP Diekmann in Weinhaus Huth

A first-class Franco-German restaurant with a large outdoor terrace, within a unique historic building in Potsdamer Platz.

Alte Potsdamer Str. 5; Tel (030) 25 29 75 24; 12.00–1.00, daily; U-/S-Bahn Potsdamer Platz.

Even though Platz means "square", this has been far more than just a square for many years. It is a brand new district with luxury apartments, offices, hotels, shops, cinemas, and restaurants in the former border area between East and West Berlin. In the 1990s, the largest European inner-city construction site attracted onlookers from around the world, but the buildings designed by internationally renowned architects are now reaching for the sky. Renzo Piano, Richard Rogers, Arata Isozaki, Hans Kollhoff, Helmut Jahn, and Giorgio Grassi have created a 21st-century urban development, which has been both admired and criticized. The foundation stone was laid in October 1994, and Daniel Barenboim directed "dancing cranes" for the topping-out ceremony in 1996. By 1998, ten streets had been constructed and 17 buildings completed. In December 2000, the red Infobox exhibition was broken up into sections and auctioned off.

THE HIGHLIGHTS: NEW CENTRAL AREA

The first impression of the Sony Center is overwhelming. The tentlike roof is illuminated at night in a series of changing hues. Inside, you can immerse yourself in the world of illusion in one of the cinemas or the Film Museum.

TIP Billy Wilder's

A chic bar with a great selection of 85 vodkas and more than 120 different cocktails. If you don't know where to start, try the cocktail of the month.

Potsdamer Str. 2; Tel. (030) 26 55 48 60; 12.00–2.00, daily; U-/S-Bahn Potsdamer Platz.

SONY CENTER 28

Top architect Helmut Jahn created his glass and steel complex of seven buildings around a central plaza, The Center is home to cinemas, restaurants, cafés, and offices. Its sweeping roof resembles a circus tent, and is supported by a ring beam and steel cables and covered with lengths of self-cleaning fabric. Thanks to the glass roof, there is a constant change of images and effects as the light alters throughout the day and it is spectacularly illuminated at night. The Kaisersaal and the Frühstückssaal, two listed rooms, dating from 1911 and belonging to the former luxury hotel Esplanade which stood on the site, were the subject of a second feat of engineering: in 1996 the 1,300-tonne (1,433-US ton) Kaisersaal was moved 75 m (246 feet) on cushions of air – at a speed of 5 m (16 feet) per minute and is now integrated into the Center. To protect this piece of architectural history, the apartments above it are supported on a bridge-like structure.

To open the film festival, every year the Musical Theater in Potsdamer Platz is transformed into the Berlinale Palast. Inset, below: Richard Gere, Catherine Zeta-Jones, Renée Zellweger, Rob Marshall, and Jon C. Reilly were among the stars who appeared on the red carpet in 2003, watched by hundreds of eager photographers.

BERLIN FILM FESTIVAL

The 50th International Film Festival in Berlin in February 2000 was a very special occasion. The red carpet was unrolled for the first time in the brand new Potsdamer Platz, which had finally arisen from an urban wasteland. The recently opened Musical Theater became the main festival venue and all the stars who had previously avoided a dismal Berlin February turned out, and not just on the chance that they would take home a Berlinale Bear, the famous 4-kg (9-lb) trophy designed by the sculptor Renée Sintenis. This was a new start. Fourteen years previously, Wim Wenders had chosen this location for his moving film *Wings of Desire*, in which the 86-year old Curt Bois had called out in the devastated former square: "Ich kann den Potsdamer Platz nicht finden..." (I can't find Potsdamer Platz...).

The IFB (Internationale Filmfestspiele Berlin), which became known as the Berlinale, was the brainchild of cabaret artist Tatjana Sais, who was a member of the first jury, in 1951. The Allies' cultural officers were keen to promote the new event in the impoverished postwar city. The first festival was a somewhat synthetic affair, with films and filmstars flown in to boost the morale of the public, hungry for a little glamour. In 1957 the newly built Zoo Palast cinema became the main venue for the Berlinale, which eventually became a competitor to the Venice and Cannes Film Festivals.

THE HIGHLIGHTS: NEW CENTRAL AREA

The Philharmonie concert hall (right) is a beacon in the otherwise unspectacular Kulturforum. Acoustic "sails" suspended over the auditorium (below) help create a unique sound. The Gemäldegalerie has an unprepossessing exterior but a well laid-out exhibition space (inset, below).

TIP Cafeteria in the Gemäldegalerie

If you're hungry or thirsty after a surfeit of culture, this is a convenient place for a short break. Light meals, pizzas, and salads are all available.

Matthäikirchplatz 8; Tel (030) 266 29 51; 10.00–18.00, daily; U-/S-Bahn Potsdamer Platz.

The Kulturforum is the area near Potsdamer Platz where a number of Berlin's cultural institutions are concentrated, including the Museum of Decorative Arts, the Museum of Prints and Drawings, and the Museum of Musical Instruments. The Gemäldegalerie contains an important collection of European paintings, with works by old masters such as Dürer, Raphael, Titian, and Rembrandt. Equally unmissable, the Neue Nationalgalerie (New National Gallery), designed by Mies van der Rohe in 1962, houses 20th-century painting and sculpture by artists from Picasso to Frank Stella. The Philharmonie, built by Hans Scharoun between 1960 and 1963, and the nearby Kammermusiksaal (Chamber Music Hall), based on designs by Scharoun and built in the 1980s, are striking. The Philharmonie auditorium has acoustic "sails" that contribute to the incomparable sound of the Berlin Philharmonic Orchestra, currently directed by Sir Simon Rattle.

Aspects of modern art: Henry Moore's *Archer* in front of Mies van der Rohe's Neue Nationalgalerie (below). A Picasso exhibition and other work in the Berlinische Galerie (insets, below). Right: A light installation makes the Hamburger Bahnhof glow from within at night.

BERLIN'S MODERN ART MUSEUMS

After reunification, combining the modern art collections from both East and West Germany under one roof proved no easy task since the national galleries of West Germany had collected European and international art, while those of East Germany had concentrated on art from the DDR. Combining the two collections in the Neue Nationalgalerie, housed in a glass and steel building designed by architect Mies van der Rohe, inevitably caused controversy and led to an examination of value judgments. A rift in the collection of works up to the 1970s is still evident, and the loss of 20th-century works rejected by the Nazi regime has been only partly rectified. However, highlights of some of the 20th-century paintings and sculptures now on display include works by the critical realists Otto Dix and George Grosz, as well as examples of Cubist, Expressionist, and Surrealist art. The Hamburger Bahnhof, a converted station, houses the Museum für Gegenwart (Museum of Contemporary Art), with works by Joseph Beuys, Anselm Kiefer, Andy Warhol, and many others; the Friedrich Christian Flick Collection is in an adjoining building. The Berggruen Museum in the Stüler building near Charlottenburg Palace is devoted primarily to Picasso and his contemporaries, while the Berlinische Galerie in Kreuzberg focuses on modern art originating from Berlin.

THE HIGHLIGHTS

CHARLOTTENBURG, WILMERSDORF

With the Kurfürstendamm and such well-known sights as Schloss Charlottenburg, the zoo, exhibition grounds, and the Olympic stadium, this part of Berlin is regarded as the epitome of its middle-class West and its second central district. Though the side streets of Charlottenburg boast some fine buildings, Wilmersdorf is the more affluent area. It is home to a fairly conservative group of people – known by Berliners as the "Wilmersdorfer widows" – who were affectionately satirized in the long-running cult musical *Linie 1*. After reunification, the historic central district (see p. 30–71) became the heart of the city, but these western areas still have plenty to offer.

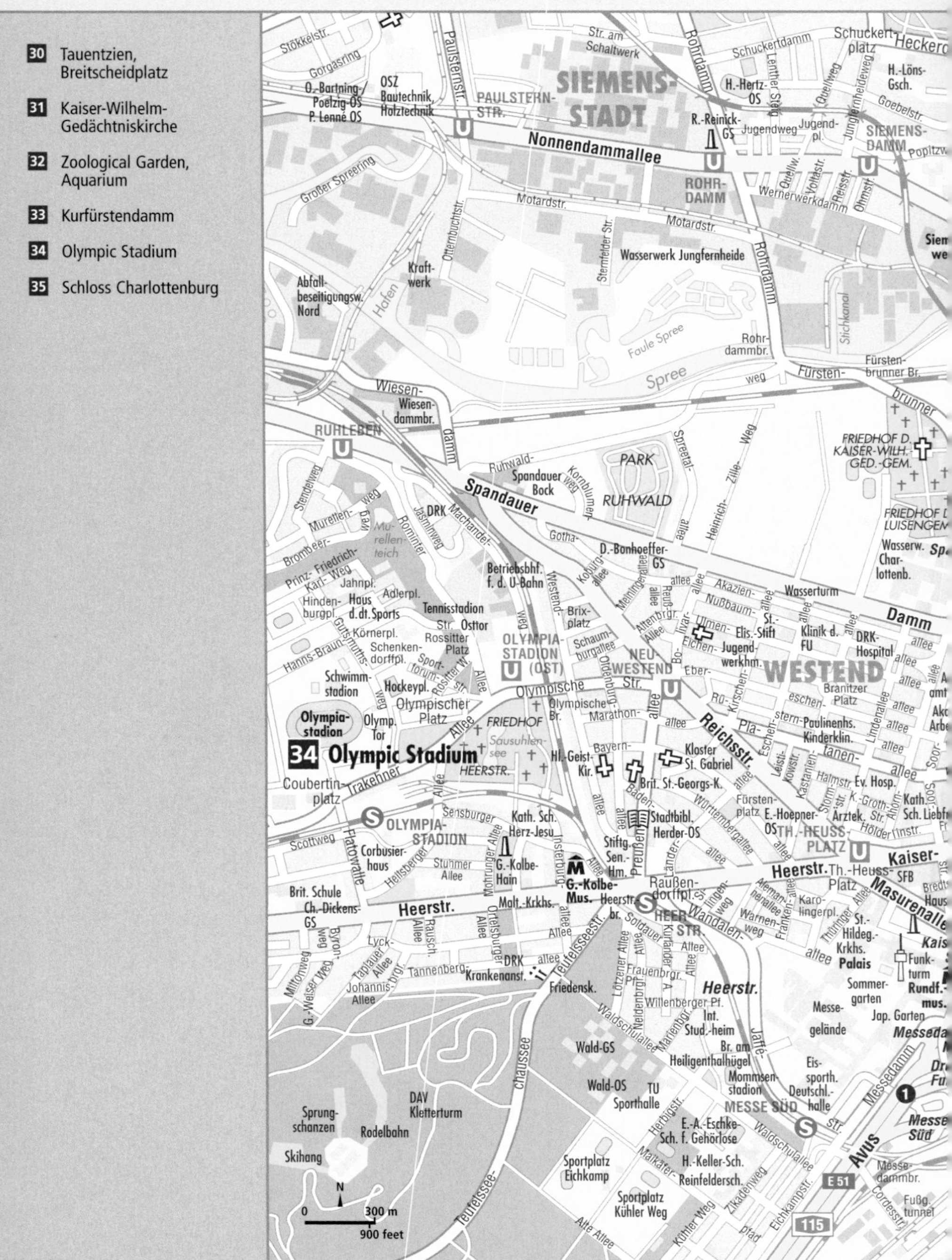
30 Tauentzien, Breitscheidplatz
31 Kaiser-Wilhelm-Gedächtniskirche
32 Zoological Garden, Aquarium
33 Kurfürstendamm
34 Olympic Stadium
35 Schloss Charlottenburg
SIEMENSSTADT
Nonnendammallee
Paulsternstr.
Rohrdamm
Motardstr.
Wasserwerk Jungfernheide
Spree
Ruhleben
Spandauer Damm
Park Ruhwald
Westend
Olympia-Stadion (Ost)
Olympischer Platz
Olympia-stadion
34 Olympic Stadium
Heerstr.
Reichsstr.
Theodor-Heuss-Platz
Kaiserdamm
Masurenallee
Funkturm
Messegelände
Messe Süd
Avus
Teufelsseechaussee
DAV Kletterturm
Rodelbahn
Sprungschanzen
Skihang
Sportplatz Eichkamp
0 300 m
900 feet

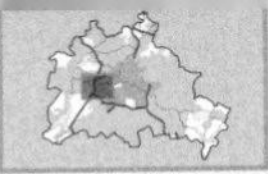

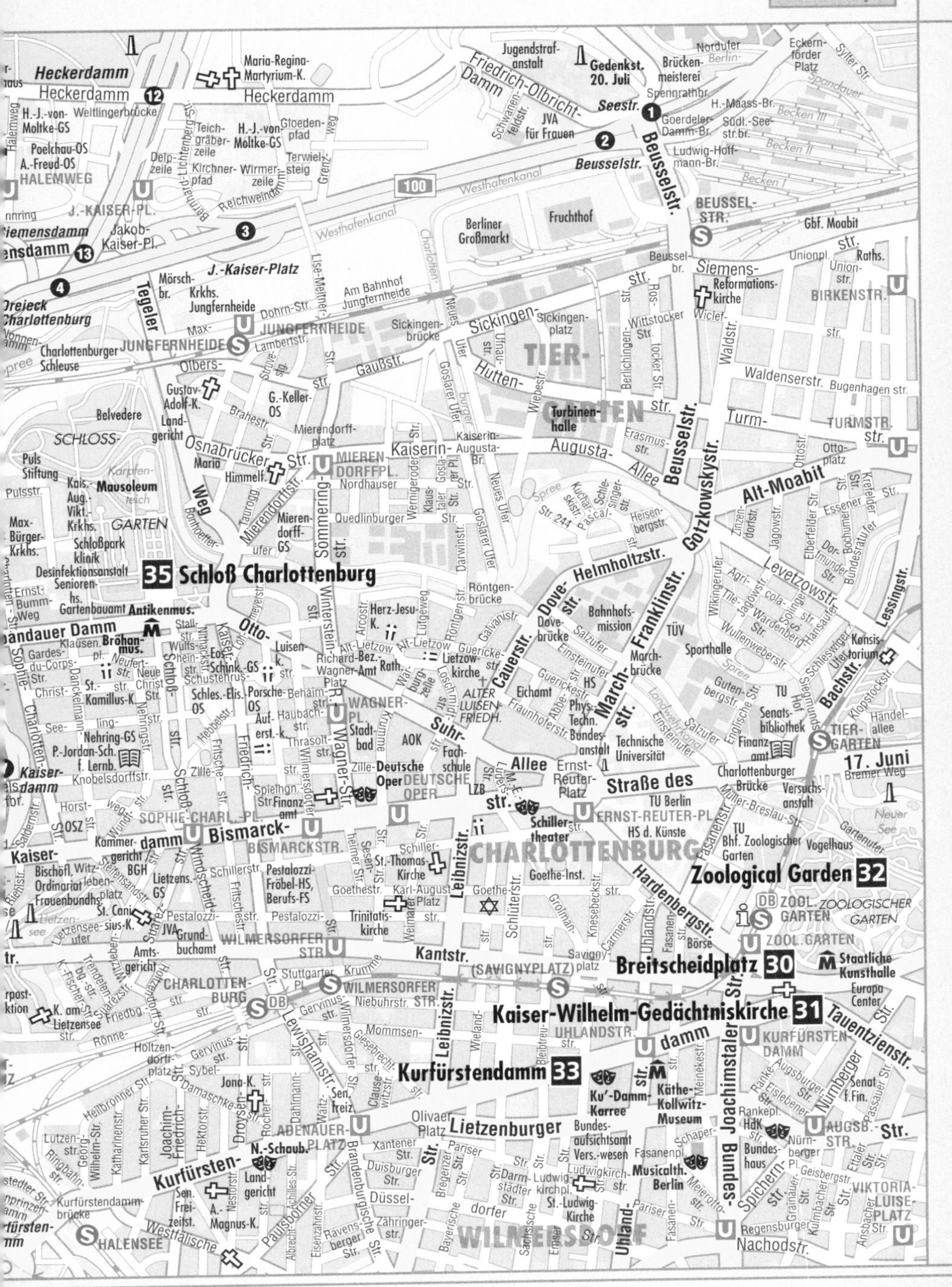
35 Schloß Charlottenburg
Zoological Garden 32
Breitscheidplatz 30
Kaiser-Wilhelm-Gedächtniskirche 31
Kurfürstendamm 33
Heckerdamm
Maria-Regina-Martyrium-K.
Jugendstrafanstalt
Gedenkst. 20. Juli
Friedrich-Olbricht-Damm
JVA für Frauen
Seestr.
Beusselstr.
Westhafenkanal
Berliner Großmarkt
Fruchthof
Gbf. Moabit
J.-Kaiser-Platz
Jakob-Kaiser-Pl.
Dreieck Charlottenburg
Tegeler Weg
Jungfernheide
Charlottenburger Schleuse
Krkhs. Jungfernheide
Sickingenstr.
Huttenstr.
Tiergarten
Turbinenhalle
Reformationskirche
Waldenserstr.
Turmstr.
Alt-Moabit
Kaiserin-Augusta-Allee
Mierendorffplatz
Belvedere
Schlossgarten
Mausoleum
Schloßpark Klinik
Landgericht
Gustav-Adolf-K.
Maria Himmelf.
Helmholtzstr.
Levetzowstr.
Franklinstr.
Gotzkowskystr.
Bahnhofsmission
Sporthalle
Antikenmus.
Bröhan-mus.
Spandauer Damm
Otto-Suhr-Allee
Richard-Wagner-Platz
Deutsche Oper
Technische Universität
Ernst-Reuter-Platz
Straße des 17. Juni
Charlottenburger Brücke
Schillertheater
Bismarckstr.
Sophie-Charl.-Pl.
Kaiserdamm
Charlottenburg
TU Berlin
HS d. Künste
Bhf. Zoologischer Garten
Vogelhaus
Goethe-Inst.
Zool. Garten
Staatliche Kunsthalle
Europa Center
Tauentzienstr.
Kantstr.
Savignyplatz
Wilmersdorfer Str.
Lietzensee
Amtsgericht
Adenauer-Platz
Lietzenburger Str.
Käthe-Kollwitz-Museum
Ku'-Damm-Karree
Musicalth. Berlin
Nürnberger Str.
Viktoria-Luise-Platz
Wilmersdorf
Halensee
Kurfürstendammbrücke
Nachodstr.
Bundesallee
Joachimstaler Str.
Uhlandstr.
Hardenbergstr.
Börse
Senat f.Fin.

THE HIGHLIGHTS: CHARLOTTENBURG WILMERSDORF

For the city's 750th anniversary in 1987, the Kurfürstendamm was transformed into an open-air art gallery. Brigitte and Martin Matschinsky-Denninghoff's steel tube sculpture, entitled *Berlin*, was left in place and still frames this view of the Kaiser-Wilhelm-Gedächtniskirche (below). The historic department store KaDeWe (inset, below).

TIP First Floor, Palace Hotel restaurant

The Palace Hotel has one of Berlin's top gourmet restaurants. It seats just 40 people, so make sure you have a reservation.

Budapester Str. 45; Tel (030) 25 02 10 20; Tues–Sat 12.00–15.00, 18.30–23.00; U-/S-Bahn Zoologischer Garten.

TAUENTZIEN, BREITSCHEIDPLATZ 30

The buildings may be new – mostly no more than 50 years old – but the spirit of the Golden Twenties lives on. To the west, the Kurfürstendamm looks almost Parisian, but the liveliest section of this famous street still lies at its eastern end, close to Breitscheidplatz, just as it did in the 1920s, before the area was devastated in World War II. Artists, musicians, and writers such as author Erich Kästner, playwright Bertolt Brecht, and film director Billy Wilder, would congregate in venues such as the Romanische Café. Russian poets in exile sang the praises of silks and satins, and easy girls. Russian writer Andrei Bely, who lived in Berlin at the start of the 1920s, summed up the atmosphere with the words "The Night! Tauentzien! Cocaine!". Years later, the area was the setting for *Wir Kinder vom Bahnhof Zoo* (*Children of Bahnhof Zoo*, also released as *Christiane F*, 1981), a film based on the true story of a young heroin addict in the 1970s.

The new church comprises four buildings grouped around the old church and its 19th-century entrance hall, while a separate hexagonal bell-tower now stands next to the old damaged tower. The chancel glows with deep-blue light, filtered through 33,000 glass bricks, produced in Chartres, France.

TIP Ranke 2

A genuine old Berlin bar with good, traditional food – knuckle of pork with sauerkraut, meatloaf, Königsberger Klöpse (meatballs), herring, etc. – and a warmhearted welcome.

Rankestr. 2; Tel (030) 883 34 48; 11.30–2.00, daily; U-/S-Bahn Zoologischer Garten.

KAISER-WILHELM-GEDÄCHTNISKIRCHE 31

"Everything passes" was the subject of the sermon in the Kaiser-Wilhelm-Gedächtniskirche at the eastern end of the Kurfürstendamm on 22 November 1943. It was the Sunday before Advent, when the dead are remembered in Germany. Shortly afterwards, bombs reduced the church to ruins, causing the damaged west tower, which lost most of its spire, to be henceforth known to Berliners as the "broken tooth". William II had the church built in 1895 to commemorate his grandfather and to form the highlight of the new area that was springing up in the west of the city. Intending the building to be a major landmark, he also wanted to counter the "radical tendencies of an anarchic and godless party" (the Social Democrats) by presenting a united front of both throne and church. Berliners did not have the heart to tear down the ruins, so in 1961 architect Egon Eiermann built a new church around the remains of the old one.

Berlin Zoo's architecture is a fascinating mix of old and new, but it is the animals who attract all the attention. Berliners love their zoo, and major events, such as the arrival of Giant Panda Bao Bao, always attract great attention. Polar bear and media star Knut, born here on 5 December 2006, is now a sturdy adult.

INFO Berlin Zoo and Aquarium

The oldest zoo in Germany has more species than any other zoo in the world. You can buy a combined ticket for the zoo and aquarium.

Hardenbergplatz 8 (Lion Gate) or Budapester Str. 32 (Elephant Gate); Tel (030) 25 40 10; Zoo 9.00–18.30, Aquarium 9.00–18.00; U-/S-Bahn Zoologischer Garten.

ZOOLOGICAL GARDEN, AQUARIUM 32

Newcomers to Berlin often wonder what the difference is between the Tierpark ("animal park") and the Tiergarten ("animal garden"). In fact there are two zoos in addition to the Tiergarten, which is actually a park. The Tierpark in Friedrichsfelde to the east is the biggest zoo, covering about 160 hectares (395 acres). However, the more famous zoo, second only to the Reichstag in terms of visitor numbers, is the Berlin Zoo in the Mitte district. Although it only covers 32 hectares (79 acres), it boasts more species than any other zoo in the world. The brainchild of naturalist Alexander von Humboldt and landscape architect Peter Joseph Lenné, it was opened in 1844 and was the first zoo in Germany. King Frederick William IV donated the first animals from the royal menagerie on the Pfaueninsel (Peacock Island). Today, the aquarium has more than 10,000 creatures: including sharks, jellyfish, amphibians, reptiles, and a coral lagoon.

After a shopping trip, relax and watch the world go by from a street café. The haute couture houses (right) are mostly based in the upper Ku'damm near Olivaer Platz, while many attractive smaller shops line the side streets. Ku'damm at night: a sea of lights (inset, below).

TIP Café Wintergarten in the Literaturhaus

An elegant café within the Berlin Literaturhaus. Sit on leather sofas and designer armchairs under ornamented ceilings, and enjoy fine, fresh bistro cuisine.

Fasanenstr. 23; Tel (030) 882 54 14; 9.30–1.00, daily; U-Bahn Uhlandstrasse.

The capital of the empire should have an impressive boulevard to equal the Champs Elysées – so decided Imperial Chancellor Otto von Bismarck upon his return from Paris after the Franco-Prussian War. Hence this magnificent avenue, 3.5 km (2 miles) long, 53 m (173 feet) wide, and lined with aristocratic residences, was developed from the original road that connected the city with the old hunting lodge in Grunewald. Many visitors never look up and so miss the imposing and often delightful, 19th-century buildings, their eyes instead glued to the shop windows with their displays of fine fabrics and fashions that change with the seasons. The Kurfürstendamm now has to compete for tourists with the rejuvenated old Mitte district, which provides strong competition, but the shoppers remain, and as far as they are concerned, the Ku'damm is still the best street in Berlin.

A timeless classic: Bertolt Brecht's *Mother Courage* is regularly performed in the city – here in a modern setting by the Berliner Ensemble (below). Far right, from top: The Berliner Volksbühne is one of the most exciting venues in Berlin; as are the Schaubühne on Lehniner Platz; and the Maxim Gorki Theater in Dorotheenstadt, the smallest of all Berlin's playhouses. Opulent revues (right) have been the trademark of the Friedrichstadtpalast since DDR times.

THE BERLIN THEATRICAL SCENE

How many drama venues are there in Berlin? Fifty? Or more? Nobody knows for sure. Many appear out of nowhere, and then disappear just as quickly. But one thing is for sure: a significant part of German theatrical history was – and will be – written in Berlin, so a visit to a theater is strongly recommended. Dramatists Gerhart Hauptmann, August Strindberg, Henrik Ibsen, and Bertolt Brecht all had major breakthroughs here. Directors such as Max Reinhardt, Erwin Piscator, and Gustaf Gründgens are well-known, and their successor Peter Stein is still causing controversy with his projects. The Berlin theatrical scene is impressive partly because it is so varied: there are German classics and modern standards, as well as plays by contemporary American, British, Russian, and French writers; highly experimental work coexists with old-fashioned whodunits, musicals, and popular drama. Additional impetus is provided by regular drama festivals, which bring together talent from Germany and around the world. The Grips Theater on Hansaplatz is famous for plays for children and young people: its most enduringly popular production, *Linie 1*, has been on the repertoire since 1986. It's an amusing but socially critical musical about a young woman who is searching the city for her friend, and who meets different Berlin characters on the U-Bahn. It is still playing to full houses.

THE HIGHLIGHTS: CHARLOTTENBURG WILMERSDORF

The transparent panels of the roof of Germany's largest stadium allow light through while protecting the spectators below. Two pillars mark the Olympische Tor to the east (inset, below). Great sporting events are often held here – including the International Stadium Festival (right) and the 2009 World Athletics Championships.

INFO Olympic Stadium

The stadium is open every day (apart from Sundays, public holidays, and scheduled event days), for individual viewing or guided tours (in German).

Olympischer Platz, visitor point at the eastern gate (Osttor); Tel (030) 25 00 23 22; U-/S-Bahn Olympiastadion.

OLYMPIC STADIUM 34

The distinctive oval shape of the Olympic stadium is based on ancient sporting arenas. Recently renovated, it succeeds in reconciling past with present – a new 21st-century stadium (the venue for the 2006 World Cup final; the World Athletics Championships will be held here in 2009) now stands on top of the old 1930s building (the 1936 Olympic Games were held here). Protected as a historic monument, 70 percent of the original structure was retained during the reconstruction. The stadium is also the home ground of Hertha BSC, one of Berlin's principal football clubs, whose blue home team strip is echoed in the blue athletics track surrounding the central pitch. To the west of the stadium, the Marathontor gateway gives a clear view of the Maifeld, the huge field used for dressage and polo matches, the stadium's bell-tower, and the Waldbühne, a vast outdoor venue for concerts and other events.

THE HIGHLIGHTS: CHARLOTTENBURG WILMERSDORF

Two warriors guard the entrance to the courtyard of Schloss Charlottenburg, with its equestrian statue of the Great Elector Frederick William (below). Inset, below: Memorial to Prince Albrecht of Prussia in Schloss-strasse. Right: lifesize statues representing the Muses.

TIP Trip on the Spree

Take a boat trip on the Spree through the middle of Berlin, from Charlottenburg palace through the government district and the historical heart to Alexanderplatz.

Departs from the Charlottenburg palace bridge; Tel (030) 342 24 31; April-Oct 10.00, 12.00 and 14.00; U-Bahn Richard-Wagner-Platz.

SCHLOSS CHARLOTTENBURG 35

This palace is the most important historic structure in western Berlin. It was built between 1695 and 1699 by Johann Arnold Nering as a royal summer residence. Originally named Lietzenburg, it was renamed Charlottenburg after the death of Queen Sophie Charlotte in 1705. Once Elector Friedrich III had been crowned King Frederick I of Prussia in 1701, he felt the baroque central building was not prestigious enough and began to extend the palace. A cupola tower was added to the orangery in 1713. Frederick the Great had new wings constructed, and in 1791 Frederick William II added a theater, which brought the total length of the palace to 505 m (1,656 feet). Schloss Charlottenburg was almost destroyed by bombing in 1943, but after many years of renovation work is now restored to its former glory and is open to the public. The ornately decorated, opulently furnished rooms contain fine works of art.

THE HIGHLIGHTS

PRENZLAUER BERG, FRIEDRICHSHAIN, KREUZBERG, TEMPELHOF

When Germans talk about Berlin, they often use the word *Kiez* – by which they mean a relatively small community with lots of style, warmth, local bars, and a distinctive mix of inhabitants. Berlin is famous for several such *Kieze*, and the most famous of all are the Prenzlauer Berg and Friedrichshain areas – traditionally working-class districts, but now trendy residential areas for well-heeled and alternative New Berliners. Much the same could be said of multicultural Kreuzberg, with all its problems and all its charm. One of the poorest areas in the city during the 1970s, it is now well known for its youth and alternative subcultures.

THE HIGHLIGHTS: PRENZLAUER BERG, FRIEDRICHSHAIN, KREUZBERG, TEMPELHOF

All kinds of cultural and artistic events are held at the Kulturbrauerei: The Theater RambaZamba (right) works with actors and artists with disabilities (inset, left), while all tastes in music are catered for, from hip hop and rock to world music; air guitar championships (inset, right).

INFO Kulturbrauerei

Culture for everyone, whether you love music or literature, dance or drama. A playground for creative types and their audiences.

Schönhauser Allee 36; Tel (030) 44 31 51; U-Bahn Eberswalder Strasse.

Built between 1890 and 1910, the Kulturbrauerei was once the headquarters of the Schultheiss brewery, and was in use as such until 1965. Then leather-clad Eastern rockers moved in, and the Franz-club, a famous East-German disco and music venue, opened in 1970, closing in 1997. The building was also listed as a historic monument. Soon after the end of the communist era, the complex became famous as the KulturBrauerei and the "threadbare space" (as one commentator described it) became hugely popular with the youth and alternative culture movements that were sweeping Berlin. The building was renovated and refurbished – out went workshops and studios and in came a cinema and bar. The venue has sufficient space to cater for all kinds of art, with stages for readings, dancefloors, a yoga studio, and the "Sonnenuhr" art and performance workshop where people with disabilities can work alongside artists, actors, and musicians.

Germany's largest synagogue in Rykestraße in the Prenzlauer Berg area. Insets below, scenes from 21st-century Jewish life, from left: dressed for a special occasion; men pray wearing the *tallit*, the traditional prayer shawl; a visit by the chief rabbi; a shop.

JEWISH LIFE

In 1933, there were 160,000 Jews living in Berlin. By 1939, half of these people had left the country. Fifty-five thousand Jews were subsequently removed during the Nazi regime, packed into cattle wagons at Grunewald station and transported to extermination camps, where they were murdered. In 1945, many of the 8,000 survivors waited in large detention camps for authorization to emigrate to Palestine or elsewhere. Berlin's oldest Jewish cemetery on the Grossen Hamburger Strasse had been destroyed, and Berlin's – and Europe's – largest Jewish cemetery in Weissensee needed major renovation. Today, Berlin's Jewish community numbers more than 12,000, but they still feel the loss of the spiritual and cultural leaders who enriched the prewar life of the city, among them the painters Max Liebermann and Lesser Ury, the philosophers Martin Buber, Ludwig Marcuse, and Walter Benjamin, the physicist Albert Einstein, the writers Kurt Tucholsky and Lion Feuchtwanger, and the publishers Samuel Fischer, Rudolf Mosse, and Leopold Ullstein. Happily, the number of Jewish institutions is increasing. The Central Council of Jews in Germany started work in Berlin in 1999, and there are now Jewish theaters, and museums that document everyday Jewish life and culture. The spectacular new Jüdisches Museum (see p. 136), opened in 2001, tells the story of two millennia of German-Jewish history.

THE HIGHLIGHTS: PRENZLAUER BERG, FRIEDRICHSHAIN, KREUZBERG, TEMPELHOF

Many a military parade marched along this avenue during the Cold War period: the 90-m (295-foot) wide Karl-Marx-Allee begins at Strausberger Platz. The workshops of Meissen were overwhelmed by the huge demand for ceramic tiles for the façades of many of the buildings lining the street.

TIP Ehrenburg Espresso Bar

A pleasant atmosphere, wonderful coffee, homemade cakes, a beautiful terrace, and friendly staff; ask if you can borrow the equipment for a game of boules.

Karl-Marx-Allee 103; Tel (030) 42 10 58 10; 10.00-2.00, daily; U-Bahn Weberwiese.

Work began on the broad avenue that was to be known as Stalinallee on 21 September 1949, the 70th birthday of the Soviet Union's dictator. The city planners wanted to give shape to the new socialist era, and naturally also demonstrate the superiority of socialism over Western capitalism. Construction of the luxurious apartments, shops and restaurants that were to line the avenue began to the sound of patriotic working songs. However, the grand scale of the building work in the so-called "wedding cake" style did not sit well with the workers and Stalinallee became the focus for the workers' uprising of 17 June 1953, which was quashed by Soviet tanks and troops. Broad and imposing, it was a fitting venue for East Germany's annual May Day Parade. Now renamed Karl-Marx-Allee, the 2.3-km (1.4-mile) long street is today protected as a historic monument.

In the autumn of 1990, 110 artists from 24 countries turned a piece of the Wall on the Eastern side of the Spree into an open-air gallery (inset below and right). Below: On 9 November, candles are lit at the memorial on Bernauer Strasse to commemorate the fall of the Wall.

THE WALL

During the night of 13 August 1961, East German border troops began building the "antifacist protective wall" encircling West Berlin, in order to stem the flow of people leaving the Eastern sector of the city. For 28 years, the Wall separated not only families but also two different worlds. In the euphoria after the fall of the Wall, this forbidding symbol of a divided city was knocked down, broken up, and pieces sold, given away, or crushed to form material for road building. The removal of the Wall was so complete that many visitors – and even Berliners themselves – wonder where it once stood. A cycle path now follows the route of the Wall and loops round part of the city for 155 km (96 miles). Berliners realized that some permanent memorials were needed, so isolated fragments have been preserved at different sites around the city – some parts of the Wall are also preserved in the USA. There are pieces at the Presidential Library in Simi Valley and at Chapman University, both in California. The awareness of everyday violence associated with the Wall has gone, but it lives on in the memories of Berliners and is hard to convey to outsiders. A concrete wall across the heart of a city, guarded by 300 watchtowers, a strip of permanently-lit wasteland, patrols, guard dogs, guns, tank traps, and a 100-m (328-foot) wide no-go area – the reality of Wall is hard to imagine now, yet several hundred defectors from the DDR died trying to cross it.

Thanks to new building development, many areas around the river are changing, with some sections undergoing a complete facelift. A riverside promenade between the Reichstag and Hauptbahnhof (below); the Trias building complex on the Michaelbrücke (inset, below); the Ministry of the Interior in the Moabit district (right).

ON THE SPREE

The River Spree, which rises in Mount Kottmar in Upper Lusatia in northern Germany, has been a useful transport route into the city for centuries and is still in use as such today – the construction sites at Potsdamer Platz and the new Hauptbahnhof were supplied with building material via the Spree. From the Weidendammer Brücke in the Mitte district, you can see the craft that ply the river, including barges for transport as well as countless passenger craft. A boat trip is a good way to explore Berlin from a different vantage point, as the city slips by quietly and peacefully. With a total of 180 km (111 miles) of river (the Spree and Havel) and canals, Berlin has more waterways than any other metropolis in Europe. Though houseboats do not exist officially, a small number of Berliners choose to live on the water, particularly in Charlottenburg and Treptow, where lines of laundry blow gently in the breeze along the banks on dry days. A number of industrial areas also line parts of the river, though once the first companies and embassies had discovered the attraction of the riverside, apartments began to appear alongside them and plans are now afoot to build floating homes. Restaurant boats rock gently in the water, and people can bathe once more in the Spree – but only in the "bathing ship", an old ship converted into a floating swimming pool (see p. 146).

Designed in the Renaissance style, the Martin-Gropius-Bau is one of the most attractive museum buildings in Germany (right). The Deutsches Technikmuseum traces the history of science and technology with exhibits such as the early Z5 computer built by computer pioneer Konrad Zuse (inset, below) and a ship's engine room (below). Right: a tugboat.

INFO Martin-Gropius-Bau

The interior provides a magnificent setting for first-class exhibitions inspired by global art history.

Niederkirchnerstr. 7/Stresemannstr. 110; Tel (030) 25 48 60; Wed–Mon 10.00–20.00; U-Bahn Potsdamer Platz.

MARTIN-GROPIUS-BAU 38
DEUTSCHES TECHNIKMUSEUM 39

Two of Berlin's finest museums are situated in Kreuzberg. The Martin-Gropius-Bau (Martin-Gropius Building), a neo-Renaissance style building by architect Martin Gropius, opened in 1881 as an arts and crafts museum and displays the work of craftsmen from around the world. The reliefs on the façade show blacksmiths, basket weavers, and glass blowers. Restored in 1978, the museum now hosts many international exhibitions. Opened in 1982, the Deutsches Technikmuseum (Museum of Technology) traces the cultural history of science and technology. Among its highlights are the world's first computer, vintage locomotives and aircraft, as well as exhibits of film technology, photography, engineering, navigation and shipping, printing, and telecommunications. Outside in the museum's park you can visit an old brewery, a blacksmith, and a windmill. The Spectrum Science Center has interactive, hands-on exhibits (see p.182).

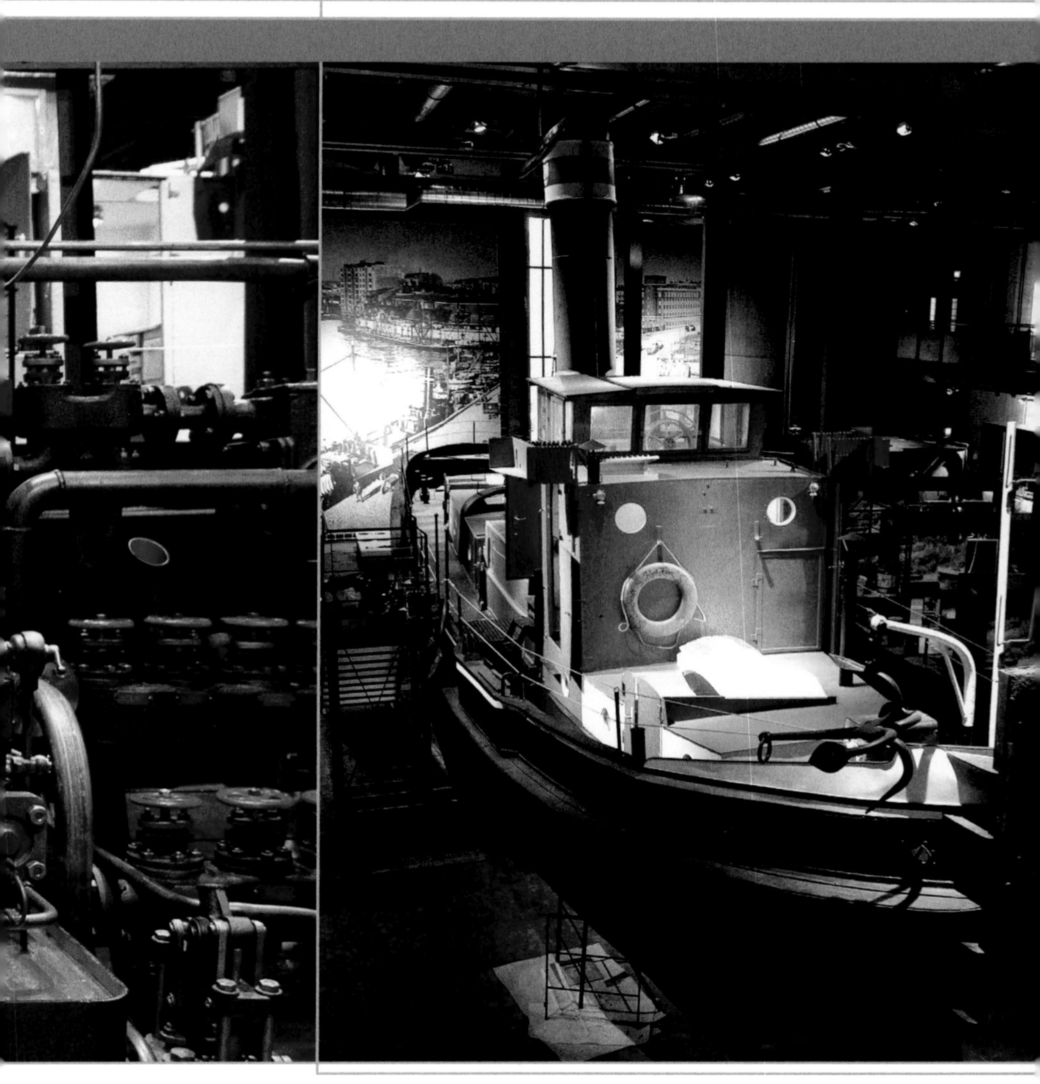

INFO Jüdisches Museum

The unusual architecture of this museum deliberately disorients the visitor with its strange, stark forms, reflecting the fate of the Jewish people. The Holocaust Tower and Garden of Exile (insets, below); light penetrates the building through slits in the walls (right); thought-provoking images and symbols from Jewish life throughout history (below).

A comprehensive permanent exhibition on German-Jewish history; there are always special exhibitions on political, artistic, and religious subjects.

Lindenstr. 9–14; Tel (030) 25 99 33 00; Mon 10.00–22.00, Tues–Sun 10.00–20.00; U-Bahn Hallesches Tor.

Even before it opened its doors, the Jewish Museum building was controversial: the design in the form of a shattered star of David certainly raised some eyebrows. The zinc skin of the building reflects the sun; slits are the only openings piercing the windowless walls, and there's no "proper" entrance. You enter the building, designed by Daniel Libeskind, through the old baroque building of the Supreme Court and then find yourself in a strangely moving space. Empty rooms, symbols of desolation, which the architect calls "voids", extend up through all the floors. Only the narrow slits let light into the building – perhaps suggesting vague rays of hope. The Holocaust Tower represents the darkness and emptiness of the war years. A garden, in which Russian olive trees grow on top of concrete pillars symbolizes hope. Some 2,000 years of German-Jewish history is presented here, from the time of the Romans to the present day.

Despite appearances, old traditions have not disappeared; Kreuzberg is the hub of a vibrant ethnic community. Turkish-owned businesses are flourishing and the market is thronged with people every day; the mosque also plays an important role in daily life (right).

TURKISH KREUZBERG

The largest Turkish community outside Turkey – about 200,000 Turks live in Berlin – is based on the far side of the Kottbusser Tor in Kreuzberg. Turkish banks, groceries, jewelers, clothing shops, bakeries, and coffee shops have the same Middle Eastern atmosphere as the market on the Maybachufer. This creates traffic chaos twice a week, when many local families shop for meat, peppers, spinach, almonds, fruit, cakes, and tea, as well as for clothing and goods for the home. There is a Turkish radio and television station and an agency for Turkish belly dancers. Until the end of the communist era, cheap apartments were still available here, not far from the Wall. Gastarbeiter ("guest workers") settled in the area, though seldom with the intention of staying for long. Between 1960 and 1970, their numbers grew from 225 to 39,000. Northern Kreuzberg, known as SO36 after the old code for the postal district, became a place to escape bourgeois Berlin, and has flourished to become a multicultural area. The legendary music club SO36 in Oranienstrasse still waves the flag for the underground music scene, people of all nationalities now meet in the Turkish baths, delicatessens sell Middle Eastern snacks, and you can puff away at a hookah in true bohemian fashion in the Orient Lounge of the Rote Harfe bar and restaurant, once a meeting place for Kreuzberger bohemians and dropouts.

THE HIGHLIGHTS: PRENZLAUER BERG, FRIEDRICHSHAIN, KREUZBERG, TEMPELHOF

Today, the echoing and empty arrival hall feels like a film backdrop. For former West Berliners, Tempelhof's significance is more emotional than economic. Now that the airport is closed to air traffic, plans are underway for the next stage in the life of the fourth largest building in the world.

INFO Tempelhof airport

The memorial in front of the airport, known as the "claw of hunger" is dedicated to the pilots of the Berlin airlift of 1948/49.

Badener Ring; Tel (01 80) 5 00 01 86; U-Bahn Platz der Luftbrücke.

In 2008, following much discussion and a referendum, it was decided that Tempelhof airport (Flughafen Tempelhof) had played its final part in the history of Berlin air transport. The last planes left just before midnight on 30 October 2008. One of Europe's major prewar airports, Tempelhof was to have formed the southern end of the north–south axis of "Germania", Hitler's grand vision for Berlin as a world capital city, but when the city was split up into occupied zones after the war, Tempelhof found itself in the American sector. An important episode in the airport's turbulent history that also helped contribute to its legend occurred in 1948, when it played a vital role during the Soviet Union's blockade of West Berlin by land. Western powers flew food, fuel, and essential goods into Berlin via Tempelhof. Berliners nicknamed the cargo aircraft that helped keep them alive "*Rosinenbombern*" (raisin bombers).

THE HIGHLIGHTS

AROUND BERLIN

Berlin is far from a desert of stone and steel – many Berliners live amid green spaces and, not far from the city, the surrounding forest and lakeland areas are easily accessible. Taking into account its open spaces and areas of water, a surprising 40 percent of the city remains undeveloped. Gardens large and small, in a variety of styles, from practical and urban to sophisticated and exotic, punctuate the inner city with areas of green. The city's woods, rivers, and lakes are popular destinations for days out. For West Berliners at least, when the Wall was in existence there was no alternative if they wanted to avoid long waiting times at the border.

42 Treptow, Friedrichsfelde

43 Schloss Glienicke, Glienicker Brücke

44 Grunewald

45 Wannsee

46 Pfaueninsel

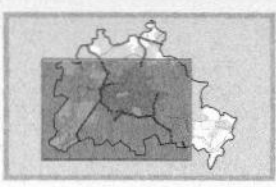

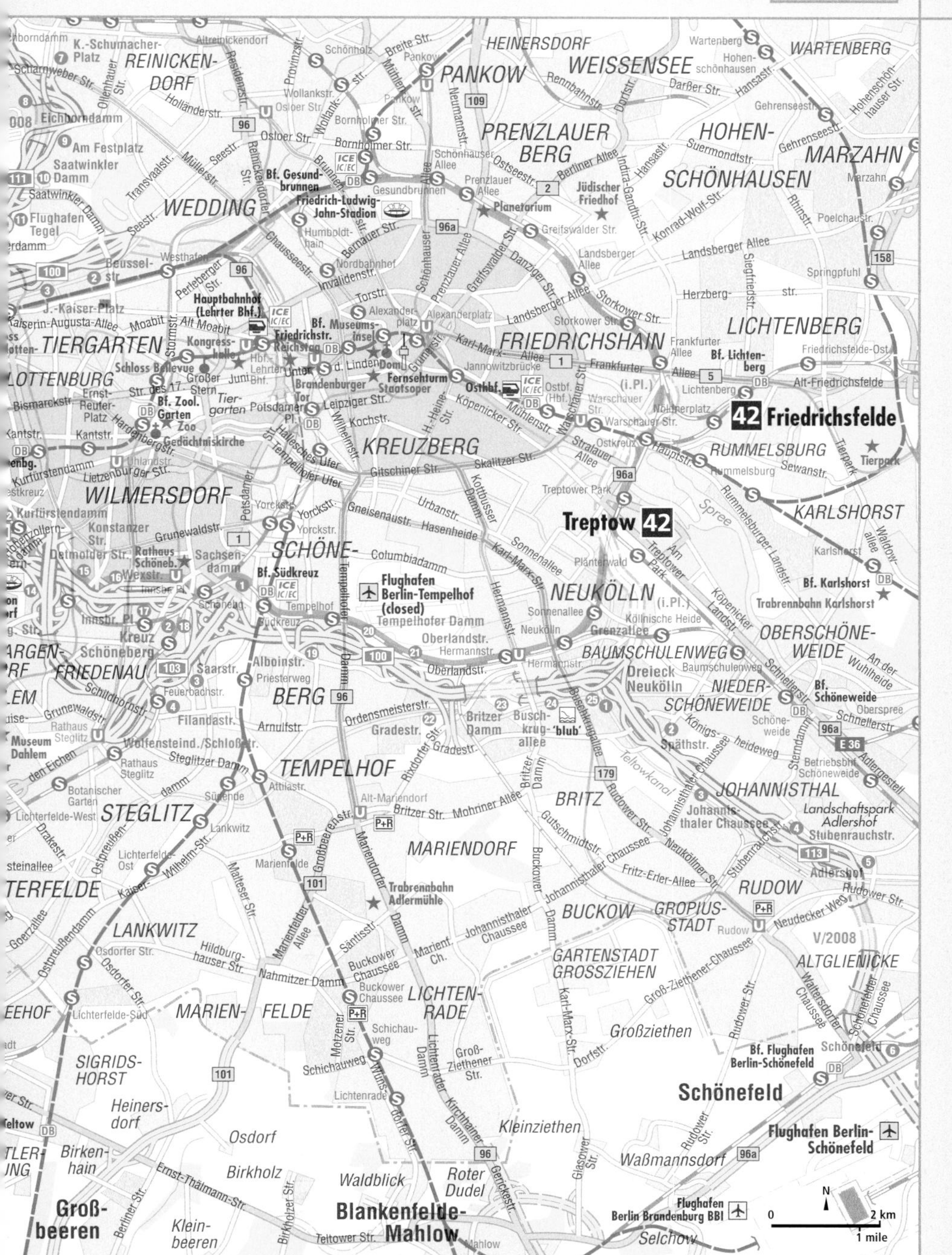

HEINERSDORF
WEISSENSEE
WARTENBERG
PANKOW
REINICKEN-
DORF
PRENZLAUER
BERG
HOHEN-
SCHÖNHAUSEN
MARZAHN
WEDDING
Bf. Gesund-
brunnen
Friedrich-Ludwig-
Jahn-Stadion
Planetarium
Jüdischer
Friedhof
Hauptbahnhof
(Lehrter Bhf.)
TIERGARTEN
Bf. Museums-
insel
Friedrichstr.
Reichstag
Kongress-
halle
Schloss Bellevue
Fernsehturm
Staatsoper
Brandenburger
Tor
FRIEDRICHSHAIN
LICHTENBERG
Bf. Lichten-
berg
Ostbhf.
42 Friedrichsfelde
RUMMELSBURG
Tierpark
Bf. Zool.
Garten
Zoo
Gedächtniskirche
KREUZBERG
WILMERSDORF
Treptow 42
KARLSHORST
SCHÖNE-
BERG
Bf. Südkreuz
Flughafen
Berlin-Tempelhof
(closed)
NEUKÖLLN
Bf. Karlshorst
Trabrennbahn Karlshorst
OBERSCHÖNE-
WEIDE
BAUMSCHULENWEG
Dreieck
Neukölln
NIEDER-
SCHÖNEWEIDE
Bf.
Schöneweide
FRIEDENAU
TEMPELHOF
'blub'
JOHANNISTHAL
Landschaftspark
Adlershof
STEGLITZ
BRITZ
MARIENDORF
Trabrennbahn
Adlermühle
RUDOW
BUCKOW
GROPIUS-
STADT
V/2008
ALTGLIENICKE
LANKWITZ
GARTENSTADT
GROSSZIEHEN
MARIEN-
FELDE
LICHTEN-
RADE
Großziethen
SIGRIDS-
HORST
Bf. Flughafen
Berlin-Schönefeld
Schönefeld
Flughafen Berlin-
Schönefeld
Kleinziethen
Waßmannsdorf
Osdorf
Birkholz
Waldblick
Roter
Dudel
Heiners-
dorf
Birken-
hain
Groß-
beeren
Klein-
beeren
Blankenfelde-
Mahlow
Flughafen
Berlin Brandenburg BBI
Selchow
0
2 km
1 mile
N

THE HIGHLIGHTS: AROUND BERLIN

At one time the Oberbaumbrücke (below), the bridge between Kreuzberg and Friedrichshain, marked the very edge of Berlin, but the city no longer ends here. People can now venture beyond and swim until midnight in the "bathing ship", or just chill out at the city beach (inset below and right).

TIP MS Hoppetosse

A café-restaurant ship with an international menu and a spectacular view of the Spree. Regular club nights, parties, and concerts.

Eichenstr. 4; Tel (030) 53 32 03 40; Mon–Fri from 12.00, Sat from 14.00, Sun from 11.00; S-Bahn Treptower Park.

The Plänterwald forest and Treptower Park both lie in the district of Treptow, just beyond the inner city, and it is here that many Berliners go to relax. They were laid out during the period of industrialization in the late 19th century, in order to provide green spaces and "to raise the senses above material existence and to soothe raw casts of mind, if present". Some remnants of industrialization on the banks of the Spree still await redevelopment. Others have already found a new role, such as the Arena Berlin with its huge, hangar-like events space, "bathing ship" (a series of pools anchored out in the middle of the river), sandy beach, and restaurant ship. A seaplane offers sightseeing flights, and from the port, boats make regular trips on the Spree. The most popular attraction in Friedrichsfelde is the Tierpark: more than a zoo, with 160 ha (395 acres), it's the largest landscaped animal park in Europe.

Called the "Bridge of Unity" or the "Agents' Bridge" by East Germans during the Cold War period, today the Glienicker Brücke (right) is once again known by its original name. Fabulous creatures crown the Greifentor gate in front of Schloss Glienicke (insets). Below: railings at the "Große Neugierde" garden pavilion.

INFO Schloss Glienicke

This Italian-style villa was largely designed by architect Karl Friedrich Schinkel. Today it houses a museum of royal gardening history.

Königsstr.; Tel (030) 805 30 41; Nov–March Sat, Sun, public hols 10.00–17.00, Apr–Oct Tues–Sun 10.00–18.00; Bus 316 Schloss Glienicke.

SCHLOSS GLIENICKE, GLIENICKER BRÜCKE 43

Schloss Glienicke (Glienicke Castle), part of the Potsdam cultural landscape, and today a UNESCO World Heritage Site, lies to the south-west of Berlin. From the 17th century onwards, the Hohenzollern rulers built parks, palaces, and villas in this area. Prince Carl of Prussia, the third son of the king, acquired Klein-Glienicke in 1824 and commissioned the famous architect Karl Friedrich Schinkel to convert the palace and garden designers Peter Joseph Lenné and Fürst von Pückler-Muskau to perfect the landscape. They created a pleasure ground that extended to the bank of the Havel. The original Glienicker Brücke (Glienicke Bridge) was also designed by Schinkel. It was replaced in 1907 by a bridge of iron and steel. During the Cold War it became known as the "Agents' Bridge", because captured secret agents were exchanged between East and West here on several occasions.

THE HIGHLIGHTS: AROUND BERLIN

A sandy beach, yachts and motorboats, a mild breeze, and the gentle splashing of the waves are part of a Berlin summer on the Wannsee (below, right). There is plenty of space and a peaceful setting for sport fans, as well as some high-class accommodation, such as the Ritz Carlton Schlosshotel in Grunewald (insets, below).

TIP Wirtshaus Schildhorn

This idyllic, 19th-century estate, a protected historic monument, has a restaurant serving modern international cuisine. In summer, you can sit in the large garden, overlooking the Havel.

Strasse am Schildhorn 4 a; Tel (030) 305 31 11; from 12.00, daily; Bus 218 Schildhorn.

GRUNEWALD 44
WANNSEE 45

Grunewald, which gives its name to a colony of villas, is Berlin's most exclusive address, just as it was one hundred years ago. This residential area was constructed on the initiative of Bismarck in the 1880s; nameplates, some dating back to Bismarck's time, still indicate the homes of prominent residents. The area south-west of Berlin has many lakes, such as the Schlachtensee and the larger Wannsee, and other colonies of country houses grew up here, in the Zehlendorf district. Politicians, industrialists, publishers, poets, and composers treasured the closeness to nature. However, this green paradise also experienced darker times: Berlin Jews, including some inhabitants of this same district, were deported from S-Bahnhof Grunewald – built in the style of an English country house – to extermination camps, and new owners moved into their beautiful homes. Today Grunewald, like the Wannsee, is a popular destination for days out.

The 18th-century castle (right) still has its original furnishings: patterned parquet floors, wall fabrics, and horsehair armchairs. With a bit of luck, you may see a shimmering display by one of the 35 peacocks that live on the island.

INFO Pfaueninsel

A paradise for fresh-air fiends and for anyone seeking peace and quiet. Dogs are banned from the Pfaueninsel, and it is forbidden to smoke or play music.

S-Bahn to Wannsee, then Bus 218 or ferry to Pfaueninsel.

Pfaueninsel (Peacock Island), the "pearl in Lake Havel" – covering 98 ha (242 acres) – became famous as the love nest of Frederick William II. He came here to meet his mistress, Wilhelmine Encke, in the small castle that he built for her on the island. Ennobled by the king as Countess Lichtenau, she bore him five children, and in 1797 he died in her arms. His son, Frederick William III, outraged, banished the Countess and used the island as a summer residence with his wife, Queen Louise. On certain days, the public was allowed to come and experience its fairy-tale world of fountains, rose gardens, palm trees, and a menagerie, which later formed the basis for the collection at Berlin Zoo. The Pfaueninsel has remained a magical place, and since 1990 has been a UNESCO World Heritage Site. The ferry crossing and walk through the magnificent landscaped park make a delightful excursion from the city.

CITY EXPLORER

COMPACT BERLIN

Berlin has a wealth of historic buildings, breathtaking modern architecture, museums, and art galleries, and it's easy to get around the city to see them all thanks to its excellent public transport system. Berlin is also a good place for shopping – you can buy whatever you want, from fashion and items for the home to the more esoteric and unusual. Events and festivals are held throughout the year, such as the Love Parade in July and the Film Festival in February, and there is a wide range of sporting facilities available. In the following pages, you will find expert tips on some of the best-known addresses, to help you enjoy your stay in one of the most exciting cities in Europe.

Living-room furniture in the DDR Museum.

Museums, music, and drama

Berlin Cathedral

This ornate, baroque-style, Protestant cathedral was consecrated in 1905, under Emperor William II; destroyed by bombs in World War II, it has been painstakingly reconstructed. In the crypt there are over 90 sarcophagi of members of the Hohenzollern dynasty, rulers of Prussia for 500 years (see p. 60).
Am Lustgarten; Tel 20 26 91 19 for guided tours; Mon–Sat 9.00–20.00, Sun 12.00–20.00, 1 Oct–31 Mar until 19.00. www.berliner-dom.de

Berliner Ensemble

Many consider this the most beautiful playhouse in Berlin. Plays by Brecht and Müller are often performed here.
Bertolt-Brecht-Platz 1, Tel 28 40 81 55. www.berliner-ensemble.de

Bode-Museum

After a long period of renovation, the Bode-Museum reopened in 2006. The building, at the tip of the Museumsinsel, houses the Museum of Byzantine Art, a sculpture collection, a coin gallery, and old master paintings from the Gemäldegalerie (see p. 56).
Bodestr. 1–3; Tel 20 90 55 77; 10.00–18.00, daily, Thurs 10.00–22.00. www.smb.spk-berlin.de

Chamäleon

A cosmopolitan venue with music, variety performances, and cabaret. Modern productions in the art nouveau atmosphere of a former ballroom in the Hackesche Höfe.
Rosenthaler Str. 40/41; Tel 40 00 59 30. www.chamaeleon-variete.de

DDR Museum

The Palace of the Republic – the seat of the East German parliament – used to be opposite; this small museum documents everyday life in the DDR, bringing it to life with interactive exhibits. Watch TV in a 1970s-style apartment, drive a Trabant on a simulated journey, open drawers and cupboards to learn more about subjects such as the Jugendweihe coming-of-age ceremony for 14-year-olds, holidays in Bulgaria, prefabricated buildings, and "gastronomy" – a menu lists the "Feuertanz" meat cocktail for 1.75 Marks.
Karl-Liebknecht-Str. 1, Tel 847 12 37 31, Mon–Sun 10.00–20.00, Sat until 22.00. www.ddr-museum.com

Deutsche Guggenheim

The ground floor of the Deutsche Bank – a building dating from 1920 – hosts three or four exhibitions of contemporary art every year; there are also lunchtime lectures, and a café.
Unter den Linden 13/15; Tel 202 09 30; 10.00–20.00, daily, Thurs until 22.00; free guided tours at 18.00, daily, lunchtime lectures every Wed 13.00; free admission on Mon. www.deutsche-guggenheim. de

Distel

A cabaret venue specializing in political satire; it was originally East Berlin's answer to West Berlin's popular "Die Stachelschweine" cabaret (see p.165).
Friedrichstr. 101; Tel 204 47 04; www.distel-berlin.de

Friedrichstadtpalast

Lavish, large-scale shows are presented in this modern, 2,000-seat auditorium.
Friedrichstr. 107, Tel 23 26 23 26. www.friedrichstadtpalast.de

Friedrichswerdersche Kirche – Schinkelmuseum

A neo-Gothic brick church (1824–30) designed by Karl Friedrich Schinkel. Inside there is a gallery detailing Schinkel's life and work, along with sculptures by his contemporaries.
Bodestr. 1–3; Tel 208 13 23; Mon–Sun 10.00–18.00. www.smb.spk-berlin.de

Galerie 0047

The Norwegian gallery is a meeting place for young artists and architects from various countries. They collaborate in themed exhibitions that examine the role of art and architecture in cultures around the world.
Tieckstr. 10; Tel 28 04 19 40.

Galerie Eigen + Art

This gallery, owned by artist Gerd Harry Lybke, shows original paintings and sculpture by contemporary artists.
Auguststr. 26; Tel 280 66 05; Tues–Sat 11.00–18.00. www.eigen-art.com

Galerie Nordenhake

Exhibitions of international contemporary art in various media, with a leaning toward Swedish artists.
Lindenstr. 34; Tel 206 14 83; Tues–Sat 11.00–18.00. www.nordenhake.com

Hamburger Bahnhof – Museum für Gegenwart

A magnificent building for the Museum for Contemporary Art, with works by Joseph Beuys, Andy Warhol, Anselm Kiefer, and many others. The Friedrich Christian Flick Collection of 20th-century work is part of the same museum; it includes paintings, photography, sculpture, and installations by Bruce Nauman, Georg Baselitz, and Pippilotti Rist, among others (see p. 100).
Invalidenstr. 50/51; Tel 39 78 34 11; Tues–Fri 10.00–18.00, Sat 11.00–20.00, Sun 11.00–18.00. www.hamburgerbahnhof.de

Informations- und Dokumentationszentrum Berlin

Though the Documentation Center would prefer not to be known informally as the Stasi Museum, it is hard to overlook the fact that the Stasi – the former East Germany's

From left: The Brandenburg Gate is the venue for many major events; the four-horse chariot crowning the Gate; Berlin's Mitte district is great for shopping, eating, and drinking; a glamorous revue in the Friedrichstadtpalast.

BERLIN'S HISTORICAL HEART

These pages give additional information for the area described in the "Highlights" chapter (pp. 30–71). (Area code for Berlin: 030.)

secret police – loom large here. The Federal office preserves Stasi documentation with plenty of background information about the former Ministry for State Security, which wielded so much power during the East German dictatorship.
Mauerstr. 38; Tel 23 24 79 51; Mon–Sat 10.00–18.00. www.bstu.de

Konzerthaus Berlin
Situated in the glorious Gendarmenmarkt square, this building is one of the masterpieces of classical architecture in Germany, built by Karl Friedrich Schinkel between 1818 and 1821. It has its own orchestra, and features concerts performed by well-known musicians.
Gendarmenmarkt 2, Tel 20 30 90. www.konzerthaus.de

KunstWerke
The Institute for Contemporary Art is located in a converted margarine factory. It maintains close links with its founder, Klaus Biesenbach – now at the world-renowned Museum of Modern Art in New York – and has an ambitious schedule of exhibitions from international artists.
Auguststr. 69; Tel 243 45 90; Tues–Sun 12.00–19.00, Thurs 12.00–21.00. www.kw-berlin.de

Maxim Gorki Theater
The building, behind the Neue Wache, was built in 1825–27. The repertoire includes Shakespeare, Ibsen, and Goethe alongside renowned and less well-known Russian authors.
Am Festungsgraben 2, Tel 20 22 11 15. www.gorki.de

Museum für Kommunikation
The Museum of Communication was formerly the imperial postal museum, founded in 1875 on the initiative of the postmaster general Heinrich von Stephan. It is therefore the oldest post museum in the world and its treasure trove of stamps includes the legendary 1847 red and blue Mauritius. But to reflect just how forms of communication have changed over the years, you are welcomed in the atrium by three robots.
Leipziger Str. 16; Tel 20 29 42 04; Tues–Fri 9.00–17.00, Sat, Sun 10.00–18.00. www.museumsstiftung.de/berlin

Neue Synagoge – Centrum Judaicum
Once the largest synagogue in Germany, with seating for around 3,000 people, the building was used by the Nazis as a storage depot, destroyed by bombs in 1943, and rebuilt since the mid-1980s. Today, only a small part of the structure is used as a place of worship. Exhibitions give an impression of Jewish life in Berlin before and after World War II (see p. 70).
Oranienburger Str. 28–30; Tel 88 02 83 00; April–Sept Sun, Mon 10.00–20.00, Tues–Thurs 10.00–18.00, Fri 10.00–17.00; Oct– March Sun, Mon 10.00–20.00, Tues–Thurs 10.00–18.00, Fri 10.00–14.00; closed on Jewish festivals. www.cjudaicum.de

Neuer Berliner Kunstverein
Contemporary art is displayed in exhibitions located over several floors. If you don't have enough money to buy the originals, you can always borrow pieces from the Artothek art library.
Chausseestr. 128/129; Tel 280 70 20; Tues–Fri 12.00–18.00, Sat, Sun 14.00–18.00. www.nbk.org

Quatsch Comedy Club
This club stages comedy shows, often featuring well-known comedians. Some shows are recorded for TV.
Friedrichstr. 107, Tel (018 05) 25 55 65. http://quatsch-comedy-club.de/berlin

Staatsoper (German State Opera) Unter den Linden
Conductor Daniel Barenboim has made the German State Opera House (the Lindenoper) one of Berlin's leading music venues. Ballet is also performed here (see p. 50).
Unter den Linden 7, Tel 20 35 45 55. www.staatsoper-berlin.org

Tipi
Singers and cabaret artistes, dancers and musicians perform in a circus-style tent near the Chancellor's Office. The Tipi is an offshoot of the more intimate, mirrored "Bar jeder Vernunft" in Schaperstrasse in Charlottenburg.
Grosse Querallee; Tel (01 80) 327 93 58. www.tipi-das-zelt.de

Topographie des Terrors
Behind one of the less well-maintained remnants of the Wall, lies Berlin's most important collection of documents from the Nazi era. The foundations of the Gestapo prison were rediscovered in 1986, beneath the former headquarters of the Nazi SS and the secret state police, where terror and genocide were planned. The persecution and murder of people throughout Europe is presented in an open-air exhibition.
Niederkirchnerstr. 8; Tel 25 48 67 03; May–Sept 10.00–20.00, Oct–April 10.00–18.00 (or until dark). www.topographie.de

Zille Museum
Centrally located in the Nikolaiviertel area, this small museum is dedicated to Heinrich Zille, who depicted Berlin's working classes at the end of the 19th and beginning of the 20th centuries. The artist's local bar has been rebuilt next to the museum.
Propststr. 11; Tel 24 63 25 00; Mon–Sun 11.00–18.00, April–Oct 11.00–19.00. www.heinrich-zille-museum.de

Festivals and events

Berlinale – International Film Festival
Every February, thousands of film professionals – actors, directors, scriptwriters, designers, and others from behind the scenes – compete in Berlin for one of the Golden (or Silver) Bears, the highest award of this international festival. The visiting actors bring Hollywood style to the Spree. The festival films are shown in many cinemas around Berlin, and there are also retrospectives and special performances. Season tickets are available at the main sales outlets in the arcades on Potsdamer Platz, and elsewhere (see p. 96).
Potsdamer Strasse 5; Tel 25 92 00; Feb. www.berlinale.de

The Alte Nationalgalerie during the Lange Nacht der Museen.

Berlin International Dance Festival
For almost two decades, this event has presented modern choreography in sensational productions from around the world. The wide-ranging schedule of events has something for every interested dance enthusiast.
Tel 25 90 04 41, Mid Aug–early Sept. www.tanzimaugust.de

Berliner Märchentage
The world's largest fairytale festival: hundreds of readings take place at different locations and squares in Berlin.
Spreeufer 5; Tel 34 70 94 78; Nov. www.berliner-maerchentage.de

Classical Open Air
Classical and popular film music is played in the evenings, against the stunning backdrop of the beautiful Gendarmenmarkt.
Early July. www.classicopenair.de

Frühschoppen
In Berlin the term *Frühschoppen* means more than just a social gathering where friends meet for a morning or lunchtime drink: those in the know expect stories and music as well. On Sundays at 13.00, a group of writers read their latest work, from the sublime to the ridiculous, covering topics from politics to fashion and traffic. Songs and drama are sometimes part of the act, and there are appearances from guest artistes.
Schlot, Chausseestr. 18; Sun 13.00. www.der-fruehschoppen.de

Lange Nacht der Museen
Twice a year, in January and in August, museums, churches, and other institutions around the city open their doors until midnight for one evening. Events include concerts, children's workshops, talks, guided tours, dance, films, video installations, and much more; it's generally so well-attended that it can be difficult to see what the museums actually have on display.
Tel 24 74 98 88; End Jan, end Aug. www.lange-nacht-der-museen.de

Maerzmusik
Berlin's festival of contemporary music offers an exciting choice of concerts, from light to serious, from chamber music, via flamenco, to electronica. Held at various venues throughout the city.
Schaperstr. 24; Tel 25 48 91 00; March. www.maerzmusik.de

MuseumsInselFestival
A potpourri of cultural events and performances. As well as the eponymous Museumsinsel, there are several other venues, including the Kulturforum near Potsdamer Platz, where there is an open-air cinema.
Tel 20 68 91 00; May–Sept.

Musikfest Berlin
In cooperation with the Berlin Philharmonic, the orchestra festival presents major works from the symphonic repertoire, as well as less well-known and new pieces. Visitors get the chance to hear composers, conductors, and soloists from the international music scene.
Schaperstr. 24; Tel 25 48 92 44; Sept. www.berlinerfestspiele.de

Sandsation
We don't know who discovered sand sculpture, but it seems to have become an internationally popular art form; the sand carvers also work as sculptors, set designers, or restorers. Sand is compacted into wooden forms using construction machinery – it can then be worked like soft stone. This event has a different theme each year, it opens in June, and the finished works remain on display for about six to twelve weeks.
Between the Hauptbahnhof and Bundeskanzleramt; Tel (01 62) 403 22 19; June–July. www.sandsation.de

Silversterparty
More than one million people gather to celebrate the end of the year at the Brandenburg Gate. The New Year is welcomed in at midnight with a spectacular firework display.
31 Dec.

UltraSchall
A festival of new music, committed to avant-garde sounds, in a venue not far from the Hackescher Markt.
Late Jan. www.sophiensaele.com

Sport and leisure

Berlin Marathon
They run in Berlin and then in New York. Or vice versa. The number of applications increases each year, so if you don't apply in time you'll be left to run circuits in the park.
SCC-RUNNING, Glockenturmstr. 23; Tel 30 12 88 10; Sept. www.berlin-marathon.com

Flying
What an experience – the helium balloon rises 150 m (nearly 500 feet) into the air, firmly tethered by a steel cable; after ten minutes, everyone has enjoyed a panoramic view of Berlin, and electric motors bring the balloon back down to earth.
Zimmer-/Wilhelmstrasse; 10.00–22.00, daily, depending on weather and wind strength. www.air-service-berlin.de

Kinderbad Monbijou
An open-air swimming and paddling pool for parents and children up to 15 years of age, located in Monbijoupark on the Spree, opposite the Museumsinsel.
Oranienburger Str. 78; Tel 282 86 52; May–Sept Mon–Fri 11.00–19.00, Sat, Sun 10.00–19.00; www.berlinerbaederbetriebe.de

From left: The lovingly restored Nikolaiviertel; the Bode-Museum; Café Barcomi (see p. 160) in the Sophie-Gips-Höfe; a production of *Faust* at the Staatsoper (State Opera House).

BERLIN'S HISTORICAL HEART

These pages give additional information for the area described in the "Highlights" chapter (pp. 30–71). (Area code for Berlin: 030.)

Puppentheater Firlefanz
Little Red Riding Hood, the Frog King, and Mozart's Magic Flute are just some of the pieces performed at this puppet venue. There are matinees for children aged four and over, and evening performances for adults.
Sophienstr. 10;
Tel 283 35 60. www.
puppentheater-firlefanz.de

Rowing
The beer garden at the Neuer See in Tiergarten may be full, but there are usually empty boats at the landing stage on the lake. It's a relatively steep price for one hour's rowing, but the enchanting bays will appeal to romantics.
Lichtensteinallee 2;
Tel 254 49 30; in summer, from 10.00, daily.

Sea Life Center
Walking through the glass tunnel set inside the aquarium, flanked by menacing rays, you could be walking through the Atlantic Ocean. The Center takes you on an underwater journey from the source of the Spree through rivers and lakes to the North Sea and away, with large tanks containing many different types of fish and other creatures in their natural environments. Finally, see the tropical fish and living coral in the world's largest aquarium from a panoramic lift.
Spandauer Str. 3; Tel 99 28 00; 10.00 to 18.00, daily.
www.sealifeeurope.com

Skate night
In May and July, skaters head out from the Brandenburg Gate into the night. The route is about 17.5 km (10 miles) long – and the pace is slow and family-friendly. If you're feeling fit you can finish with a 6.5-km (4-mile) sprint along the Strasse des 17 Juni.
May and July.
http://www.berlin.skate-bynight.de

Tango under the colonnades
On summer nights, music plays and tango dancers meet under the colonnades of the Alte Nationalgalerie. What began in a small way with tealights placed on the ground and music from CD players has escalated into something grander. Now there's often a small orchestra playing. If you want to dance, join in. Or just sit in a deckchair and watch.
Bodestr. 1; in summer, every other Fri at 24.00.
http://tangoberlin.de

Shopping

Berliner Bonbonmacherei
It smells wonderful as soon as you step through the door. You can watch as the sweets and candies are made: the ingredients are boiled, the molten mixture is poured out, kneaded, then pressed into delicate shapes.
Oranienburger Str. 32;
Tel 44 05 52 43; Sept–June Wed–Sat 12.00–20.00 (closed July/Aug and Christmas until early/mid Jan).
www.bonbonmacherei.de

Departmentstore
Quartier 206 is an exclusive shopping address that contains a number of haute couture boutiques, along with the vast single store known simply as "Departmentstore". It's one of the most fashionable and luxurious department stores in Europe; many international designers are represented here.
Friedrichstr. 71; Tel 20 94 68 00; Mon–Fri 11.00–20.00, Sat 10.00–18.00.
www.departmentstore-quartier206.com

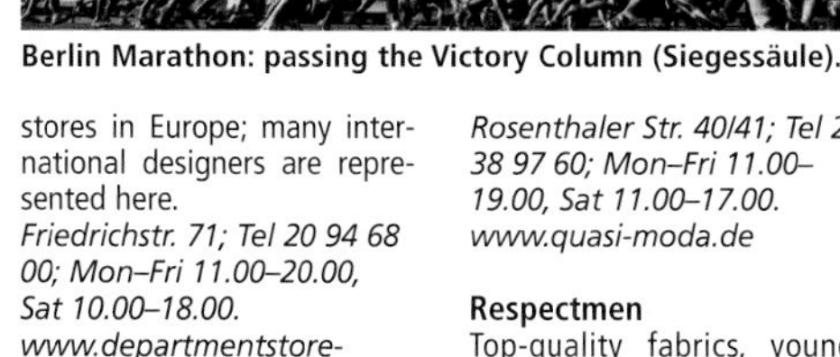

Berlin Marathon: passing the Victory Column (Siegessäule).

Konk
Berlin fashion is not always about clubwear. At Konk, you will find the elegant designs of Schultze & Lotz, two graduates from the Letteschule (Berlin's school of design), along with creations from other designers.
Kleine Hamburger Str. 15;
Tel 28 09 78 39;
Tues–Sat 12.00–20.00.
www.konk-berlin.de

Kunst- und Nostalgiemarkt
A weekend art and antiques market selling antiquarian books, pictures, hats and clothing, jewelry, and crafts.
Am Zeughaus/Kupfergraben; Sat, Sun 11.00–17.00.

Quasi Moda
Two designers, Cmok and Ziegler, aim for designs that won't date, using fabrics and shapes that they themselves love. Wearable everyday fashions, or something special for the evening. The shop is located in the fourth court of the Hackesche Höfe.
Rosenthaler Str. 40/41; Tel 28 38 97 60; Mon–Fri 11.00–19.00, Sat 11.00–17.00.
www.quasi-moda.de

Respectmen
Top-quality fabrics, young, bold, elegant designs, for men who know what they want.
Neue Schönhauser Str. 14;
Tel 283 50 10; Mon–Fri 12.00–20.00, Sat 12.00–19.00.
www.respectmen.de

Specler Store
Individual works of art, based on a vast film archive. There's a huge number of images to choose from, all based on film stills that have been painted or digitally processed in various styles. Alternatively, if you have a particular film scene in mind, they can produce a quality print to your specification.
Auguststr. 28; Tel 32 29 90 47; Tues–Sat 14.00–19.00.
www.specler.de

Trippen
Handmade shoes, boots, and sandals for men, women, and children; stylish and comfortable, in stunning shapes.
Rosenthaler Str. 40/41;
Tel 28 39 13 37; Alte Schönhauser Str. 45;
Tel 24 63 22 84; Knaackstr. 26, Tel 40 50 03 92.
www.trippen.com

Elegance and tradition at the new version of the Hotel Adlon.

Unikat
Having won awards for their designs, Unikat's two owners are now designing bags to cater for all tastes, with the result that nothing is too eccentric. They work with a wide range of materials, ranging from wool to crocodile leather, and produce just about everything from iPod covers to suitcases.
Auguststr. 86; Tel 97 89 45 04; Mon–Fri 12.00–19.00, Sat 12.00–16.00.
www.unikat-bag.de

Eating and drinking

Barcomi's Deli
The owner is an American who was so successful with her café in Kreuzberg that she set up this branch in the Sophie-Gips-Höfe, next to the Sophienkirche. They roast 13 different coffees on the premises, and all the cakes and snacks are homemade.
Sophienstr. 21; Tel 28 59 83 63; Mon–Sat 9.00–22.00, Sun and public holidays 10.00–22.00.
www.barcomis.de

Café Cinema
A narrow, cozy, traditional-style café-bar located next to the Hackesche Höfe, brimming with fascinating movie memorabilia.
Rosenthaler Str. 39; Tel 280 64 15; from 12.00, daily.

Ganymed
Before the fall of the Wall, the Ganymed was one of East Berlin's top eateries. Still popular, this French brasserie specializes in fish and shellfish, alongside classic French dishes such as cassoulet and sauerkraut.
Schiffbauerdamm 5, Tel 28 59 90 46, daily 11.30–2.00.
www.ganymed-brasserie.de

Kasbah
Embroidered silk cushions, brass lamps, and the fragrance of roses: you can rinse your hands with rosewater before settling back to enjoy a little taste of Morocco in the heart of Berlin. Exotic spices, many different varieties of couscous, tagines, Moroccan wines, and fresh mint tea to finish.
Gipsstr. 2; Tel 27 59 43 61; Tues–Sun 18.00–24.00.
www.kasbah-berlin.de

Suppenbörse
The frequently changing menu is inspired by dishes from around the world. Fresh and nutritious soups – many of them a meal in themselves – and more besides.
Dorotheenstr. 43; Tel 20 64 95 98; Mon–Fri 11.00–18.00, Sat 12.00–18.00.
www.suppenboerse.de

Unsicht-Bar dark restaurant
Eating in the dark is said to sharpen the other senses. This restaurant was founded by an association for the blind and partially sighted, to give its guests a whole new sensory experience.
Gormannstr. 14; Tel 24 34 25 00; Mon–Sun 18.00–1.00.
www.unsicht-bar-berlin.de

Weinstein Mitte
Wonderful wines, mostly from Germany and Austria, with snacks or more substantial food, served in a charming art nouveau setting.
Mittelstr. 1; Tel 20 64 96 69; Mon–Fri 12.00–1.00, Sat 17.00–1.00.
www.t-d-g.de/restaurant-weinstein.html

Accommodation

Hotel Adlon Kempinski
This first-class luxury hotel is one of Germany's most famous. The Adlon, one of the best-known addresses in Berlin, is located on Pariser Platz (see p. 36).
Unter den Linden 77; Tel 226 10. www.hotel-adlon.de

Arte Luise Kunsthotel
Located not far from the Brandenburg Gate, the main building of this hotel is a neoclassical townhouse dating from 1825. Each of the 48 rooms was designed by a different artist – you can sleep like a prince, or like an artist or poet.
Luisenstr. 19; Tel 28 44 80.
www.luise-berlin.com

Artist Riverside Hotel
Hotel and day spa located on the banks of the River Spree; unusually, rooms range from very affordable to luxurious suites with water beds and whirlpools.
Friedrichstr. 106, Tel 28 49 00.
www.tolles-hotel.de

Art'otel
This beautiful historic building is in the heart of the city, near the ship museum (Museumshafen). Original works by Georg Baselitz hang on the walls of the salon, forming the largest display of this contemporary artist's work in the whole of Germany.
Wallstr. 70–73; Tel 24 06 20.
www.artotel.de

The Circus
If you're looking for a place to stay in Berlin on a budget, The Circus hostel and its sister hotel have bright, modern rooms with comfortable beds, internet connection, and places to eat. Both are near Rosenthaler Platz.
Weinbergsweg 1a; Tel 20 00 39 39; www.circus-berlin.de

Honigmond Garden Hotel
A little paradise, with a fairytale atmosphere, is hidden behind the entrance to number 122 Invalidenstrasse. Guests who have experienced the relaxed atmosphere and excellent service of this stylish hotel come back time and again.
Invalidenstr. 122; Tel 28 44 55 77.
www.honigmond-berlin.de

The Regent Berlin
An exquisite and luxurious five-star hotel (formerly the "Four Seasons") located on

From left: The neoclassical Altes Museum on the Museumsinsel; the Friedrichstrasse shopping mile; an atmospheric open-air concert in the Gendarmenmarkt; the Staatsoper (State Opera House).

BERLIN'S HISTORICAL HEART

These pages give additional information for the area described in the "Highlights" chapter (pp. 30–71). (Area code for Berlin: 030.)

the Gendarmenmarkt, with excellent cuisine. According to the American trade press, this is one of the best hotels in the world.
Charlottenstr. 49; Tel 203 38.
www.theregentberlin.com

Nightlife

Ballhaus Mitte
This famous old ballroom, also known as "Clärchens Ballhaus", closed in 2004 after 91 years – now it's back, and doesn't seem to have changed much, although it's now popular with a younger set. There are ballroom, salsa, and tango nights, live swing music, and on Fridays and Saturdays there's disco. People also come at lunchtime to eat, and in summer the German-Italian menu is served in the secluded garden.
Auguststr. 24; Tel 282 92 95; from 10.00, daily.
www.ballhaus-mitte.de

Newton Bar: nudes on the wall, cocktails in the glass.

Dante am Hackeschen Markt
RnB, soul, and house – and a huge dance floor that's crowded until the small hours. There's a great selection of cocktails at the bar.
Am Zwirngraben 8–10; Tel 24 72 74 01.
www.dante-club.de

Felix
A stylish club and restaurant just behind the Hotel Adlon – apparently it's a great place for celebrity-spotting. On Wednesdays there's live jazz; on Thursday it's the afterwork crowd; on Fridays and Saturdays you can dine, and then dance the night away.
Behrenstr. 72; Tel 206 28 60; Wed–Sat from 18.00.
www.felixrestaurant.de

Greenwich
An elegant bar, with designer sofas where artists hang out and discuss their new projects until the small hours.
Gipsstr. 5; Tel 28 09 55 66; from 19.00, daily.

Grüner Salon
The "Green Room" club of the popular Volksbühne theater has a lively schedule, including comedy and live music from swing to salsa and tango. On the first and third Friday in the month, the theme is "Swinging Century Ballroom". Newcomers can try out their dance steps to equally new bands in the Grüner Salon's counterpart, the Rote Salon ("Red Room").
Rosa-Luxemburg-Platz 2; Tel 28 59 89 36.
www.gruener-salon.de

h2o-Club
There's a strong emphasis on hip-hop, soul, RnB, and dancehall, presented by some of Berlin's top DJs. The themed club nights are always popular.
Dircksenstrasse; Tel (01 63) 315 05 80.
www.h2o-club.com

Kaffee Burger
The name is somewhat misleading: this isn't actually a café, but a club that is well known for its Russian disco night every second and fourth Saturday in the month. Decades of smoke have yellowed the curtains, and the brown-patterned wallpaper dates back to the days of the DDR. Some nights begin with a literary event, followed by live music, and finish with a DJ party.
Torstr. 60; Tel 28 04 64 95; Sun from 19.00, Mon–Thurs from 20.00, Fri, Sat from 21.00. www.kaffeeburger.de

Newton Bar
A high-profile bar in the Gendarmenmarkt, with a classy atmosphere. Giant black and white nudes by legendary Berlin-born photographer Helmut Newton decorate the walls. Liveried waiters serve first-class cocktails and drinks, which you can enjoy in a comfortable leather armchair while you puff on a Cuban cigar.
Charlottenstr. 56; Tel 202 95 40; Sun–Thurs 10.00–3.00, Fri–Sat 10.00–4.00.
www.newton-bar.de

Schokoladen
Angels look down from gilt frames on the walls, and the velvet sofas from the early 1990s are well worn. People usually drink beer here, but on Tuesdays it becomes a cocktail lounge. There are singers on Thursdays, readings on Sundays, and on Fridays and Saturdays there are occasionally live bands: some newcomers, others better known.
Ackerstr. 169; Tel 282 65 27; from 20.00, daily.
www.schokoladen-mitte.de

2BE Club
A popular club, with a main floor large enough for 1,000 people, and a lounge. The young, mixed crowd loves hip-hop, RnB, and dancehall. Regular party nights, special events, and occasional live shows.
Ziegelstr. 23; Tel 89 06 84 10; Fri from 23.00, Sat from 2.00. www.2be-club.de

Weekend
You can choose from three different parties here: on the ground floor there is techno from the No Ufo team, at the back there's Sternradio, a classic rave club, and the elevator at the front of the building takes you to the twelfth floor, where there is house and electro music, and a fantastic view over the city.
Alexanderplatz 5; Tues, Wed, Sun from 20.00, Fri, Sat from 23.00.
www.week-end-berlin.de

Windhorst
The Windhorst is rather hidden away, but it's only two minutes from the revitalized boulevard of Unter den Linden. Police guard the nearby US embassy, but not the entrance to the bar, which boasts some of the best cocktails in Berlin.
Dorotheenstr. 65, Tel 20 45 00 70, Mon–Fri from 18.00, Sat from 21.00.

If you like it hot, you'll love the SAGE Club.

Museums, music, and drama

Bauhaus-Archiv/Museum für Gestaltung

The Bauhaus, founded by Walter Gropius in 1919, was the 20th century's most important school of art, architecture, and design. This design museum holds a large collection of Bauhaus-related items, such as furniture, crafts, and architectural models.
Klingelhöferstr. 14; Tel 254 00 20; Wed–Mon 10.00–17.00; www.bauhaus.de

Berliner Philharmonie

The renowned concert hall of a world-class orchestra, which has been a musical institution for more than 100 years. Throughout its history, the Berlin Philharmonic has been led by famous conductors, including Wilhelm Furtwängler, Herbert von Karajan and – today – Simon Rattle (see p. 98).
Herbert-von-Karajan-Str. 1; Tel 25 48 81 78. www.berliner-philharmoniker.de

C/O Berlin

C/O Berlin, an international forum for photography, is an important part of the cultural landscape of Berlin. The former Royal Post Office building shows the work of renowned photographers from around the world.
Oranienburger Str./Tucholskistrasse; Tel 28 09 19 25; 11.00–20.00, daily. www.co-berlin.com

Gaslaternen-Freilichtmuseum

An open-air, round-the-clock, free exhibition of gas lanterns from all over Europe, dating from 1826 to 1950. You'll find it at the western end of the Tiergarten park.
From Parkweg at the Berlin Pavillon on the Strasse des 17 Juni, to the Schleusenbrücke, and on Joseph-Haydn-Weg.

Gedenkstätte Deutscher Widerstand

A memorial to those involved in the resistance to the Nazis, including the assassination attempt on Hitler on 20 July 1944, on the site of the former Bendlerblock, today the Federal Ministry of Defence.
Stauffenbergstr. 13–14; Tel 26 99 50 00; Mon–Fri 9.00–18.00, Thurs 9.00–20.00, Sat, Sun 10.00–18.00. www.gdw-berlin.de

Komische Oper

Since comic opera is traditionally devoted to popular, everyday subjects and is lighter in style than the loftier and grander classic Western opera, the performances here are always sung in German. The building itself, seriously damaged during the war and now rebuilt, is quite simple, but the charming neobaroque auditorium is protected as a historic monument.
Behrenstr. 55/57; Tel 20 26 00; www.komische-oper-berlin.de

Martin-Gropius-Bau

Martin Gropius was an architect and great-uncle of the Bauhaus founder Walter Gropius; he built this museum in 1881. It now holds fascinating exhibitions on cultural history (see p.134).
Niederkirchnerstr. 7; Tel 25 48 60; Wed–Mon 10.00–20.00. www.gropiusbau.de

Museum für Film und Fernsehen

A museum of film and television within the Sony Center. The permanent exhibitions on film and television history naturally have a strong German focus, but also reference Hollywood and important milestones in the history of world broadcasting. The building is also home to the Arsenal, an arthouse movie theater. There's pretty much everything here for film fans.
Potsdamer Str. 2; Tel 300 90 30; Tues–Sun 10.00–18.00, Thurs to 20.00. www.deutsche-kinemathek.de

Musikinstrumenten-Museum

A collection of hundreds of musical instruments, from the 16th century to the present day. The most impressive piece is demonstrated only on Saturdays: the "Mighty Wurlitzer" is the largest cinema organ in Europe. It was never used in a cinema: the jukebox pioneer Wurlitzer built it in 1929 for a concert hall for the Siemens family of industrialists. Not only can it play any melody (of course), it can also twitter, roar like thunder, and imitate the chimes of London's Big Ben.
Tiergartenstr. 1 (entrance on Ben-Gurion-Strasse); Tel 25 48 11 78; Tues–Fri 9.00–17.00, Thurs 9.00–22.00, Sat–Sun 10.00–17.00; guide with musical demonstrations Sat 11.00; presentation of the Wurlitzer organ Sat 12.00; entrance free after 18.00. www.sim.spk-berlin.de

Neue Nationalgalerie (New National Gallery)

Art fans queue in front of the Mies van der Rohe building not just for the spectacular temporary exhibitions, but also for the New National Gallery's permanent collection of work by classic artists of the 20th century. Important examples of European sculpture are on display both inside the building and in the sculpture garden (see p. 180).
Potsdamer Str. 50; Tel 266 26 51; Tues, Wed 10.00– 18.00, Thurs 10.00–22.00, Fri–Sun 10.00–18.00. www.smb.spk-berlin.de

Wintergarten

Red carpets, a starry sky full of twinkling lights. This beautiful cabaret venue opened in 1992 and is already legendary. You can watch top variety acts while you dine.
Potsdamer Str. 96, Tel 25 00 88 88. www.wintergarten-variete.de

From left: The Reichstag building with its impressive dome; the Holocaust Memorial; the Tiergarten – one of the many delightful green spaces in the city.

NEW CENTRAL AREA

The expert tips in these pages give additional information for the area described in the "Highlights" chapter (pp. 72–101). (Area code for Berlin: 030.)

Festivals and events

Christopher Street Day
Christopher Street Day (CSD), the German equivalent of the Gay Pride parades held all over the world, commemorates the first demonstrations by homosexuals and other minorities against police persecution, which took place in Christopher Street in Greenwich Village in New York on 27 June 1969. The protests continued for several days. The first Gay Pride marches were held in New York and Los Angeles in 1970 and now take place every year on the last Saturday in June. The first CSDs took place in Berlin and Bremen in 1979. The carnival-style parade with its outrageous costumes attracts thousands of spectators.
June; www.csd-berlin.de

Sport and leisure

Boat trips
Strolling beside the river, you could be forgiven for thinking that Berlin has more boat jetties than S-Bahn stations. There are a number of companies operating cruises in Berlin, the largest being Stern und Kreisschifffahrt. Enjoy a leisurely trip along the Spree and the Landwehrkanal. Pick up a boat up at the Jannowitzbrücke, and get off at the Corneliusbrücke near the Bauhaus-Archiv.
Tel 536 36 00.
www.sternundkreis.de

Ice skating
If you come to Berlin in winter, you can skate in the Gendarmenmarkt, and in several other locations, including the Potsdamer Platz. But the toboggan run in Potsdamer Platz, with views of the Brandenburg Gate, is quite unique. The snow is delivered in early November.
Potsdamer Platz,
Tel 25 75 57 00.
www.eisbahnen-berlin.de

IMAX
With a screen ten times larger than a standard cinema, what makes this cinema special are the 3-D films – for which you need to wear 3-D spectacles. Amazing sound from the 6-channel system, with some 25,000 Watts digital output.
Potsdamer Str. 4; Tel 26 06 64 00. www.cinestar-imax.de

Shopping

Swatch-Store
There's a huge range of Swatch watches and straps at this shop in the Potsdamer Platz arcades. You can also have older models repaired, or have scratches removed.
Alte Potsdamer Str. 7,
Tel 25 29 71 06,
Mon–Sat 10.00–20.00.
www.swatch.com

Junk and art market
The term "junk" is not really appropriate for most of the items on offer here, they could easily be described as antiques.
Strasse des 17 Juni; Tel 26 55 00 96; Sat, Sun 10.00–17.00.

Eating and drinking

Café Viktoria
This small, friendly café is opposite the Siegessäule (Victory Column) and is reached through a tunnel. Ideal for weary Tiergarten visitors.
Strasse des 17 Juni;
Tel 39 74 62 90; 11.00–23.00, daily (winter 11.00–18.30).

Caffè e Gelato
Long queues at the counter, and the tables are always occupied – everyone's waiting for the excellent Italian ice cream.
Potsdamer Platz; Tel 25 29 78 32; Mon–Thurs 10.00–22.30, Fri, Sat 10.00–24.00, Sun 10.30–22.30.
www.gelato-berlin.de

Lindenbräu
In the heart of the Sony Center, Bavarian Weisswürst sausages and pretzels are served with Weissbier (wheat beer) – all the genuine article from Munich.
Bellevuestr. 3–5; Tel 25 75 12 80; Sun–Thurs 11.00–1.30, Fri, Sat 11.00–2.30.
www.lindenbraeu-berlin.de

Accommodation

Grand Hotel Esplanade
Comfortable rooms and suites. Rated by some as one of the best hotels in Germany, if not in Europe. There's a fitness studio, spa, pool, bars, a restaurant, and the hotel has its own restaurant ship.
Lützowufer 15; Tel 254 78 82 55; www.esplanade.de

Grand Hyatt
If you want somewhere to relax after a strenuous day in the city, this hotel has a fitness area and pool overlooking the rooftops of Berlin.
Marlene-Dietrich-Platz 2,
Tel 25 53 12 34.
www.grand.hyatt.com

Ritz-Carlton
The exterior is New York, the interior is art-deco glitter, and the furniture in the breakfast room/brasserie came from Mâcon in France. Guests can take advantage of a butler who will run their bath to the perfect temperature. If you spend the night here, you're almost certain to bump into a celebrity or two.
Potsdamer Platz 3,
Tel 33 77 77.
www.ritzcarlton.com

Nightlife

ADAGIO
This glamorous nightclub with its sumptuous baroque interior is a playground for the rich and famous.
Marlene-Dietrich-Platz 1,
Tel 258 98 90,
Thurs 19.00–2.00, Fri 22.00–5.00, Sat 22.00–5.00, Sun–Wed closed.
www.adagio.de

SAGE Club
One of the hottest party locations in Berlin. The club is in the former Heinrich-Heine-Straße U-Bahnhof, and has five different dancefloors: Dragon Floor, Mainhall, Separée, SAGE Garden, and VIP Lounges. Various club nights throughout the week feature different sounds, such as rock, funk, house, and techno.
Köpenicker Str. 76,
Tel 278 98 30.
www.sage-club.de

Spielbank Casino
Once you've warmed up on the slot machines in the basement, you can relocate to the ground floor casino to play roulette and blackjack. If you're still having a lucky streak, you can move up to the Casino Royal.
Marlene-Dietrich-Platz 1; Tel 255 99; slot machines 11.30–3.00, Casino Leger until 5.00, Casino Royal until 3.00.
www.spielbank-berlin.de

The chancel of the Kaiser-Wilhelm-Gedächtniskirche.

Verdi's *Simon Boccanegra* at the Deutsche Oper.

Museums, music, and drama

Berggruen Collection
Berlin-born art patron Heinz Berggruen (1914–2007) lived in Paris after World War II, and was a friend of Pablo Picasso and other major artists of the 20th century. His collection, which is on display here, includes work by Picasso, Matisse, Paul Klee, and Alberto Giacometti.
Schlossstr. 1; Tel 32 69 58 15; Tues–Sun 10.00–18.00. www.smb.spk-berlin.de

Berliner Kabarett Klimperkasten
Komm'se rinn, könn'se zugucken! (Come on in and have a look!) is the motto of this musical-literary cabaret in the restaurant under the Charlottenburg town hall. It has been entertaining people since 1971, with appearances from famous German comedians such as Jürgen von der Lippe, and the German cult singer Max Raabe.
Otto-Suhr-Allee 102; Tel 785 64 77; www. kabarett-klimperkasten.de

Brusberg
This well-known gallery on the corner of the Ku'damm and Uhlandstrasse focuses on modern figurative art by artists such as Botero and Altenbourg, as well as work from up-and-coming sculptors and graphic artists.
Kurfürstendamm 213; Tel 882 76 82; Tues–Fri 10.00–18.30, Sat until 14.00, Mon by arrangement. www.brusberg-berlin.de

Camerawork
With around 500 works by world-famous photographers, including Helmut Newton, Peter Lindbergh, and Diane Arbus, this gallery has one of the largest collections of popular photos and photography books in the world.
Kantstr. 149; Tel 310 07 76; Tues–Sat 11.00–18.00. www.camerawork.de

Deutsche Oper
The Deutsche Oper (German Opera) was opened in 1912 as a democratic alternative to the royal Opernhaus Unter den Linden, primarily with the aim of performing the works of Richard Wagner in a suitable setting. Destroyed in 1943, this large, modern opera house reopened in 1961. The repertoire includes mainly international classics, with occasional rediscovered forgotten works.
Bismarckstr. 35, Tel 3 43 84 01. www.deutscheoperberlin.de

Galerie Aedes
Founded in 1980, this was the first private gallery of architecture in Europe. Its exhibitions focus on the subject of urban construction.
Savignyplatz, Else-Ury-Bogen 600–601, and Christinenstr. 18–19; Tel 282 70 15; 10.00–20.00, daily. www.aedes-arc.de

GRIPS Theater
One of Germany's best-known theaters for children and young people – mainly thanks to the musical *Linie 1*, which was first produced here in 1986 and has since become one of the most-performed plays in the German-speaking world.
Altonaer Str. 22, Tel 39 74 74 77. www.gripstheater.de

Kaiser-Wilhelm-Gedächtniskirche
A poignant symbol of prewar Berlin, the ruins of the old church still stand proudly beside the new church and bell-tower designed by architect Egon Eiermann – a new beginning after the destruction of war (see p. 108).
Breitscheidplatz; Tel 218 50 23; church 9.00–19.00, daily, evening music Sat 18.00. www.gedaechtniskirche.com

Käthe Kollwitz Museum
One of the few private museums in the city. Devoted to the artist Käthe Kollwitz (1867–1945), it contains a collection of her politically inspired and socially critical graphic work and sculptures.
Fasanenstr. 24; Tel 8 82 52 10; Wed–Mon and public holidays 11.00–18.00. www.kaethe-kollwitz.de

Museum für Fotografie – Helmut-Newton-Stiftung
The Museum of Photography and Helmut Newton Foundation are housed in a neoclassical building located just behind the zoo station. Photographs by Helmut Newton (1920–2004) – his gift to the city – are shown in changing exhibitions; his images, with their cool eroticism, are modern classics.
Jebensstr. 2; Tel 266 21 88; Tues–Sun 10.00–18.00, Thurs until 22.00. www.smb.spk-berlin.de

Renaissance Theater
Built in 1902, the building was not used as a theater until 1922 and today it is the only completely intact art deco theatrical venue in Europe. The theater's repertoire includes modern and

From left: Kaiser-Wilhelm-Gedächtniskirche; KaDeWe stands for Kaufhaus des Westens; café on the Kurfürstendamm; the imported art of haute couture – at home on the Ku'damm.

CHARLOTTENBURG, WILMERSDORF

The expert tips in these pages give additional information for the areas described in the "Highlights" chapter (pp. 102–119). (Area code for Berlin: 030.)

contemporary drama and comedy by such renowned writers as Alan Ayckbourn and Samuel Beckett.
Knesebeckstr. 100; Tel 312 42 02. www.renaissance-theater.de

Schaubühne on Lehniner Platz
Artistic Director Thomas Ostermeier has received great acclaim for his productions of contemporary pieces, as well as plays by greats such as Ibsen, Schiller, and Shakespeare. The building is by Berlin architect Erich Mendelsohn (1887–1953).
Kurfürstendamm 153; Tel 89 00 23. www.schaubuehne.de

Die Stachelschweine
One of Berlin's best-known cabaret venues, in the basement of the Europa-Center. The company was originally formed in 1949; one of its driving forces was Wolfgang Gruner, who made this West Berlin ensemble famous throughout Germany.
Europa-Center, Am Breitscheidplatz; Tel 261 47 95. www.diestachelschweine.de

***Standing Woman* by Alberto Giacometti, in the Berggruen museum.**

Theater des Westens
Berlin's much-loved Performing arts venue is housed in a beautiful building, more than 100 years old.
Kantstr. 12; Tel 31 90 30; www.stageentertainment.de

Theater und Komödie am Kurfürstendamm
A famous playhouse on the Ku'damm, where film and TV stars often appear on stage in popular plays.
Kurfürstendamm 206/209, Tel 88 59 11 88. www.komoedie-am-kurfuerstendamm.de

Die Wühlmäuse
The list of artistes who have performed here reads like a *Who's Who* of German comedy, cabaret, and entertainment. The owner is comedian Dieter Hallervorden, who founded this cabaret venue more than 40 years ago.
Pommernallee 2–4; Tel 30 67 30 11. www.wuehlmaeuse.de

Zaubertheater Igor Jedlin
Igor Jedlin, the star magician from the renowned Moscow State Circus, who is a great exponent of illusion and magic, runs the only continuously showing theater of magic in Europe.
Roscherstr. 7; Tel 323 37 77; Thurs–Sun 15.30 for children, Thurs–Sat 20.00 for adults. www.zaubertheater.de

The Schaubühne in Lehniner Platz – a must for drama fans.

Festivals and events

Art Forum Berlin
Displaying fresh, vibrant, high-quality contemporary art, Art Forum Berlin is an international art fair held at Berlin's exhibition grounds.
Messe Berlin, Messedamm 22; Tel 30 38 20 76 or 30 38 18 33; Oct. www.art-forum-berlin.de

International Literature Festival, Berlin
Around 120 prose and poetry writers from all over the world come to Berlin to read from their works and take part in discussion groups. Approximately 300 events are held at different locations: museums and cafés, even cemeteries and prisons.
Chausseestr. 5; Tel 27 87 86 20; Sept/Oct. www.literaturfestival.com

JazzFest Berlin
November has been *the* month for Berlin's jazz fans since 1964. Musical styles range from traditional to progressive jazz, with performances from established stars as well as newcomers. In recent years the festival has also opened up to pop, world, and new music.
Schaperstr. 24; Tel 25 48 90; Nov. www.jazzfest-berlin.de

Spielzeiteuropa
The Berliner Festspiele's drama season runs from October to January, staging first-class productions of drama and dance from around the world.
Schaperstr. 24; Tel 25 48 90; Oct–Jan. www.spielzeiteuropa.de

Theatertreffen
In May every year, drama professionals, critics, and fans from home and abroad visit the most important festival in German-language theater. Ten outstanding productions are staged over a three-week period and at a "festival within the festival", a selection of new plays by unpublished authors are presented at the Stückemarkt.
Schaperstr. 24; Tel 25 48 90; May. www.berlinerfestspiele.de

Sport and leisure

Internationale Grüne Woche
Just about everything on the subject of food, agriculture, and horticulture – one of the best-known exhibitions in Germany and, with its many stands offering samples, surely one of the tastiest.
Late Jan. www.gruenewoche.de

The elegant Schlosshotel im Grunewald.

Internationale Tourismusbörse
An event to trigger (and satisfy) your wanderlust. The travel show is a trade exhibition that's open to the public, attracting thousands of visitors every year.
Early March.
www.itb-berlin.de

Popkomm
Germany's largest music exhibition, aimed equally at people in the music business and members of the public. Live concerts are held at the Messe Berlin exhibition site and in numerous other locations and bars.
Sept. www.popkomm.de

Spa at the Europa-Center
From outside, this spa oasis is rather unprepossessing, but the large open-air terrace gives it the edge over its competitors. There is a variety of steam baths and saunas – such as a biosauna with aromatherapy oils and gently changing fibre-optic lights, plunge pools at different temperatures, and a saltwater swimming pool with a large outdoor area, as well as quiet lounge areas and good food.
Nürnberger Str. 7;
Tel 257 57 60; Mon–Sat 10.00–24.00, Sun to 21.00.
www.thermen-berlin.de

Shopping

Berliner Zinnfiguren
From Frederick the Great to Rameses, these hand-cast, hand-painted, historically accurate, miniature tin figures represent every period in history, some new, some second-hand. Also an extensive range of books on military and cultural history.
Knesebeckstr. 88; Tel 315 70 00; Mon–Fri 10.00–18.00, Sat 10.00–15.00.
www.zinnfigur.com

Finns
A small boutique selling sophisticated designer shoes, bags, ladies clothing, and accessories.
Bleibtreustr. 47;
Tel 883 22 02; Mon–Wed 11.00–19.00, Thurs, Fri to 20.00, Sat to 18.00.
www.finns-mode.de

Grandezza
Beautiful, high-quality shoes for women with larger-than-average feet (considered size 41 and over).
Passauer Str. 8; Tel 21 91 24 83; Mon–Fri 10.00–19.00, Sat 11.00–18.00.

KaDeWe
The Kaufhaus des Westens has been serving customers for more than 100 years. With 60,000 sq m (645,834 sq feet) of floor space, it is the largest department store in continental Europe – with an amazing gourmet food hall and a fantastic range of luxury goods and services.
Tauentzienstr. 21–24;
Tel 212 10; Mon–Fri 10.00–20.00, Sat 9.30–20.00.
www.kadewe-berlin.de

Lean Selling
This shop considers itself a luxury supermarket – though you may be forgiven for thinking it's an "everything must go" sale. Haute couture is presented without any of the usual fuss: pullovers stacked on tables, shoes piled up in cardboard boxes, etc.
Schlüterstr. 42; Tel 88 71 82 96; Mon–Fri 11.00–19.00, Sat 11.00–18.00.
www.lean-selling.de

Linkshändler – Everything for left-handers
Everything in this store is designed for left-handed people: writing materials, scissors, pocket knives, household equipment, musical instruments, watches, etc.
Schmargendorfer Str. 34;
Tel 78 71 39 35; Mon–Fri 10.00–13.00, 15.00–18.00, Sat 10.00–13.00.
www.der-linkshaender-laden.de

Stilwerk
Four floors of designer lifestyle: furniture, flooring, lighting, and accessories, from classic to avant-garde. If you can't find what you're looking for here, you won't find it anywhere.
Kantstr. 17; Tel 31 51 50;
Mon–Fri 10.00–20.00, Sat 10.00–18.00.
www.stilwerk.de

Eating and drinking

Daitokai
As you enter, there's a sunken goldfish pond and a bridge. Each table has an inset griddle on which the Japanese chefs can prepare teppanyaki food in a flash, and flambé ice cream for dessert: a gastronomic experience in the Europa-Center.
Tauentzienstr. 9–12;
Tel 261 80 90; 12.00–15.00 and 18.00–24.00, daily.
www.daitokai.de

Namaskar
This Indian restaurant's sophisticated cuisine has been praised by *Gault Millau*, one of the most influential French restaurant guides; the food is matched only by the stylish interior.
Pariser Str. 56/57; Tel 88 68 06 48; Tues–Sun 2.00–24.00, Mon 17.00–24.00.
www.restaurantnamaskar.de

Petrocelli
Petrocelli has some famous regulars, and Mama Ada's delicious pasta is renowned. You will need to book in advance if you want to dine in this trattoria, the third of the family's outlets. Fortunately, the kitchen is open until late in the evening, but they are also busy all day thanks to their reasonably priced business lunches and pizza happy hour from 12.00 until 18.00, as well as their cheery, helpful serving staff.
Kurfürstendamm 36,
Tel 88 92 64 80,
Mon–Sat 12.00–23.00.
www.petrocelli-berlin.de

Tian Fu
This restaurant's name is the Chinese term for the province

From left: Industrial gas tanks and water tower; the Olympic Stadium is the home of Berlin's Hertha BSC soccer club; the former tram depot; Schloss Charlottenburg at night.

CHARLOTTENBURG, WILMERSDORF

The expert tips in these pages give additional information for the areas described in the "Highlights" chapter (pp. 102–119). (Area code for Berlin: 030.)

of Sichuan, and it also means "the overflowing land". The food, especially the dim sum, is much appreciated by gourmets of Chinese food.
Uhlandstr. 142; Tel 861 30 15; 11.30–15.30, 17.30–2.00, daily.
www.tianfu.de

Waldmann
It may sound bizarre – blood sausage and apple strudel, tomato and strawberry soup with green pepper – but basically, it's just German cuisine.
Fasanenstr. 42; Tel 32 29 47 17; Mon–Fri from 12.00, Sat, Sun from 18.00.

Accommodation

Art Nouveau
This hotel is housed in an art nouveau building located not far from the Kurfürstendamm. The individually decorated rooms are tasteful, modern, and elegant.
Leibnizstrasse 59, Tel 327 74 40.
www.hotelartnouveau.de

KaDeWe, a shopping paradise in Wittenbergplatz.

Askanischer Hof
A cozy, family-run hotel that boasts excellent service. It's popular with artists and nostalgia fans alike, who will love the "Golden Twenties" atmosphere.
Kurfürstendamm 53, Tel 881 80 33.
www.askanischer-hof.de

Bleibtreu
A renovated 19th-century hotel just off the Kurfürstendamm, with an inviting courtyard. The furnishings are a harmonious combination of natural wood, warm tones, terrazzo floors, and mosaics.
Bleibtreustr. 31; Tel 88 47 40.
www.bleibtreu.com

Brandenburger Hof
An elegant five-star hotel not far from the Kurfürstendamm, with an excellent restaurant and Japanese-style courtyard.
Eislebener Str. 14, Tel 21 40 50.
www.brandenburger-hof.com

Frauenhotel Artemisia
A three-star hotel with 12 rooms in a great location just south of the Kurfürstendamm; it's only open to women and children.
Brandenburgische Str.18, Tel 873 89 05.
www.frauenhotel-berlin.de

Hotel Quentin Berlin Design
Minimalist furnishings, lots of cherrywood, Tibetan prayer stools, and oriental vases contribute to the atmosphere of this boutique hotel. It's practically next door to the Kurfürstendamm, Europa-Center, the Gedächtniskirche, and the famous KaDeWe department store.
Kalckreuthstr. 12, Tel 51 06 30.
www.quentinhotels.com/berlindesign

Hotel Seehof Berlin
Four-star hotel on the Lietzensee, with a lake terrace, restaurant, swimming pool, and Ayurveda spa.
Lietzensee Ufer 11, Tel 32 00 20.
www.hotel-seehof-berlin.de

Ku'damm 101
The spacious lobby of this hotel makes a statement about the minimalist design concept that continues throughout the 170 rooms, meeting rooms, wellness suite, and lounge bar. A new building, the hotel stands out from the traditional Kurfürstendamm residences that surround it.
Kurfürstendamm 101, Tel 520 05 50.
www.kudamm101.com

Q!
This award-winning hotel looks rather unprepossessing, and the discreet, grey façade has no nameplate, but the interior is an amazing piece of minimalist/futuristic design: there are no right angles to be seen, and the walls and floors seem to flow into one another. The design philosophy continues in the rooms, where the bathtub snuggles up to the bed. The spa offers a tempting menu of different massage treatments.
Knesebeckstr. 67, Tel 810 06 60.
www.loock-hotels.com

Schlosshotel im Grunewald
A romantic palace, not 5 km (3 miles) from the Kurfürstendamm, in the villa district of Grunewald. This five-star hotel has 53 rooms and suites, each individually designed under the direction of Karl Lagerfeld, and equipped with the latest technology. You can have breakfast in the conservatory, dine in the wood-panelled Vivaldi gourmet restaurant, and enjoy pleasant evenings in the bar.
Brahmsstr. 10; Tel 89 58 40.
www.schlosshotelberlin.com

Nightlife

Cabaret Chez Nous
Men let the women do the asking here. This famous drag cabaret has been going since 1958; stars such as Hildegard Knef, Ella Fitzgerald, Shirley Bassey, and Romy Schneider have all enjoyed the acts.
Marburger Str. 14, Tel 213 18 10.
www.cabaret-chez-nous.de

Quasimodo
One of the oldest jazz cellars in the city, founded in 1975; it's still the top spot for live music from jazz to blues, soul, funk, and rock. Nowhere else will you get such a great opportunity to enjoy an evening with top artists from the world of music. Meet for a drink in the café above the jazz club.
Kantstr. 12a; Tel 312 80 86.
www.quasimodo.de

Universum Lounge
Located in the Mendelsohn building (also home to the Schaubühne, originally a cinema), this stylish bar has pebble-covered walls and curtains made from chains.
Kurfürstendamm 153; Tel 89 06 49 95.
www.universumlounge.com

Museums, music, and drama

Berliner Kriminaltheater
This playhouse is the place for whodunit fans: three or four exciting plays are performed every week; Agatha Christie's *The Mousetrap* has been staged several hundred times.
Palisadenstr. 48,
Tel 47 99 74 88.
www.kriminaltheater.de

Berlinische Galerie
The State Museum of Modern Art, Photography, and Architecture focuses on art produced in Berlin from 1870 to the present day.
Alte Jakobstr. 124–128,
Tel 78 90 26 00,
Mon–Sun 10.00–18.00.
www.berlinischegalerie.de

Gorillas
One of the best improvisational theater groups in the city. The group appears on stages across Berlin, but is based at the Kreuzberg Ratibor Theater, where they usually give performances on Fridays and Saturdays.
Cuvrystr. 20; Tel 618 61 99.
www.ratibor-theater.de;
www.die-gorillas.de

Prater der Volksbühne
A branch of the Volksbühne Theater; the productions are often controversial or political, as well as entertaining.
Kastanienallee 7–9,
Tel 24 06 55.
www.volksbuehne-berlin.de

Schaubude
No puppet theater clichés here: this playhouse is a creative meeting place for all kinds of independent glove puppet and marionette companies, with a varied repertoire for children, teenagers, and adults. The venue no longer has its own ensemble, although its productions are performed in playhouses throughout the city.
Greifswalder Str. 81–84,
Tel 423 43 14.
www.schaubude-berlin.de

Theater RambaZamba
People with learning difficulties find a role as artistes at the Theater RambaZamba located in the KulturBrauerei. The Sonnenuhr association, founded in 1990, provides the creative platform.
Schönhauser Allee 36–39,
Tel 43 73 57 44.
www.sonnenuhr-berlin.de

Festivals and events

Fête de la Musique
An event to mark the start of summer in around 100 cities across the world, the Fête de la Musique has been part of Berlin's cultural calendar since 1995. Hundreds of musicians from many countries play in locations around the city, usually open-air, always free of charge.
Schönhauser Allee 163;
Tel 41 71 52 89; 21 June.
www.fetedelamusique.de

Karneval der Kulturen
A carnival to celebrate multicultural Berlin. Festivities and street parties take place over a period of four days; the main parade is on Whitsunday, when decorated floats and participants from Berlin's many ethnic groups pass along the Hasenheide in costume, playing their music, watched by thousands of spectators lining the streets.
Whitsun.
www.karneval-berlin.de

Sport and leisure

Mauerpark
Part of the area where the Wall once stood, marking the border between the eastern and western parts of the city, has now become a park with play areas and sports facilities. Mauerpark (Wall Park) connects the districts of Prenzlauer Berg and Wedding. There's also a famous fleamarket.
Oderbergerstrasse,
Bernauer Strasse.
www.mauerpark.info

Skatehalle-Berlin
Skateboarders' heaven. A giant hall with the largest halfpipe in Germany. Professional skateboarders train here and there are courses for beginners.
Revaler Str. 99; Tel 29 36 29 66; Mon, Thurs 14.00–22.00, Tues, Wed, Fri 14.00–24.00, Sat, Sun 11.30–20.00 (in summer from 14.00, Sat until 24.00).
www.skatehalle-berlin.de

Trabrennbahn Mariendorf
Trotting races provide a spectacle for horse enthusiasts, and guaranteed fun for the whole family – especially as children can take part in a mini competition.
Mariendorfer Damm 222;
Tel 740 12 12; some Sun, Mon and public holidays.
www.berlintrab.de

Shopping

DIM Die Imaginäre Manufaktur
For over 120 years, brushes, brooms, and wicker chairs have been manufactured at this institute for the blind. More recently it has also begun to produce designer goods, and has gained an international reputation.
Oranienstr. 26; Tel 285 03 01 21; Mon–Fri 10.00–19.00, Sat 10.00–14.00.
www.u-s-e.org

Extrafein
Selling clothing for men and women, this shop is particularly known for its fabric bags. With the slogan "jute instead of plastic", the bags have become a hot accessory for environmentally aware purchasers, with avant-garde designers creating some of the designs.
Kastanienallee 55; Tel 46 60 69 20; Mon–Sat 12.00–20.00.
www.extrafein.com

Knopf Paul
In Berlin, anyone looking for the perfect button comes to this shop. If you can't find it here, it probably doesn't exist.
Zossener Str. 10; Tel 694 15 00; Tues, Fri 9.00–18.00, Wed, Thurs 14.00–18.00.
www.paulknopf.de

Mondos Arts
Nostalgia for the DDR is the tongue-in-cheek theme here: T-shirts, mugs, bags, and gifts with revolutionary slogans, images of Lenin and Marx, the Ampelmännchen (traffic-light-man) motif, and more.
Schreinerstr. 6; Tel 42 02 02 25; Mon–Fri 11.00–20.00, Sat 11.00–6.00.
www.mondosarts.de

Türkenmarkt
The Turkish market is the brightest and liveliest market in Berlin; you'll find fresh fruit and vegetables, ready-to-eat food, household items, fabrics, and clothing.
Maybachufer; Tues and Fri 12.00–18.00.

From left to right: the Kulturbrauerei; Berlin's hottest areas have clubs for (almost) every taste; a section of the Wall on display in the East Side Gallery; the fashionable Orient Lounge in Kreuzberg.

PRENZLAUER BERG, FRIEDRICHSHAIN, KREUZBERG, TEMPELHOF

The expert tips in these pages give additional information for the areas described in the "Highlights" chapter (pp. 120–141).

Eating and drinking

Anna Blume
During the day this is a flower shop and cozy café selling fine, homemade cakes and pastries; in the evening it becomes a restaurant.
Kollwitzstr. 83; Tel 44 04 87 49; 8.00–2.00, daily. www.cafe-anna-blume.de

Bergmann 103
A café on several floors in one of the most beautiful shopping streets in Kreuzberg. It's open for breakfast, lunch, and evening cocktails.
Bergmannstr. 103; Tel 694 83 23; daily 9.00–1.00. www.bergmann103.de

Café am Ufer
Cafés and restaurants are lined up one beside the other on this section of the Landwehrkanal, and almost all have front gardens overlooking the canal. The one belonging to this café is enchanting – the perfect place for a leisurely breakfast in summer.
Paul-Lincke-Ufer 42; Tel 61 62 92 00; from 10.00, daily. www.cafe-am-ufer.de

Café Sowohlalsauch
Everything is just perfect here: the cakes and tarts, and the setting, and even the prices are reasonable.
Kollwitzstr. 88; Tel 442 93 11; 8.00–2.00, daily. www.tortenundkuchen.de

Chez Maurice
French country cooking at its best – good and filling; rustic yes, but also surprisingly refined.
Bötzowstr. 39; Tel 425 05 06; from 18.00, daily, Tues–Sat 12.00–16.00 (lunch in the adjacent delicatessen).

Freischwimmer
A fun, floating bar and restaurant on the Treptow-Ufer in Kreuzberg. There's also an area for children.
Vor dem Schlesischen Tor 2; Tel 61 07 43 09; Mon–Fri from 16.00, Sat, Sun from 11.00; www.freischwimmer-berlin.de

Gugelhof
Bill Clinton and Gerhard Schröder ate sauerkraut here, as many other lovers of cuisine from Alsace. At weekends the restaurant is open for breakfast. The evening menu kicks in at 16.00, and includes Tarte Flambée, a pizza-like dish covered with onions, bacon, and cheese.
Knaackstr. 37; Tel 442 92 29; Mon–Fri 16.00–1.00, Sat, Sun 10.00–1.00. www.gugelhof.de

Hasir
This restaurant in Kreuzberg, beside the Kottbusser Tor, has been serving sophisticated Turkish cuisine since 1981. It now boasts other branches, including one near the Hackesche Höfe in Oranienburger Strasse in Mitte.
Adalbertstr. 10; Tel 614 23 73; www.hasir.de

Noiquattro
Whether you are looking for sophisticated Italian cuisine or a down-to-earth trattoria, Noiquattro fits the bill. Each month there's a special event, such as a poetry reading or wine tasting.
Südstern 14; Tel 32 53 45 83; Mon–Sat 12.00–24.00. www.noiquattro.de

Offenbach Stuben
There's a cabbage roulade called "Orpheus in the Underworld", and the sounds of opera accompany your meal, just as they did in DDR times, when people invited their guests from non-socialist countries to this restaurant.
Stubbenkammerstr. 8; Tel 445 85 02; from 18.00, daily.

Pfefferberg Sommergarten
The site of the former Pfeffer brewery; now there's a large garden with trees and leaf-covered columns where you can drink beer, eat freshly barbecued food, and enjoy music on summer evenings.
Schönhauser Allee 176; Tel 44 38 33 42; from 12.00, daily. www.pwag.net

Voland
In one of his books, writer Mikhail Bulgakov named the devil Voland, which signals to readers of Russian literature that the cuisine here is Russian – and devilishly good.
Wichertstr. 63; Tel 444 04 22; from 18.00, daily. www.voland-cafe.de

Accommodation

Ackselhaus
Sophisticated hotel in a renovated 19th-century building, close to the hot spots of the district. The rooms are individually designed, for example in African or Venetian style, and there's a beautiful garden.
Belforter Str. 21, Tel 44 33 76 33. www.ackselhaus.de

East Seven
A charming hostel in a side street off Kastanienallee. The reception area resembles the living room of a multicultural commune, and the rooms and dorms are bright and modern.
Schwedter Str. 7; Tel 93 62 22 40. www.eastseven.de

Myer's Hotel
Within a 19th-century building, the hotel combines classic interior design with a touch of nostalgia. Central location, yet quiet.
Metzer Str. 26; Tel 44 01 40. www.myershotel.de

Nightlife

Icon Club
Electro, hip-hop, funk, soul, with drum'n'bass every Saturday. Light shows play on the walls of the dance floor.
Cantianstr. 15; Tues from 23.00, Fri, Sat from 23.30. www.iconberlin.de

KulturBrauerei
A former brewery complex, now a venue for film, drama, dance, readings, exhibitions, and festivals.
Schönhauser Allee 36; Tel 44 31 51 52. www.kultur-brauerei-berlin.de

Orient Lounge
The Rote Harfe bar/restaurant located in the basement was once the meeting place of Kreuzberger revolutionaries. Their less politically minded successors now sit on soft cushions and enjoy the sweet smoke of the hookahs.
Oranienstr. 13; Tel 69 56 67 62; from 17.00, daily. www.orient-lounge.com

Würgeengel
Good selection of cocktails, whiskys, and music. The food comes from the nearby Gorgonzola Club, which is also legendary in Berlin.
Dresdener Str. 122; Tel 615 55 60; from 19.00, daily. www.wuergeengel.de

Party until dawn at the 90 Grad club.

Museums, music, and drama

AlliiertenMuseum
The Allied Museum tells the story of the soldiers of the Western powers stationed in Dahlem during the Cold War, with images, audio and video stations, a spy tunnel and airplane, and special exhibitions.
Clayallee 135; Tel 818 19 90; Thurs–Tues 10.00–18.00. www.alliiertenmuseum.de

Atze Theater- und Konzerthaus für Kinder
A theater and concert hall designed for children – the only one of its kind in Germany – with an auditorium seating 500. Drama, musicals, and rock and pop music to suit even the youngest children. For German speakers.
Luxemburger Str. 20, Tel 81 79 91 88. www.atze.net

Brücke Museum
This museum, in a modernist building, displays the work of die Brücke ("the bridge"), the German expressionist group formed by Karl Schmidt-Rottluff, Ernst Ludwig Kirchner, and Erich Heckel, in Dresden in 1905. Other artists linked with the movement include Otto Mueller and Max Pechstein. Changing exhibitions focus on various aspects of their life and work.
Bussardsteig 9; Tel 831 20 29; Wed–Mon 11.00–17.00. www.bruecke-museum.de

Dahlem museums
Berlin's ethnological collections are united in the museums at Dahlem, south-west of the city. The Museum of Asian Art combines treasures from India – stone sculptures, terracottas, bronzes, and paintings from the 2nd century BC to the 19th century – with the collection of East Asian art, including ancient Chinese silk paintings, Japanese wood cuts, and a Japanese tearoom. Some of its most significant exhibits come from the Turfan Collection, with wall paintings and sculptures from Buddhist monasteries. The nearby Ethnological Museum displays ethnic cultural items including Maya and Aztec gold objects, a boat from Tonga, and native North American crafts.
Arnimallee 27; Tel 830 13 61; Tues–Fri 10.00–18.00, Sat, Sun 11.00–18.00. www.smb.spk-berlin.de

Hofgärtnermuseum
In the 18th century, exotic foods such as pineapples and melons were wrested from the Brandenburg soil for the delight of the wealthy. The design and maintenance of these royal gardens were entrusted to privileged court gardeners. This museum tells the tale of their work, their expeditions to discover new plants, the importance of their discoveries, and the changing fashions in garden design.
Schloss Glienicke; Königsstr. 36; Tel 969 42 00; April–Oct Tues–Sun 10.00–18.00. www.spsg.de

Kleines Theater
The "little theater" is aptly named: it has just 99 seats. You can see a selection of Berlin premieres, musical productions, and revues in an intimate atmosphere.
Südwestkorso 64; Tel 821 20 21. www.kleines-theater.de

Liebermann Villa at Wannsee
Max Liebermann, the great German impressionist painter, acquired a piece of land on the bank of the Grosser Wannsee in 1909, where he had this house and its gardens built. The gardens, in particular, inspired much of his later work.
Colomierstr. 3; Tel 80 58 38 30; April–Oct Wed–Mon 11.00–18.00; Thurs 11.00–20.00. www.max-liebermann.de

Neuköllner Oper
The most unconventional of the four Berlin opera houses – in outlook, stage design, and repertoire. It offers up to ten new productions per season: from experimental music, through classical opera, to operetta and musicals.
Karl-Marx-Str. 131–133; Tel 68 89 07 77. www.neukoellneroper.de

Rathaus Köpenick
The main claim to fame of this large, red-brick, neo-Gothic city hall is the Hauptmann von Köpenick (Captain of Köpenick) affair. In 1906 Friedrich Voigt, a thief and conman, dressed up as a captain, commandeered some soldiers, and occupied the building. He had the mayor and treasurer arrested, confiscated the funds, then jumped on a train and disappeared with the money. Documents illustrate this daring act, as well as a display on the architecture of the building.
Alt-Köpenick 21; Tel 655 75 50; 10.00–18.00, daily. www.koepenick.net/rathaus-koepenick

Schloss Köpenick
The Köpenick palace was commissioned by Prussian king Frederick William III, and built between 1677 and 1689. Today it is home to a collection of historic furnishings and decorative arts.
Schlossinsel; Tel 65 66 17 49; Tues–Sun 10.00–18.00. www.smb.spk-berlin.de

Festivals and events

Berliner Frühlingsfest
Berlin's spring fair is held at the main fairground in the Wedding district. It's loud, lively, and lots of fun. Wednesday is family day.
Kurt-Schumacher-Damm; late March–mid April. www.schaustellerverband-berlin.de

Berliner Oktoberfest
Berlin's own version of the Munich beer festival.
Kurt-Schumacher-Damm; late Sept–mid Oct. www.berlineroktoberfest.de

From left: The "bathing ship" draws crowds in summer; the design of the Oberbaumbrücke, completed in 1896, was inspired by the Middle Ages; the idyllic Wannsee; the small castle on Pfaueninsel.

AROUND BERLIN

The expert tips in these pages give additional information for the areas described in the "Highlights" chapter (pp. 142–153). (Area code for Berlin: 030.)

Deutsch-Amerikanisches Volksfest
From the 1960s, West Berliners celebrated with American troops stationed in Berlin. After the fall of the Wall, most of the troops went home, but the fair still takes place every year, with a different US state providing the theme. People eat, drink, dance, and enjoy traditional fairground rides.
Tel (01 63) 390 09 30; late July–early Aug. www.deutsch-amerikanisches-volksfest.de

Deutsch-Französisches Volksfest
This French-themed fair dates back to when French troops were stationed in Berlin; there's French food, accordion music, and fireworks.
Kurt-Schumacher-Damm; mid June–mid July. www.schaustellerverband-berlin.de

Sport and leisure

Badeschiff
The bathing ship is a pool made from a converted ship, so it's like swimming in the Spree itself. You can splash around until midnight, lie on the beach, and drink cocktails.
Eichenstr. 4, Treptow; Tel 533 20 30; summer bathing season 8.00–24.00. www.badeschiff.de

Botanischer Garten (Botanical Garden)
The Botanical Garden in Dahlem covers an area of 43 ha (106 acres), and is home to 2,000 varieties of flowers and plants from all over the world.
Königin-Luise-Str. 6–8; Tel 83 85 01 00; Nov–Jan 9.00–16.00, daily, Feb 9.00–17.00, March, Oct. 9.00–18.00, Sept 9.00–19.00, April, Aug 9.00–20.00, May–July 9.00–21.00. www.botanischer-garten-berlin.de

FEZ Berlin
This forum for children and families has a space travel experience, cinema, theater, and interactive museum.
An der Wuhlheide 197; Tel 53 07 10; Tues–Fri 9.00–22.00, Sat 13.00–18.00, Sun 10.00–18.00 (different opening hours during holiday periods). www.fez-berlin.de

Figurentheater Grashüpfer
A small puppet venue, with plenty of opportunities to join in and be creative.
Puschkinallee 16a; Tel 53 69 51 50. www.theater-grashuepfer.de

Golf
The Berlin-Wannsee Golf Club, founded in 1895, is the oldest in Germany. It has an 18-hole course and a 9-hole course.
Golfweg 22; Tel 806 70 60; 8.00–17.00, daily. www.glcbw.de

Museumsdorf Düppel
This reconstruction of a medieval village shows what life was like 800 years ago. People dressed in peasant costumes work in the fields, bake bread, and tend sheep. A cart pulled by Willibald the ox takes children around the site.
Clauertstr. 11; Tel 802 66 71; Easter–start Oct Sun and public holidays 10.00–17.00, Thurs 15.00–19.00. www.dueppel.de

Pedalos
You can hire a pedalo on the Spree between the Zenner beer garden in Treptower Park and the sea plane jetty.
Near S-Bahnhof Treptower Park; Tel (01 77) 299 32 50; 10.00–20.00, daily.

Rowing
Hire a boat and travel along the canals of the old city of Köpenick between the Müggelspree and Dahme.
Aquaris, Katzengraben 19/ Spindlergasse; Tel 67 81 80 84; Mon–Fri 12.00–18.00, Sat, Sun 10.00–18.00. www.aquaris.info

Tierpark
The largest landscaped animal park in Europe requires a bit of stamina. The elephant kindergarten is very popular.
Am Tierpark 125, Friedrichsfelde; Tel 51 53 10; mid Oct–mid March 9.00–16.00, April–10 Sept until 18.00, otherwise until 17.00. www.tierpark-berlin.de

Wannsee beach
The sandy beach on the lake is 1 km (0.5 mile) long, dotted with wicker beach chairs.
Wannseebadweg 25; Tel 70 71 38 33; May–Aug Mon–Fri 10.00–19.00, Sat, Sun 8.00–20.00; www.berlinerbaederbetriebe.de

Shopping

Domäne Dahlem
A 15-ha (37-acre) organic farm and open-air agricultural museum. Produce is sold in the farm shop. At harvest festival and at weekends during advent, medieval-themed market festivals are held.
Königin-Luise-Str. 49; Tel 666 30 00; Wed–Mon 10.00–18.00; farm shop Mon–Fri 10.00–18.00, Sat 8.00–13.00. www.domaene-dahlem.de

Eating and drinking

Blockhaus Nikolskoe
This Russian-style log cabin has a large terrace, with a view of the Pfaueninsel and its small castle. The menu features German dishes, such as pork knuckle with pea purée.
Nikolskoer Weg 15; Tel 805 29 14; 12.00–22.00, daily. www.blockhaus-nikolskoe.de

Diekmann in the Chalet Suisse
A pretty setting in Grunewald between Clayallee and the Grunewaldsee lake, serving gourmet cuisine and, in summer, grilled chicken, pork, and sausages in the beer garden.
Im Jagen 5; Tel 832 63 62; 12.00–1.00, daily. www.j-diekmann.de

Remise in Schloss Glienicke
Dine in style and make the most of a visit to this restaurant serving haute cuisine in the grandest of surroundings.
Königstr. 36; Tel 805 40 00; Wed–Sun from 12.00. www.schloss-glienicke.de

Nightlife

Arena
An interesting venue on the banks of the Spree hosting various events including concerts, drama, and dance.
Eichenstr. 4, Treptow, Tel 533 20 30. www.arena-berlin.de

90 Grad
This is where the rich and famous come to party through the night. Every party has a different theme.
Dennewitzstr. 37, Tel (01 76) 10 09 23 47. www.90grad.com

CITY EXPLORER

MAJOR MUSEUMS

If you like visiting museums, Berlin is the place for you. After reunification, the city even found itself with doubles of some, though these have now been restructured. Berlin is rich in world-class art collections, while its historical museums bring alive ancient cultures from many parts of the world and narrate Germany's history up to the present day. Other museums trace the progress of technology and natural science. From gigantic dinosaur skeletons, through finds from ancient Egypt, to vast airships, Berlin has something to interest most visitors. The greatest difficulty will be in deciding which ones to choose, and then allowing sufficient time to do justice to them.

After a long period of restoration, the Alte Nationalgalerie was the first museum to reopen on Berlin's famous Museumsinsel, in December 2001. Its exhibits are based around the collection of Johann Heinrich Wagener, who in 1861 bequeathed to the Prussian state more than 260 paintings by both German and foreign artists.

INFO

Alte Nationalgalerie, Bodestr. 1–3, Tel (030) 20 90 58 01, Tues–Wed and Fri–Sun 10.00–18.00, Thurs 10.00–22.00, U-/S-Bahn Friedrichstr.

Caspar David Friedrich

The Alte Nationalgalerie has many works by the German Romantic artist Caspar David Friedrich. Born in Greifswald in 1774, he died in Dresden in 1840. His powerfully symbolic and religiously inspired imagery helped to define the Romantic style. Two of his best-known works hang side by side: the *Monk by the Sea* (1808–10) and the *Abbey in an Oak Forest* (1809–10). Typical of Friedrich are his meticulously accurate representation and the haunting stillness of his uniquely atmospheric works. The images are mysterious and defy direct interpretation. The viewer's sense of the grandeur of nature in Friedrich's work is often heightened by the presence of figures, dwarfed by the landscape, identified only as an outline. Friedrich sought to convey a subjective and emotional response to the natural world in which man was frequently seen as diminished.

Friedrich's *Monk by the Sea* – a masterpiece of German Romanticism.

Classicism, Biedermeier, and beyond

The Alte Nationalgalerie has three exhibition floors filled with numerous works of art from the period between the French Revolution and World War I, encompassing early classicism, Romanticism and the Biedermeier period, realism and symbolism, through to mature impressionism and the beginning of the modern period. The works on display form part of the extensive collection of the Nationalgalerie, which also includes the Neue Nationalgalerie (see p. 180), the Friedrichswerder Kirche, and Hamburger Bahnhof museums, and the Berggruen Collection. The idea of constructing a national gallery took root in 1815, although the building was not officially opened until 1876. The original collection was based on contemporary art from Prussia and Germany; Impressionist art was added later, after which the focus on German artists was abandoned.

The 19th century has at times been a rather unpopular period in terms of art history, but a visit to the Alte Nationalgalerie shows the true wealth of this period – such as in classical sculpture, with the enchantingly graceful *Double Statue of the Princesses Luise and Friederike of Prussia* (1795–97) by Johann Gottfried Schadow, or Christian Daniel Rauch's *Seated Victory* (1838–45), both sculpted from white marble.

From the Romantic period to symbolism

One of the highlights of the Alte Nationalgalerie are the works of the German Romantics. There are a number of important paintings by Caspar David Friedrich, as well as by Friedrich Overbeck, Philipp Otto Runge, and Joseph Anton Koch. Anselm Feuerbach's *Ricord di Tivoli* (1866–67) is an idyllic, classicist landscape, while the Swiss-born symbolist Arnold Böcklin's *Isle of the Dead* (1883) is a darkly visionary work. Uniting elements of Romanticism and classicism, Böcklin often used mythological and allegorical motifs. Despites its title, his *Self-portrait with Death Playing the Fiddle*

There are many important 19th-century sculptures in the Nationalgalerie.

ALTE NATIONALGALERIE

The Alte Nationalgalerie (Old National Gallery) constructed on the Museumsinsel (Museum Island) to designs by Friedrich August Stüler and Johann Heinrich Strack, was opened in 1876. The initial sketches for the building were made by King Frederick William IV of Prussia, whose equestrian statue greets visitors at the museum's entrance. The fine neoclassical building provides a worthy setting for art from the 18th and 19th centuries (see p. 58).

(1872) does not threaten: the artist depicts himself with a brush and palette, listening to death playing his violin; his peaceful, relaxed face suggests that he has interrupted his work to listen to his muse.

Prussian genius: Schinkel and Menzel

The museum also includes several paintings by Prussia's greatest architect. The classicist Karl Friedrich Schinkel's architectural legacy generally far outweighs his artistic one, though he was a very talented painter. In *Gothic Church on a Cliff by the Sea* (1815), the church rises majestically against the setting sun – the motif is not quite in the classical spirit, nor the Romantic, while the Middle Ages appear idealized. Schinkel's *Glimpse of Greece's Golden Age* (1825), on the other hand, is a classicist painting: naked heroes erect an Ionian temple in an idealized ancient landscape; unfortunately the painting was lost in World War II, and only a copy by Wilhelm Ahlborn (1836) remains.

The first floor of the Alte Nationalgalerie holds a large body of work by Adolph von Menzel. Seventy works by the great realist are owned by the museum, the most important being *Flute Concert of Frederick the Great at Sanssouci* (1852) and the *Iron Rolling Mill* (1875). The former painting depicts an enlightened ruler, not sitting formally on his throne, but making music as a private individual for his sister. The *Iron Rolling Mill* is based on many preliminary studies, and shows workers casting iron in a smoke-filled, sooty hall – an early image of industrialization, which, for all of the celebration of technical advancement, clearly depicts the harsh conditions and the difficulty of the work.

"The whole room smells of spray"

Gustave Courbet's *The Wave* (1869/70) is an outstanding masterpiece. Courbet, generally considered a realist, depicted a stormy sea under a wildly racing sky, which Cézanne praised as "the wonder of the century" with the words "the whole room smells of spray".

The gallery has a large collection of paintings by Max Liebermann; he often took the world of work as his subject, but both the *Cobbler's Workshop* (1881) and the *Flax Barn in Laren* (1887) were criticized because Liebermann painted them in an impressionist, less realistic, style.

Among the numerous Impressionists represented in the Alte Nationalgalerie, the French painters Edouard Manet, Claude Monet, Auguste Renoir, Edgar Degas, and the Germans Max Slevogt and Lovis Corinth deserve particular mention, and significant works by all these artists are on display here. The post-Impressionist genius Paul Cézanne is also represented.

Friedrich Drake created this statue of Karl Friedrich Schinkel in 1869.

The Gemäldegalerie building appears restrained and almost retiring behind the striking Neue Nationalgalerie in the Kulturforum, but its modest exterior belies the immense artistic riches inside. The Gemäldegalerie contains some of the most beautiful and significant works in European art history. It is one of the most underrated galleries in Berlin.

INFO
Gemäldegalerie, Matthäikirchplatz 4/6, Tel (030) 266 29 51, Tues–Wed and Fri–Sun 10.00–18.00, Thurs 10.00–22.00, U-/S-Bahn Potsdamer Platz.

German Renaissance painting

The collection of German painting from the 13th to the 16th century brings together the most important artists of the German Renaissance. In the post-medieval period, landscapes in painting had become more realistic as artists used mathematical perspective. Portraits were less stereotyped and showed real individuals – as can be seen, for example, in the powerful portrait of senior burgomaster Hieronymus Holzschuher by Albrecht Dürer (1526) or in the portrait of the

Jakob Fugger II, painted by Albrecht Dürer in 1518.

merchant Georg Gisze painted by Hans Holbein the Younger (1532). Holbein depicts the merchant in lavish clothing, surrounded by objects that represent not only his status as a merchant, but also his private situation; the carnation in the vase indicates that Gisze is soon to marry.

European masters from the 13th to the 18th century

Originally housed in what is currently the Altes Museum, the Gemäldegalerie was opened in 1830. It was based on the art collections of Frederick William of Brandenburg, the so-called Great Elector, and of Frederick the Great – collections that were later considerably expanded, primarily under the directorship of Wilhelm von Bode (1845–1929). Bode made many important new acquisitions and since his directorship the museum has been able to present an almost complete overview of European painting from the 13th to the 18th century.

During World War II, the Gemäldegalerie lost more than 400 works, mainly large-format paintings. During the Cold War period, there were two exhibition sites: in the West in Dahlem, and in the East in the Bode-Museum on the Museumsinsel. After reunification, the collections were brought together, and there was initially a dispute about where they should be displayed. Since 1998, they have been on show in a new building designed by Heinz Hilmer, Christoph Sattler, and Thomas Albrecht at the Kulturforum – the space was originally planned for just the Dahlem exhibits, and is therefore much too small for the complete collection. Around 1,000 paintings are on permanent display in a total of 72 rooms; a complete tour forms a 2-km (1.2-mile) long circuit. On the lower ground floor, originally planned as a restoration workshop and now a study gallery, there is an additional collection of 400 paintings. Around 150 paintings have been relocated; they hang on permanent loan in the sculpture collection in the Bode-Museum.

Highlights of the collection in the Gemäldegalerie are German and Italian paintings from the 13th to the 16th century, as well as Dutch paintings from the 15th and 16th centuries. The German paintings include works by Martin Schongauer, Hans Holbein the Elder and the Younger, Albrecht Dürer, Albrecht Altdorfer, and Lucas Cranach the Elder, whose *Fountain of Youth* (1546) depicts old women climbing into a fountain and leaving rejuvenated and radiant. The early baroque period in Germany is represented by Adam Elsheimer, among

Baroque city views and landscapes from the 18th century by Giovanni Paolo Pannini.

GEMÄLDEGALERIE

One of the best and most comprehensive collections of European art from the 13th to the 18th century can be found in the Gemäldegalerie (Painting Gallery) at the Kulturforum. Among the important masterpieces here are paintings by Bruegel, Caravaggio, Cranach, Dürer, Holbein, Raphael, Rembrandt, Rubens, van Eyck, and Vermeer. The main gallery alone has around 1,000 superb paintings (see p. 98).

***Man with the Golden Helmet*, from the studio of Rembrandt.**

others, and the later baroque period by the engraver Daniel Chodowiecki.

A wealth of Rubens, Rembrandts, and masterpieces from Italy

The Gemäldegalerie has a sizable collection of Flemish and Dutch painting from the 14th to the 17th century, including works by Jan van Eyck, Rogier van der Weyden, Hugo van der Goes, Hans Memling, Pieter Bruegel the Elder, and Hieronymus Bosch. Seventeenth-century Flanders and the Netherlands are well represented: there are 17 paintings by the baroque master Peter Paul Rubens, and no fewer than 16 by Rembrandt – one of the world's most important collections of his work, it includes the self-portrait of 1634 and *Samson Threatens his Father-in-Law* (1635). In addition, there are works by, among others, Jacob Jordaens, Pieter Bruegel the Younger, and Jan Vermeer, whose masterpiece *The Glass of Wine* (1661/62) shows his fantastic handling of perspective and light.

Italian painting from the 13th to the 18th century forms a large part of the Gemäldegalerie collection. Works that deserve particular attention include Fra Angelico's *The Last Judgment* (*c.*1432), Botticelli's *Madonna with the Saints* (1484/85), Titian's *Venus and the Organ Player* (*c.* 1550), and Caravaggio's *Amore Vincitore* (1601/02).

Art from Spain, France, and England

The collections of Spanish painting from the 15th to the 18th century, French painting from the same period, and English painting from the 18th century are not as extensive as those from Germany and Italy. However, they deserve attention, as there are some celebrated masterpieces, including paintings by Murillo and Velázquez in the Spanish collection, *The Draughtsman* (1737) by Jean-Baptiste Chardin and the self-portrait by Nicolas Poussin (1649) in the French section. English painting is the smallest collection in the Gemäldegalerie – but it is the largest collection of 18th-century British art in Germany. There are five paintings by Thomas Gainsborough, including *The Marsham Children* (1787).

Sensuous Renaissance art: the female form represented by Lucas Cranach the Elder.

Like the other institutions on the Museumsinsel (Museum Island), the popular Pergamon Museum will be converted during the renovation of the whole museum complex that is due to take place over the next few years. Plans drawn up by the architect O. M. Ungers include a fourth wing that will extend the exhibition space of the museum.

INFO

Pergamonmuseum, Am Kupfergraben 5, Tel (030) 20 90 55 77, Tues–Wed and Fri–Sun 10.00–18.00, Thurs 10.00–22.00, U-/S-Bahn Friedrichstr.

The Pergamon Altar

This Hellenistic-style altar was built in the 2nd century BC in the citadel of the city of Pergamon, in what is now modern-day Turkey. The altar, some 36 m (117 feet) wide and 33 m (109 feet) deep, has a flight of steps almost 20 m (65 feet) wide. Its base is decorated in high relief, depicting the battle of the Titans against the gods; there is also a frieze representing the legend of Telephos, son of the hero Hercules, and the mythical founder of the city of Pergamon. For many centuries, the site lay forgotten, its stones plundered for building materials by locals, but Germany requested an excavation permit from Turkey in 1871. The Pergamon Altar was unearthed in 1878. Under an agreement with the authorities in Constantinople (now Istanbul), the altar was carefully removed and reassembled in Berlin.

The gigantic dimensions of the Pergamon Altar.

An ancient Greek masterpiece

The dramatic frieze of figures on the Pergamon Altar (see left), a beautiful Hellenistic work, attracts many thousands of visitors; it is part of the collection of classical antiquities in the Pergamonmuseum. Two other important collections can be seen here: the Museum of Islamic Art and the Museum of the Ancient Near East.

The city of Miletus: the Market Gate and fortifications

Part of the collection of classical antiquities, the Market Gate of Miletus is an outstanding example of Roman architecture. Dating from the 2nd century AD, it once formed the imposing southern entrance to the market in Miletus, a city on the west coast of Asia Minor (modern-day Turkey). It is thought to have been built on the occasion of a visit by the Roman Emperor Hadrian in the year 129, and was probably part of a prestigious building complex in a magnificent boulevard. Miletus was later converted into a fortress to repel the Persians, and the gate was integrated into the fortifications. It was excavated in sections from 1899 onward by German archeologists; it has undergone several phases of restoration to reinstate original pieces (new restoration work is currently being carried out).

Next to the Pergamon Altar and the Market Gate, other exhibits are rather overshadowed, but they deserve more than a passing glance. Particularly worth seeing are the reconstruction of the propylon (gate structure) to the Temple of Athena from Pergamon, and the columns of the Temple of Artemis from Magnesia on the Maeander, another ancient Greek city in Asia Minor.

There are also smaller items, such as Greek and Roman sculptures. Of particular interest are the *Reclining Lion* from Miletus (around 550 BC), the statue of a woman with a pomegranate (around 580 BC), and the *Seated Goddess* from Taranto in southern Italy (around 460 BC).

The imposing Market Gate of Miletus has Greek and Roman stylistic elements.

PERGAMONMUSEUM

Berlin's most-visited museum is named after its most important exhibit: the Pergamon Altar from the 2nd century BC, uncovered between 1878 and 1886 during excavations in what is now Turkey, and brought to Berlin. The building was constructed between 1909 and 1930 to plans by Alfred Messel and Ludwig Hoffmann. As well as the famous altar, the Pergamon also contains a collection of the world's finest antiquities (see p. 54).

Lion relief on Babylon's Processional Way.

Ishtar Gate and the Processional Way

The Museum of the Ancient Near East is housed in the south wing of the Pergamonmuseum. Some of the exhibits are several thousand years old – they were excavated by German archeologists, particularly in Mesopotamia. The museum documents the history of the Sumerian, Babylonian, and Assyrian cultures with architectural monuments, reliefs, jewelry, and items of ritual and everyday use. The main attractions are the largest exhibits: the impressive Ishtar Gate and parts of the Processional Way from Babylon, the capital of the ancient Babylonians on the Euphrates (in modern-day Iraq), constructed under the rule of Nebuchadnezzar II (605–562 BC). The Processional Way was used during Babylon's new year festival, held each year in spring. Originally between 20 and 24 m (65 and 78 feet) wide and about 250 m (820 feet) long, it led through parts of the city – as can be seen in a model also on display. Located at the end of the Processional Way, was the magnificent Ishtar Gate, named after the female ruler of the sky, the goddess of love, and the protector of troops. People passed through this gate on their way to the 90-m (295-foot) high ziggurat, a stepped temple similar to a pyramid.

The Processional Way and the Gate were clad in glazed clay bricks, predominantly blue, with geometric patterns and representations of lions, bulls, and dragons, each embodying one of Babylon's divinities. The lion stands for the goddess Ishtar; the bull for Adad, the god of weather; and the snake-like dragon for the god of fertility, the patron of the city, Marduk.

Other archeological finds are of major cultural significance, including the world's earliest example of writing from the Sumerian culture in the 4th millennium BC, and the façades from the Inanna temple in Uruk from the 3rd millennium BC.

The Palace of Mshatta and the Aleppo Room

The Museum of Islamic art on the top floor of the Pergamon Museum, contains many other architectural treasures that draw in the visitors. The 33-m (108-foot) long, 5-m (16-foot) high façade of the Palace of Mshatta (south of Amman, Jordan), with two gate towers and decorated with reliefs, dates from the 8th century. The Aleppo Room is a reconstruction of a richly-decorated, early 17th-century, wood-panelled reception room from the north Syrian city of Aleppo.

Greek statues in the classical antiquities collection.

The Neue Nationalgalerie (New National Gallery) was the first museum to be opened in the Kulturforum, in 1968. This glass palace has almost 5,000 sq m (53,819 sq feet) of exhibition space and around 800 sq m (8,611 sq feet) of wall space. It attracts numerous visitors, not only for its permanent collection, but also, in recent years, for its special exhibitions.

INFO

Neue Nationalgalerie, Potsdamer Strasse 50, Tel (030) 266 26 51, Tues–Wed and Fri–Sun 10.00–18.00, Thurs 10.00–22.00, U-/S-Bahn Potsdamer Platz.

Kronprinzenpalais

The Kronprinzenpalais on Unter den Linden, established by museum director Ludwig Justi in 1919, assumed the role of National Gallery during the interwar period, with its collection of contemporary art. Works by great German expressionist painters such as Karl Schmidt-Rottluff, Max Pechstein, Otto Mueller, Erich Heckel, Franz Marc, and Oskar Kokoschka were included, as well as sculptures by Ernst Barlach and Wilhelm Lehmbruck. The collection was soon expanded with works by the French Impressionists. After the Nazis seized power, expressionist art was considered "degenerate". Initially, it was just individual works in this style that were removed, then almost all the exhibits were confiscated and shown in the exhibition of "degenerate art" mounted by the Nazis in 1937, in which the art was ridiculed.

***Spring* by Erich Heckel, painted in 1918.**

A rum beginning

In the 1930s, celebrated German architect Ludwig Mies van der Rohe worked from an office located in this part of Berlin, before he emigrated to America. In 1961, when the decision was made to build a new 20th-century gallery in the Kulturforum, the great modernist architect was invited back on site in a leading role.

Mies van der Rohe based the design for the gallery on plans he had created in the mid-1950s for the administrative buildings of Bacardi, the rum manufacturer, in Santiago de Cuba. The Bacardi offices were never built. The gallery of the 20th century, which later became the Neue Nationalgalerie, was finally completed in 1968, just one year before the architect's death.

A bold, innovative modern building

For his design for the Neue Nationalgalarie, Mies van der Rohe looked to classical models in Berlin, such as Karl Friedrich Schinkel's Altes Museum (1823–30). Mies' contemporary interpretation of classicism resulted in the modern equivalent of an ancient temple. In the museum's interior he perfected his architectural ideal of large, open spaces, delineated by barely visible boundaries that separate them from the environment outside. The building is a square pavilion of steel and glass mounted on a granite base measuring 105 x 110 m (344 x 360 feet). The coffered steel roof is supported on eight pylons rather than on walls, the walls themselves consisting almost entirely of glass. Opened in 1968, the structure was the largest cantilevered steel construction in Europe at the time. The steel roof, measuring exactly 64.8 x 64.8 m (212.5 x 212.5 feet) and overhanging the inner space by more than 7 m (22 feet) all round, was lifted using hydraulic rams, so that the supporting structure could be placed underneath. Most of the museum's exhibition space is underground. The main hall, originally intended as a lobby and ticket sales area,is a large, well-proportioned, unified space. It began to be also used for temporary exhibitions – initially very hesitantly – and over time has come to be recognized as an ideal place for displaying installation art – such as by Jenny Holzer (2001) and Jörg Immendorff (2005–06).

A clean, uncluttered, temple of light and space: Mies van der Rohe's modernist building.

NEUE NATIONALGALERIE

Although not originally designed as an art gallery, Ludwig Mies van der Rohe's modernist building is an appropriate home for the Neue Nationalgalerie's collection; the famous "temple of light and glass" looks more like a modernist sculpture than a solid structure. Each year, a number of special exhibitions are on show but during temporary exhibitions, the permanent collection is not on view.

***The Archer* (1964), Henry Moore's monumental bronze in front of the Neue Nationalgalerie.**

Art that defines the epoch

The permanent collection covers a fantastic range of art, from the beginning of the 20th century to the 1960s and beyond. German expressionism is well represented in the Neue Nationalgalerie. Originating before World War I, this artistic movement and style rebelled against the academic conception of art and instead used simple forms – reminiscent of woodcuts – and luminous, strangely dissonant, or often unmixed, paints; its subject matter was also often in stark contrast to the acceptable themes of the time. Ernst Ludwig Kirchner's *Potsdamer Platz* (1914), for example, is an almost lifesize image of two prostitutes towering over their potential clients in a Potsdamer Platz of uncomfortably distorted perspective. *Self Portrait with Monocle* (1910) is an expressive likeness of the 26-year-old Karl Schmidt-Rottluff. There are later works by the lone wolf Max Beckmann, painted during his period of exile in Amsterdam. *The Frieze of Life* (completed in 1907) by the great Norwegian artist Edvard Munch is a highlight of the gallery, as are Pablo Picasso's cubist *Seated Woman* (1909) and Juan Gris' *Still Life.*
The Pillars of Society (1926) is a brutal caricature in which George Grosz held a mirror up to the elite of the Weimar Republic. The work of Otto Dix is similarly consciously "ugly" and disturbing for the viewer, revealing in its social comment rather than painterly.
Abstract work from the post-war period by Wols, Ernst Wilhelm Nay, and Willi Baumeister are as much part of the gallery's collection as *IKB 49* (1960) by Yves Klein, one of this artist's great monochrome blue images. The various artistic movements of the 1960s and 1970s are represented by paintings such as Barnett Newman's *Who's Afraid of Red, Yellow and Blue* and Francis Bacon's *Portrait of Isabel Rawsthorne, Standing in a Street in Soho*; Gerhard Richter's *Atelier* (1985) is also part of the permanent collection.
Outside, there is more great art: three large sculptures are displayed in front of the Neue Nationalgalerie: Henry Moore's *Archer*, Richard Serra's *Berlin Block for Charlie Chaplin*, and Alexander Calder's *Têtes et Queue.*

***Green Girl* by Karl Schmidt-Rottluff and *Seated Female Nude* by Max Pechstein show the typically bold, primitive style of the German expressionists.**

With 25,000 sq m (269,097 sq feet) of exhibition space, the Deutsches Technikmuseum has too much to see in one day – not just because of the wealth of exhibits, but also because almost every department lures you in with demonstrations and activities. The museum is currently being extended, which will double its exhibition area and make it the largest museum of technology in the world.

INFO

Deutsches Technikmuseum, Trebbiner Str. 9, Tel (030) 90 25 40, Tues–Fri 9.00–17.30, Sat, Sun 10.00–18.00, S-Bahn Anhalter Bahnhof, U-Bahn Möckernbrücke.

Science – a hands-on experience

Directly next to the Deutsches Technikmuseum is Spectrum, the Berlin Science Center, where visitors can make their own scientific experiments. There are more than 250 hands-on experiments: for example, you can make music with a "laser guitar" without touching the strings, and children can lift their parents using a "people lifter". There are also demonstrations, such as showing how a hovercraft works, or how the earth rotates on its axis. In the atrium, you'll find a 17-m (55-foot) long Foucault pendulum, with its 48-kg (105-pound) weight that swings leisurely back and forth every eight seconds, knocking down blocks set in a circle. The Center addresses all kinds of science-related questions, from natural phenomena and the laws of physics, to how technical equipment works.

Optical illusions – technology or art?

One of Europe's largest museums of technology

Developed from the Museum of Transport and Technology (Museum für Verkehr und Technik) set up in 1982, the Deutsches Technikmuseum today presents an overwhelming wealth of objects and materials in 14 subject areas – including inland and ocean navigation, rail transport, aviation and space travel, photography, textiles, and many other areas of technical history. The collection is one of the largest in Europe and it is continually being expanded.

Navigation and aviation

The new building houses two major collections: navigation and air travel. The navigation collection is one of the largest in the world, with around 1,500 exhibits – from models to large-scale and full-size exhibits – covering more than 1,000 years of history and every branch of navigation, from trade and war to sport and leisure. Among the interesting larger exhibits are the *Kurt Heinz*, a Brandenburg tug from 1901 that worked on on the River Oder for many years, and the 33-m (108-foot) long Kaffenkahn, a historic cargo sailboat from 1840, with its tall central mast. It was rescued in Berlin during work on the port and has been reconstructed using many original parts. "Kaffe" is the term for the front and rear parts of the boat, which extend into long points, providing an aid to orientation for the sailors when steering. The aviation collection tells the story of mankind's dream of flying, from the first balloon ascents and the daredevil air pioneers, through airships and military aircraft for attack and rescue, to space exploration. There are some surprising early exhibits, such as a glider developed by Otto Lilienthal in the 19th

Rosinenbombers **like this Douglas C 47 supplied Berlin during the blockade of 1948–49.**

DEUTSCHES TECHNIKMUSEUM

Technical history in action – the historic machines and models in the Deutsches Technikmuseum (Museum of Technology) present technology from early times to the present day, with an emphasis on the early industrial age. On the site of the old Anhalt goods station, the museum consists of a series of buildings, including locomotive sheds, a water tower, a reconstruction of a brewery from 1910, and the museum park (see p. 134).

A model ship made from mother-of-pearl.

century, and the only surviving example of the so-called Jeannin Stahltaube, produced in 1914 and used in World War I. There is a Junkers Ju 52 commercial aircraft, better known to Germans as *Tante Ju* (Aunty Ju), as well as information on how the Nazis used the public fascination with flying in their propaganda. The collection also includes one of the *Rosinenbomber*, used by the Allies in the Berlin airlift of 1948–49.

The fascination of rail travel

As the capital of the empire, Berlin was the central junction of the German railway network for many years. So it's not surprising that a large part of the museum of technology is devoted to railway history. In the historic locomotive sheds, built in 1874, there are no fewer than 40 original rail vehicles on 34 tracks. Dating from the early 19th century, the collection includes steam locomotives and carriages (with wooden benches in third class and comfortable upholstered armchairs in first), as well as modern carriages from the 1980s. Smaller items illustrate some of the social developments linked with rail travel. There is also a model railway showing the site as it would have looked in 1938, with the Anhalt passenger and freight station, and all the railway lines.

From print and film, to beer and computers

The Deutsches Technikmuseum includes many other interesting collections, such as road transport (with a depot of vintage vehicles) and computing and automation (with the world's first computer, built by Konrad Zuse). The transport collection is open only on special occasions so it is best to check in advance. Writing and printing technology are also covered, as well as paper production, textiles, the history of film, telecommunications and news technology, and suitcase and jewelry production. The museum complex includes the Spectrum Science Center (see p. 182, left) and a park with a historic brewery and two windmills. There are additional branches of the museum in Berlin: the Archenhold-Sternwarte (observatory) in Treptow (founded in 1896), the Zeiss Planetarium in Prenzlauer Berg, and the Sugar Museum in Wedding.

Top: In the locomotive shed. Below: A model of a Friesian sailing boat.

CITY EXPLORER

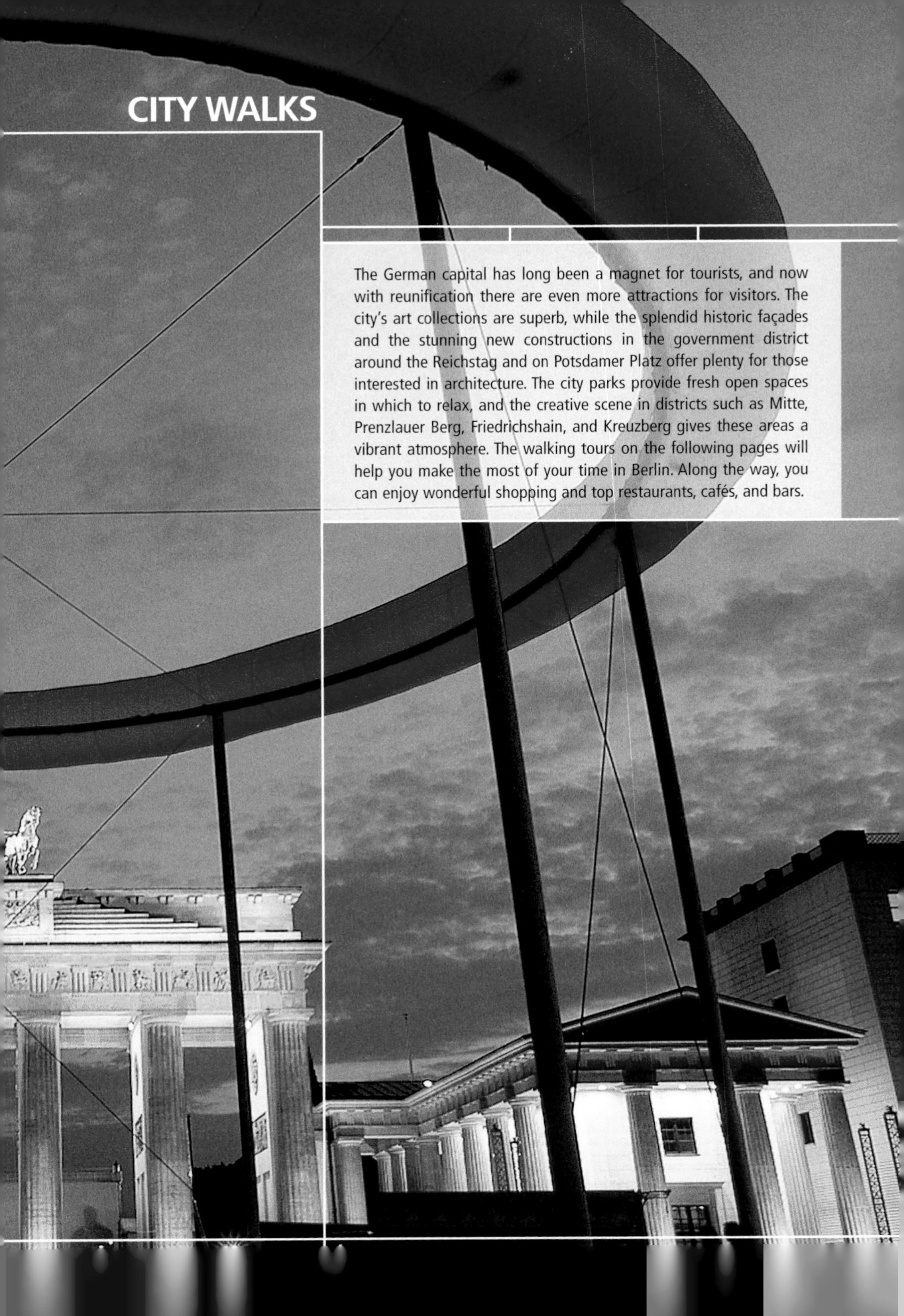

CITY WALKS

The German capital has long been a magnet for tourists, and now with reunification there are even more attractions for visitors. The city's art collections are superb, while the splendid historic façades and the stunning new constructions in the government district around the Reichstag and on Potsdamer Platz offer plenty for those interested in architecture. The city parks provide fresh open spaces in which to relax, and the creative scene in districts such as Mitte, Prenzlauer Berg, Friedrichshain, and Kreuzberg gives these areas a vibrant atmosphere. The walking tours on the following pages will help you make the most of your time in Berlin. Along the way, you can enjoy wonderful shopping and top restaurants, cafés, and bars.

Sights

❶ Zoo
The Elephant Gate at the Zoo entrance on Budapester Strasse is eyecatching – it is a reconstruction of the original, which was destroyed in the war. Stars at the oldest zoo in Germany include Knut, the polar bear who was born here, as well as lions, pandas, gorillas, and hippopotamuses. The giant bird house and the aquarium are also worth a visit (see p. 110).

❷ Kaiser-Wilhelm-Gedächtniskirche
This church is a Berlin landmark. Built at the end of the 19th century, it was bombed in 1943, but in 1961, a new tower and chancel were built around the ruins. Lined with thousands of tiny stained-glass panels that fill the interior with a magical blue light, the chancel is an oasis of calm in the hectic Breitscheidplatz (see p. 108).

❸ Kurfürstendamm
This magnificent boulevard was built along the road to Grunewald in the late 19th century. Solid Wilhelminische façades line the street – called the Ku'damm for short – but it is known primarily as a shopping mile: some parts are very chic, others are more downmarket (see p. 108, 112).

❹ Savignyplatz
Savignyplatz was one of the central meeting points for artists and intellectuals in West Berlin. Cafés and bars line the square and shops huddle beneath the arches of the S-Bahn; there are also numerous interesting galleries nearby.

❺ Deutsche Oper
At first glance, you'd never know this was an opera house: the exterior is uniform, drab, and uninteresting, some 70 m (229 feet) long and 12 m (39 feet) high. But behind this sober, square facade, with traffic rushing by, lies one of the great stages of Berlin, with outstanding acoustics and space for an audience of some 1,900 (see p. 164).

❻ Berggruen Collection
Heinz Berggruen (1914–2007) was born in Berlin, and emigrated to the United States in 1936. Returning to Europe at the end of World War II, he became a successful art dealer (and collector) in Paris. In 1996, he returned to Berlin, bringing with him his magnificent art collection. It includes important works by Picasso, Klee, Matisse, Braque, Giacometti, among others. He generously gave 165 works as a gift to the Prussian Cultural Heritage Foundation in December 2000 (see p. 164).

The Kaiser-Wilhelm-Gedächtniskirche at night.

❼ Bröhan Museum
This museum specializes in French, Belgian, German, and Scandinavian art nouveau, as well as French art deco, with an emphasis on interior design, along with paintings and drawings from the late 19th and early 20th centuries. Furniture, lighting, glass, ceramics, and other items are grouped together by style and designer, displayed in a series of room interiors.

❽ Schloss Charlottenburg
The largest and most beautiful palace in Berlin has a façade of more than 500 m (1,640 feet) in length; the mid-section is crowned with a decorative domed tower. The palace is the work of several architects and has been extended many times since it was built in the late 17th century, but its architecture still retains a unified appearance. Inside the palace are many splendidly decorated rooms, as well as the Museum für Vor- und Frühgeschichte (Museum of Pre- and Early History). In front of the building, standing on a plinth, is Andreas Schlüter's imposing equestrian statue of the Great Elector (see p. 118).

❾ Schlosspark
The palace has extensive grounds, part laid out as a baroque garden and part as a landscaped park created in the English-style. A new design combining elements of the original French baroque garden – designed in 1697 – with the less formal English park that was created in 1787 was introduced after World War II (see p. 118). A mausoleum contains the remains of several notable members of the Prussian nobility.

Shopping

❶ Showroom Berlin
Creative clothing and accessories from Scandinavia, proving that interesting fashion is not confined to the catwalks of Paris and Milan. Urban style for women, from designer brands such as Filippa K, Noa Noa, and Tiger of Sweden.
Kurfürstendamm 69; Tel 214 01 70; Mon–Wed 10.00–19.00, Thurs, Fri 10.00–20.00, Sat 10.00–18.00;

From left: Night on the Kurfürstendamm; Schloss Charlottenburg; Bücherbogen, the specialist art and design bookshop; the Asian restaurant Nu eatdrinkmanwoman.

FROM THE ZOO TO THE PALACE

Starting at the zoo, this walk takes you along the Kurfürstendamm to Schloss Charlottenburg (area code for Berlin: 030).

U-Bahn Adenauerplatz. www.showroomberlin.de

❷ Van Ravenstein

Fashion from Holland and Belgium has gained an outstanding international reputation in recent years. This shop has the best selection in Berlin, but with top names such as Ann Demeulemeester and Spijkers & Spijkers, it's not cheap.
Leibnizstr. 42; Tel 31 00 46 02; Mon–Fri 10.30–19.00, Sat 10.30–16.00; U-Bahn Adenauerplatz. www.van-ravenstein.nl

❸ Platten Pedro

A small shop, stuffed to the ceiling with vinyl records. From Marlene Dietrich to the Beatles, if you're looking for old treasures and you can't find them here, then you won't find them anywhere.
Tegeler Weg 102; Tel 344 18 75; Mon–Fri 10.00–18.00, Sat 10.00–13.00; U-Bahn Mierendorffplatz. www.platten-pedro.de

❹ Bücherbogen in Savignyplatz

Under the arches of the S-Bahn lies one of the largest and best antiquarian bookshops in Berlin. The range of titles is superb – on art, architecture, photography, film, fashion, and design. They also sell new books.
Stadtbahnbogen 593, Savignyplatz; Tel 31 86 95 11; Mon–Fri 10.00–20.00, Sat 10.00–18.00; S-Bahn Savignyplatz. www.buecherbogen.com

Eating and drinking

❶ Café Swingdiele

An atmospheric café, furnished in elegant 1930s' art deco style. Swing music plays in the background, and delicious, homemade cakes and snacks are on offer.
Goethestr. 5; Tel 54 71 04 24; Mon–Fri 10.00–19.00, closed Sat, Sun, and public holidays, also closed on Mon in winter. www.swingdiele.de

❷ Nu eatdrinkmanwoman

Modern Asian cuisine, which successfully fuses different elements from all over Asia – Japan, Thailand, Vietnam, etc. The restaurant's clean, modern style is given an eccentric twist with manga cartoons on the walls and translucent panels of pulsating light.
Schlüterstr. 55; Tel 88 70 98 11; S-Bahn Savignyplatz. www.nu-eat.de

❸ Café Reet

A beautiful location opposite Charlottenburg palace, with light meals and wonderful pastries from probably the best baker in town. The blueberry and raspberry cakes are particularly recommended.
Klausenerplatz 5; Tel 322 48 22; Mon–Fri 8.00–20.00, Sat, Sun 9.00–20.00; S-Bahn Westend.

❹ Natural Mente

The only macrobiotic restaurant in Berlin. Creative meat-free food, using tofu, lentils and beans, plus a range of generous salads.
Schustehrusstr. 26; Tel 341 41 66; Tues–Fri 12.00–15.30, Sun from 11.00; U-Bahn Richard-Wagner-Platz. www.naturalmente.de

Sights

1 Chancellor's Office
A large and costly building, the Bundeskanzleramt (German Chancellery), designed by Axel Schulte and Charlotte Frank, was completed in 2001. It houses 300 offices, the most important being that of the Chancellor (see p. 82).

2 Reichstag
From the top you have fantastic views over the city – hence the Reichstag dome has become one of the most popular tourist attractions in Berlin. Architect Norman Foster's innovative new Reichstag building sits behind the historic façade (see pp. 76–79).

3 The Brandenburg Gate
The Brandenburg Gate (Brandenburger Tor) was once a symbol of the division of Germany, but today it symbolizes the country's unity. The grand boulevard Unter den Linden stretches east from the 26-m (85-foot) high, 65-m (213-foot) wide gate (see p. 34).

4 Holocaust Memorial
Controversial even before it was built, the Holocaust Memorial, or Memorial to the Murdered Jews of Europe, consists of 2,711 concrete slabs of different sizes. The concept was not universally acclaimed, but walking among the stark, bare stones is an intensely moving experience for many (see p. 86).

5 Gendarmenmarkt
The most beautiful square in Berlin, with magnificent classical buildings: the Schauspielhaus, the Deutscher Dom, and the Französischer Dom; in the middle is a statue of the poet and dramatist Schiller, surrounded by allegorical figures representing poetry, drama, philosophy, and history. Concerts are held in the square in July (see p. 42).

6 Staatsoper
The German State Opera House, known as the Lindenoper, was built between 1741 and 1743 in classical style. It has a well-deserved reputation as one of the best ballet and opera houses in Europe (see p. 50).

7 Humboldt University
Built between 1748 and 1765 as a palace for Frederick II's brother, it became home to the university founded by Wilhelm von Humboldt in 1810. Statues of Wilhelm and his brother watch over the university entrance (see p. 44).

8 Neue Wache
In 1816–18 Karl Friedrich Schinkel built the Neue Wache to house the guards of the nearby Kronprinzenpalais. Today is the Central Memorial of the Federal Republic of Germany to the Victims of War and Tyranny (see p. 46).

***Mother with her Dead Son,* the bronze pietà by Käthe Kollwitz.**

9 Kronprinzenpalais
Originally built as a palace for the heir to the Prussian throne, the building has recently become more historically important as the place where the unification treaty between East and West Germany was signed in 1990 (see p. 50).

10 Zeughaus – Deutsches Historisches Museum
Once it was the greatest weapons depot in Prussia, but today the building is used as a museum – covering 2,000 years of German history. The architect Ieoh Ming Pei has created a striking new extension (see p. 48).

11 Altes Museum
The Altes Museum (Old Museum), designed in 1823 by Karl Friedrich Schinkel, is an embodiment of the purest architectural classicism. The Greek-style portico has 18 Ionic columns; an interior rotunda is reminiscent of the Roman Pantheon (see p. 52).

12 Berlin Cathedral
Berlin's cathedral is impressive. Emperor William II commissioned architect Julius Carl Raschdorff to produce a prestigious place of worship. Drawing inspiration from the baroque and the Italian Renaissance, Raschdorff's cathedral combines differing architectural styles (see p. 60).

13 Museumsinsel
The northern part of this island in the Spree forms Berlin's principal museum district. A number of historic buildings contain works of art spanning several millennia – from ancient Egypt and ancient Greece to the 19th century (see pp. 52–59, 174, 178).

Shopping

1 KPM – Königliche Porzellan-Manufaktur
The royal blue insignia is the seal of quality of Germany's top porcelain manufacturer. The company has been painstakingly producing luxury porcelain by hand for nearly 250 years.
Unter den Linden 35; Tel 302 06 41 50; Mon–Sun 10.00–18.00; S- and U-Bahn Unter den Linden. www.kpm-berlin.de

From left: The new Chancellor's Office on the Spree in Berlin's new government district; open-air classical concert in the Gendarmenmarkt; Galeries Lafayette; Café Einstein.

FROM THE REICHSTAG TO THE MUSEUMSINSEL

This walk begins at the political heart of Germany and ends with the treasures of the Museumsinsel (area code for Berlin: 030).

2 Galeries Lafayette

Parisian-style shopping in the heart of Berlin: five floors are arranged around a central cone-shaped space. The goods on offer include elegant French fashions and accessories, a wide range of beauty products and cosmetics, a French bookstore and, of course, an excellent food department (see p.40).
Friedrichstr. 76; Tel 20 94 80; Mon–Sat 10.00–20.00; U-Bahn Französische Strasse. www.galerieslafayette.de

3 Berlin Story

A specialist book and media store devoted exclusively to the city of Berlin. Everything written about the city can be found here: the history, art and architecture, detective novels, children's books, as well as DVDs. There are also special exhibitions and a film presentation.
Unter den Linden 40; Tel 20 45 38 42; Mon–Sun 10.00– 19.00; S- and U-Bahn Unter den Linden. www.berlinstory.de

4 Fassbender & Rausch

This chocolate shop located in Berlin Mitte offers confectionery of outstanding quality; it's also a contender for the longest counter of truffles and pralines in Germany. You even can buy a chocolate Reichstag or Brandenburg Gate to take home – far too good to eat.
Charlottenstr. 60; Tel 20 45 84 40; Mon–Sat 10.00–20.00, Sun 11.00–20.00; U-Bahn Stadtmitte. www.rausch-schokolade.de

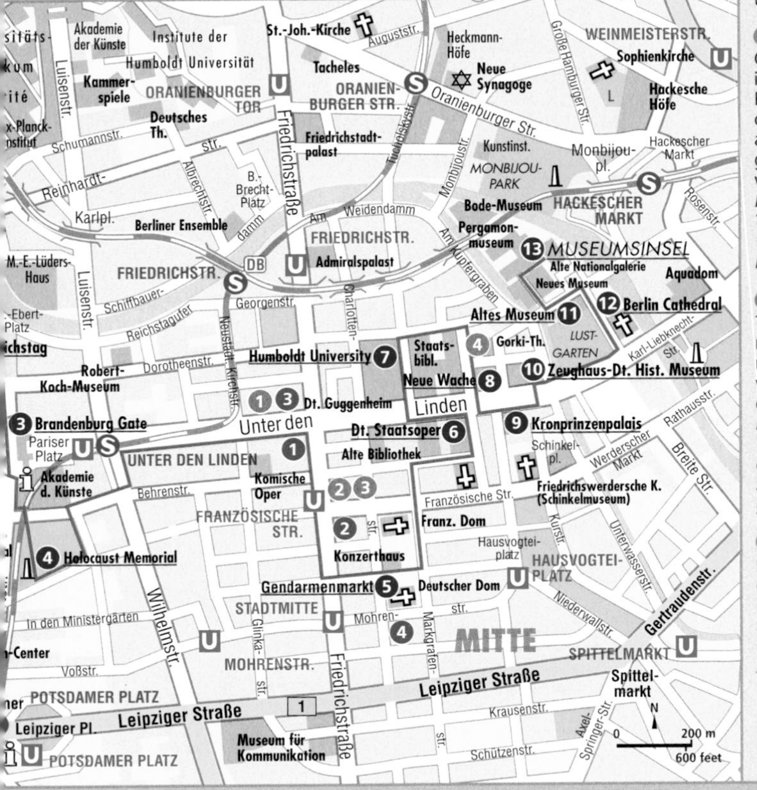

Eating and drinking

1 Einstein Unter den Linden

Opened in 1996, this cafe is one of the best-known coffee shops in Germany. Thanks to its location close to the Reichstag and the government district, it has become a meeting place for politicians, journalists, and the cultural elite.
Unter den Linden 42; Tel 204 36 32; 7.00–24.00, daily; S- and U-Bahn Unter den Linden. www.einsteinudl.com

2 Borchardt

Good Franco-German cuisine in a beautiful setting makes Borchardt popular with celebrities. Typical dishes such as Wiener schnitzel and foie gras are not cheap, and reservations are essential.
Französische Str. 47; Tel 81 88 62 62; Mon–Sat 12.00–24.00; U-Bahn Französische Strasse.

3 Aigner

The best of Austrian and German cuisine, in a pleasant art nouveau setting. You can buy wine from the restaurant's own Horcher estate.
Französische Str. 25; Tel 203 75 18 50; 12.00–2.00, daily; U-Bahn Französische Strasse. www.aigner-gendarmenmarkt.de

4 Tadschikische Teestube

Kick off your shoes, sit on cushions, and enjoy your tea in Tajikistan style in these tearooms on the first floor of the Donner'schen Palais.
Am Festungsgraben 1; Tel 204 11 12; Mon–Fri 17.00–24.00, Sat, Sun 15.00–1.00; S- and U-Bahn Friedrichstrasse.

Candles at the memorial to the Wall.

Sights

1 Nikolaiviertel
The Nikolaiviertel area looks old – but it was largely built in 1987 on the 750th anniversary of Berlin. Historic houses were transported here from other sites, and new ones with old-style gables and oriels were added – a beautiful illusion of the old city and a pleasant place to stroll. The twin-towered Nikolaikirche is a reconstruction of the 13th-century original, severely damaged in World War II. Some authentic old buildings, cafés, and restaurants can still be found (see p. 62).

2 Rotes Rathaus
The "red town hall" gets its name from its red bricks – it has nothing to do with any political persuasion. It was built between 1861 and 1869 as the meeting place of the Berlin municipal assembly; today it is the seat of the governing mayor and the senate. The tower is supposedly reminiscent of the Campanile di Giotto of Florence cathedral (see p. 64).

3 Marienkirche
A church was first built here in 1270, but the current building dates mainly from the 14th and 15th centuries. In the interior, don't miss the pulpit (1703) by Andreas Schlüter.

4 Alexanderplatz/ Fernsehturm
Alexanderplatz is an undistinguished large city square, surrounded by concrete office blocks and department stores; its most interesting feature is the world time clock. At 368 m (1,207 feet), the Fernsehturm (Television Tower) is the tallest building in Berlin: the view from the top is breathtaking (see p. 66).

5 Hackesche Höfe
The largest, most beautiful courtyard complex in Berlin: apartments, studios, shops, restaurants, cinemas, and galleries are grouped around eight inner courtyards. They were built in the early 20th century, decorated in the art nouveau style, and clad in glazed tiles. Today the complex has been lovingly and lavishly restored (see p. 68).

6 Alter Jüdischer Friedhof
The oldest Jewish cemetery in Berlin was founded in 1672 and was destroyed by the Gestapo in 1943. Only a few memorials remain, including the gravestone of the Jewish philosopher Moses Mendelssohn (1729–1786).

7 Neue Synagoge
With seating for 3,000, the Neue Synagoge was the largest synagogue in Germany when it was built in the mid-19th century. It survived Hitler's attacks in 1938, but was bombed during World War II. The exterior has now been restored, and the synagogue officially reopened in 1995. The Centrum Judaicum includes an exhibition of prewar Jewish life (see p. 70).

8 Tacheles
This 100-year-old building, originally a department store, was damaged during World War II, but has been in more or less continuous use since it was built. It is now an artists' collective and cultural base.

9 Naturkundemuseum
Visitors to the Natural History Museum are greeted by the 23-m (75-foot) long dinosaur skeleton of a *Brachiosaurus brancai*. Other highlights include the *archaeopteryx* fossil – only seven examples of this primitive type of bird exist – and the stuffed animals. The museum houses both permanent and temporary exhibitions, and an animal sound archive for research.

10 Hamburger Bahnhof
Berlin's Museum of Contemporary Art is located in a former railway building. The permanent collection of important 20th-century work is enriched by special exhibitions (see p. 100).

11 Berlin Wall Documentation Center
The Dokumentationszentrum Berliner Mauer forms part of the memorial complex on the former site of the Wall, which ran along Bernauer Strasse. It includes an exhibition that uses photos, film, and sound recordings to bring to life the time when the Wall loomed over a divided city (see p. 130).

Shopping

1 Whisky & Cigars
Over 1,000 types of whisky are kept in stock, as well as hand-rolled cigars from Cuba and the Dominican Republic, specialist literature, and other items for the general enjoyment of smokers and whisky drinkers.
Sophienstr. 8–9; Tel 282 93 76; Mon–Fri 11.00–19.00, Sat 11.00–18.00; S-Bahn Hackescher Markt. www.whisky-cigars.de

From left: Hamburger Bahnhof; the Neue Synagoge has regained its former magnificence; Sarah Wiener's restaurant – top-class cooking with an Austrian influence.

FROM THE NIKOLAIVIERTEL TO THE NEW CENTRAL AREA

From "medieval" Berlin to the Fernsehturm to enjoy the view – then on to the Berlin Wall Documentation Center (area code for Berlin: 030).

2 Fishbelly

Luxurious and extravagant underwear from Fishbelly's prizewinning and exclusive collection presented together with other renowned designers. There is also a selection of swimwear and nightwear in fun designs.
Sophienstr. 7 a (entrance Hackesche Höfe); Tel 28 04 51 80; Mon–Fri 12.30–19.00, Sat 12.00–19.00 and by arrangement; S-Bahn Hackescher Markt. www.fishbelly.de

3 Aus Berlin

A range of unique products from more than 400 Berlin-based designers and companies, from Berlin kitsch items to drinks, unusual fashions, accessories, and cosmetics. They also stock furniture, tools, CDs, books, magazines, postcards, games, food, and tobacco.
Karl-Liebknecht-Str. 17; Tel 41 99 78 96; Mon–Sat 12.00–19.00; S- and U-Bahn Alexanderplatz. www.ausberlin.de

4 Hugo Store

It's hard to say what is the most attractive feature in this store: the stylish designer fashions from Boss, or the chic interior with its mirrored changing rooms that close at the touch of a button. Or perhaps it's the beautiful bamboo grove in the inner courtyard.
Rosenthaler Str. 49, Tel 28 88 45 50, Mon–Sat 11.00–20.00, U-Bahn Weinmeisterstrasse. www.bossshops.com

Eating and drinking

1 Sarah Wiener in the Hamburger Bahnhof

Sarah Wiener is a TV cook who owns this tastefully furnished, light, and airy restaurant in the Hamburger Bahnhof museum. The menu changes every month and features modern international cuisine with an Austrian slant.
Invalidenstr. 50–51; Tel 70 71 36 50; Tues–Fri 10.00–18.00, Sat 11.00–20.00, Sun 11.00–18.00, U-Bahn Zinnowitzer Strasse. www.sarahwiener.de

2 Beckers Fritten

People are happy to queue at the painted snack cart opposite Tacheles – because these are the best French fries in the city. There is a good selection of dips and sauces.
Oranienburger Str. 43a; Sun–Thurs 12.00–1.00, Fri, Sat 12.00–4.00; U-Bahn Oranienburger Tor.

3 Pan Asia

Bright, friendly, with a strictly minimalist layout, and a great selection of Chinese, Japanese, and Thai dishes.
Rosenthaler Str. 38; Tel 27 90 88 11, Sun–Thurs 12.00–24.00, Fri–Sun 12.00–1.00; S-Bahn Hackescher Markt. www.pan-asia.de

4 Kadima

Inventive Jewish-Russian cuisine in an elegant restaurant near the Neue Synagoge. Once a month there's an evening of readings, music, and films.
Oranienburger Str. 28; Tel 27 59 42 51; 12.00–24.00, daily; S-Bahn Oranienburger Strasse. www.kadima-restaurant.com

Sights

1 Potsdamer Platz
This is more than a square – it's a gigantic space full of glitzy new buildings, sparkle, and glass. Architects of international renown competed to create the boldest buildings, and succeeded with many ambitious structures, the most impressive of which is probably the Sony Center with its tentlike roof (see pp. 92–95).

2 Filmmuseum
The Museum of Film and Television, located in the Sony Center, documents German film from its earliest days at the end of the 19th century, with photos, posters, models, and other exhibits. Three rooms are devoted to Marlene Dietrich, with costumes, photographs, and footage from her films (see p. 162).

3 Musikinstrumenten-Museum
Around 800 instruments from more than 500 years of musical history are on permanent display in this museum, but the star of the show is the "Mighty Wurlitzer", the largest cinema and theater organ in Europe. It is demonstrated every Saturday morning from 11.00. Some of the musical instruments are played at concerts at the museum (see p. 162).

4 Staatsbibliothek
The Berlin State Library, part of the Prussian Cultural Heritage Foundation, was built between 1967 and 1978 by Hans Scharoun and his colleague Edgar Wisniewski. The library has a wonderful reading hall, flooded with light, with terraced study areas.

5 Philharmonie
The Philharmonie concert hall in the Kulturforum resembles a circus tent built of stone. Built between 1960 and 1963 by Hans Scharoun, it is striking from the outside and truly spectacular within. The large auditorium has a central orchestra podium surrounded by over 2,200 seats (see p. 98).

6 Gemäldegalerie
It is a little hard to find, but is well worth the effort: this gallery is home to one of the world's finest collections of European art. All of the great names of European art history from the 13th to the 18th century are represented here (see p. 176).

7 Neue Nationalgalerie
This building is spectacular, built between 1965 and 1968 to a design by Ludwig Mies van der Rohe, the former head of the Bauhaus school of design. Spacious, airy, and transparent, the building almost seems to float. The art on display is no less wonderful, with works from the start of the 20th century to the 1960s (see p. 180).

8 German Resistance Memorial Center
A memorial to the failed assassination attempt on Hitler in 1944 – and to others involved in the resistance against the Nazis – with both a permanent and temporary exhibitions. The Gedenkstätte Deutscher Widerstand is in the former general staff building of the Wehrmacht, Hitler's armed forces.

9 Bauhaus-Archiv
The Bauhaus Archive is a museum of design devoted to the Bauhaus movement, with numerous examples of the influential work of its students and teachers. The building itself was planned by Walter Gropius (1883–1969), founder of the Bauhaus, although he did not live to see its completion. Its distinctive shape is a Berlin landmark (see p. 162).

10 Nordische Botschaften
The embassies of the five Nordic countries (Sweden, Norway, Denmark, Finland, Iceland) are united in this modern architectural complex; a sixth building is open to the public, with exhibitions and films.

11 Victory Column
The Victory Column (Siegessäule) rises 67 m (219 feet) above the Great Star, the point where the five avenues in the Tiergarten meet. Erected in 1873, it was originally situated in front of the Reichstag, to commemorate Prussia's victories against Denmark, Austria, and France, but was moved to its current position in 1938. Inside the column, 238 steps lead to a viewing platform beneath the golden angel of Victory, known to Berliners as "Goldelse" (see p. 88).

The Berlin State Library contains around ten million printed items.

Shopping

1 Potsdamer Platz Arkaden
A shoppers' paradise in Potsdamer Platz, with 40,000 sq m (430,556 sq feet) and more than 140 shops, including the fashion chains Benetton, Mexx, Zara, Wöhrl, Esprit, and Mango. There are food shops in the basement, and a very good ice-cream shop on the top floor.
Alte Potsdamer Str. 7; Tel 25 59 27-0; Mon–Sat

From left: After the fall of the Wall, Potsdamer Platz was completely rebuilt; shopping in the arcades; Facil, a gourmet restaurant on Potsdamer Platz.

FROM POTSDAMER PLATZ TO THE TIERGARTEN

From the modern architecture of Potsdamer Platz to the greenery of the Tiergarten surrounding the Victory Column (area code for Berlin: 030).

10.00–21.00; S- and U-Bahn Potsdamer Platz. www.potsdamer-platz-arkaden.de

❷ cultix

Smart gift ideas inspired by cult design and technology, and games, as well as a selection of fun souvenirs – such as a happy families card game based on Berlin's currywurst stands.
Passageway in the Sony Center, Potsdamer Platz 2; Tel 26 10 19 57; Mon–Sat 10.00–20.00, Sun 12.00–18.00; S- and U-Bahn Potsdamer Platz.

❸ Ave Maria

The Spirit moves where it will – says the owner of the only shop in Protestant Berlin selling Catholic devotional aids. The customers vary from faithful Catholics to a more secular clientele, such as clubbers looking for something unusual to wear at the disco. Lovers of incense will find around 40 types available here.
Potsdamer Str. 75; Tel 265 22 84; Mon–Fri 12.00–18.00, Sat 12.00–15.00; U-Bahn Kurfürstenstrasse. www.avemaria.de

❹ Tiergarten flea market

The largest, best-loved, and best-attended flea market in Berlin, with an adjacent arts and crafts market.
Strasse des 17 Juni; Tel 26 55 00 96; Sat 10.00–17.00, Sun 10.00–16.00. www.berliner-troedel-markt.de

Eating and drinking

❶ Facil

Gourmet restaurant on Potsdamer Platz, located on the 5th floor of the Mandala Hotel. Excellent cuisine in a simple, elegant setting: in summer the glass roof can be slid aside for open-air dining.
Potsdamer Str. 3, Tel 590 05 12 34, Mon–Fri 12.00–15.00 and 19.00–23.00. www.facil.de

❷ Maoa

The food here is a fusion of Asian, Australian, and North American cuisine – crocodile and kangaroo meat feature on the menu.
Leipziger Platz 8; Tel 22 48 80 87; Mon–Sat 17.00–1.00, Sun, public holidays 11.30–1.00; U- and S-Bahn Potsdamer Platz. www.maoa.de

❸ Joseph-Roth-Diele

A restaurant lovingly created by a great Joseph Roth fan, with bookshelves and a 1920s' atmosphere. Try a snack of bread with tasty onions or smoked sausage – or choose one of the hot dishes, such as Flammkuchen (bacon and onion tart). Good value at lunchtime.
Potsdamer Str. 75; Tel 26 36 98 84; Mon–Fri 10.00–24.00; U-Bahn Kurfürstenstrasse. www.joseph-roth-diele.de

❹ We Love Coffee

Cozy coffee bar in the Sony Center with a choice of coffees and snacks.
Passageway in the Sony Center, Potsdamer Platz 2; Tel 23 00 35 66; Mon–Fri 7.00–20.00, Sat 10.00–20.00. www.welovecoffee.de

Battered BMW Isetta in the Haus am Checkpoint Charlie.

Sights

1 Deutsches Technikmuseum
Aircraft suspended from the ceiling; a barge raised from the river bed; rail transport, telecommunications, power engineering, photo and film technology, aerospace and computing, working models and demonstrations – the wealth of exhibits here provide an overview of several hundred years of technical history (see p. 134, 182).

2 Riehmers Hofgarten
This enormous estate of 20 apartment blocks, each with five floors, grouped around a dozen courtyards, was built between 1881 and 1900 by Wilhelm Riehmer. Beautiful ornamented façades, grand entrances, and green courtyards are typical of homes for the bourgeoisie at the end of the 19th century.

3 Viktoriapark
Laid out in the late 19th century, this park is on one of the highest points in Berlin, the 66-m (216-foot) high Kreuzberg. The hill is crowned with the Denkmal für die Befreiungskriege (a memorial to Prussian victories in the 1817–21 "wars of liberation"), designed by Schinkel. From here, you can enjoy a beautiful panoramic view of the district.

4 Chamissoplatz/ Bergmannstrasse
Kreuzberg showing its best face: lovingly restored buildings from the late 1800s, with large apartments, quiet, tree-lined streets, small squares with cafés, and interesting antiques shops. One of the most beautiful residential areas of Berlin.

5 Jüdisches Museum
This spectacular museum was designed by architect Daniel Libeskind in the shape of a contorted star of David. There are no windows, but light is admitted through a series of angular slits surrounded by zinc and concrete. Entrance to the museum is through the adjacent baroque building, the former Collegienhaus, via an underground passageway. Inside, the exhibition of German-Jewish history illustrates cooperation and conflict over the last 2,000 years. Several passageways intersect: the "Axis of Continuity" leads one way to the "Garden of Exile", the other way to the "Holocaust Tower", which commemorates the fate of the murdered Jews (see p. 136).

6 Checkpoint Charlie
After the Wall was erected in 1961 there were initially just three border controls between East and West Germany: one in Helmstedt between the DDR and the BRD named Alpha; the Dreilinden (DDR/ West Berlin) checkpoint called Bravo, and the control between West and East Berlin on Friedrichstrasse famously known as Charlie.

7 Haus am Checkpoint Charlie
This small museum documents the history of the division of Berlin and Germany, as well as the history of the Wall, the area known as "no man's land", and the attempts to escape from East Berlin to the West (see p. 38).

8 Topographie des Terrors exhibition
The chilling history of persecution and the Nazi policy of extermination is documented in this open-air exhibition set among the ruins of the Gestapo and SS offices, near a surviving section of the Wall (see p. 157).

9 Martin-Gropius-Bau
In neo-Renaissance style, this building was constructed between 1877 and 1881 to the designs of Martin Gropius, a great-uncle of the Bauhaus director Walter Gropius. It is used today to stage temporary exhibitions (see p. 134).

10 Anhalter Bahnhof
This was once the largest rail terminus in Europe, constructed between 1875 and 1880 to plans by the architect Franz Schwechten and the engineer Heinrich Seidel. Now, all that's left of the station is a piece of the façade. The original entrance arch is displayed in the nearby Deutsches Technikmuseum (Museum of Technology).

Shopping

1 Marheineke-Halle
Berlin's most beautiful market hall, built in 1892, is in Kreuzberg. It reopened in December 2007 and is once again buzzing with people buying vegetables, fruit, bread, meat, and cheese – a wide range of local and organic produce – as well as snacks. There's also a wine merchant and a coffee shop.
Marheinekeplatz, Mon–Sat 9.00–20.00, U-Bahn Gneisenaustrasse.

2 Exil-Wohnmagazin
Designer furniture, sofas, shelving systems, cupboards, and lamps, the art of cool living displayed in a spacious old brick building.
Yorckstr. 24; Tel 21 73 61 90; Mon–Fri 11.00–19.00, Sat 11.00–17.00; S-Bahn Yorckstrasse. www.exil-wohnmagazin.de

3 Grober Unfug
The best comic shop in Germany. International comics and cartoons from around the world, both old and current issues; lots of manga, plus books and games.
Zossener Str. 32/33; Tel 69 40 14 90; Mon–Fri 11.00–19.00, Sat 11.00–16.00; U-Bahn Gneisenaustrasse. www.groberunfug.de

4 Holzapfel
An unusual shop selling knives, saws, and scissors – anything with a blade – including tools for cooks, carpenters, and gardeners.
Bergmannstr. 25; Tel 78 99 06 10; Mon–Fri 11.00–19.00, Sat 11.00–16.00; U-Bahn Gneisenaustrasse. www.holzapfel-berlin.de

From left: Daniel Libeskind's impressive architecture at the Jüdisches Museum; designer furniture in Exil-Wohnmagazin; Liebermanns restaurant.

FROM THE TECHNIK-MUSEUM TO KREUZBERG

This walk takes in museums, architecture, and reminders of a dark period in German history (area code for Berlin: 030).

Eating and drinking

1 Liebermanns
The restaurant in the Jüdisches Museum pampers its guests with modern Israeli, oriental, and Mediterranean dishes. If you just want a snack, there are bagels, falafel, and delicious salads. There's no pork, but it's not strictly kosher. On Monday evenings there's an oriental buffet and live traditional Jewish music.
Lindenstr. 9–14; Tel 25 93 97 60; Mon 10.00–22.00, Tues–Sun 10.00–20.00; U-Bahn Kochstrasse. www.liebermanns.de

2 Curry 36
This sausage stand is an institution, serving Berlin's famed currywurst (hot and spicy sausages), both day and night.
Mehringdamm 36; Mon–Sat 9.00–4.00, Sun 10.00–4.00; U-Bahn Mehringdamm.

3 Austria
Deservedly one of the best-known Austrian restaurants in Berlin. The cuisine is authentic: boiled beef and large, tender wiener schnitzel that hang over the sides of the plate. Reservations are essential.
Bergmannstr. 30; Tel 694 44 40; from 18.00, daily; U-Bahn Gneisenaustrasse.

4 E.T.A. Hoffmann
A very stylish yet welcoming restaurant serving new German and international cuisine. The menu makes the most of the freshest seasonal ingredients.
Yorckstr. 83; Tel 78 09 88 09; Wed–Mon from 17.00; U-Bahn Mehringdamm. www.restaurant-e-t-a-hoffmann.de

Berlin has a comprehensive public transport system. The S-Bahn also stops in the magnificent Hauptbahnhof, which opened in May 2006.

KEY

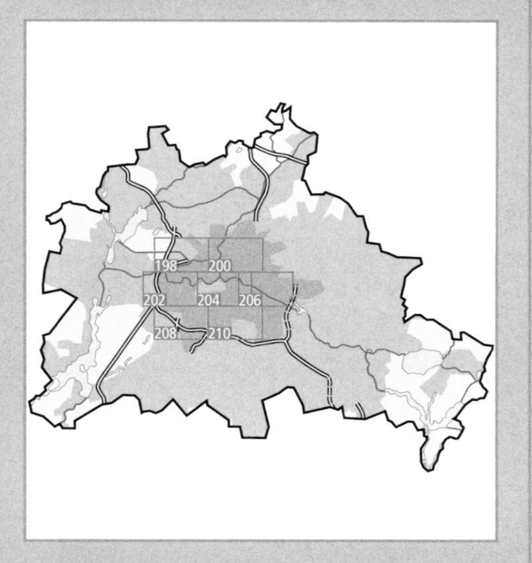

- Motorway (freeway)
- Primary route (arterial road)
- Other road
- Side (local) road
- Footpath
- Pedestrian zone
- Railway (railroad)
- Industrial railway (railroad)
- Regional/suburban railway (railroad)
- Underground/subway (under construction/planned)
- Car ferry; Passenger ferry

CITY ATLAS

The maps in the City Atlas section give detailed practical information to help make your stay more enjoyable. Clear symbols indicate the position of buildings and monuments of note, facilities and services, public buildings, the transport network, and built-up areas and green spaces (see the key to the maps below).

- Densely built-up area; Thinly built-up area
- Public building
- Building of note; Industrial building
- Green space; Wooded area
- Cemetery; Jewish cemetery
- Principal train station
- Express train station
- Regional and main line train station
- Suburban train station
- Underground (subway) station
- Car rail terminal

- Motorway (freeway) number
- Primary route (arterial road) number
- Motorway (freeway) interchange
- One-way street
- Airport
- Stadium
- Exhibition hall
- Park and Ride
- Car park; Multi-story car park
- Bus station
- Information
- Post office
- Hospital
- Radio/television tower
- Church
- Synagogue
- Mosque
- Column/monument
- Theater
- Museum
- Library
- Viewpoint
- Embassy
- Docks

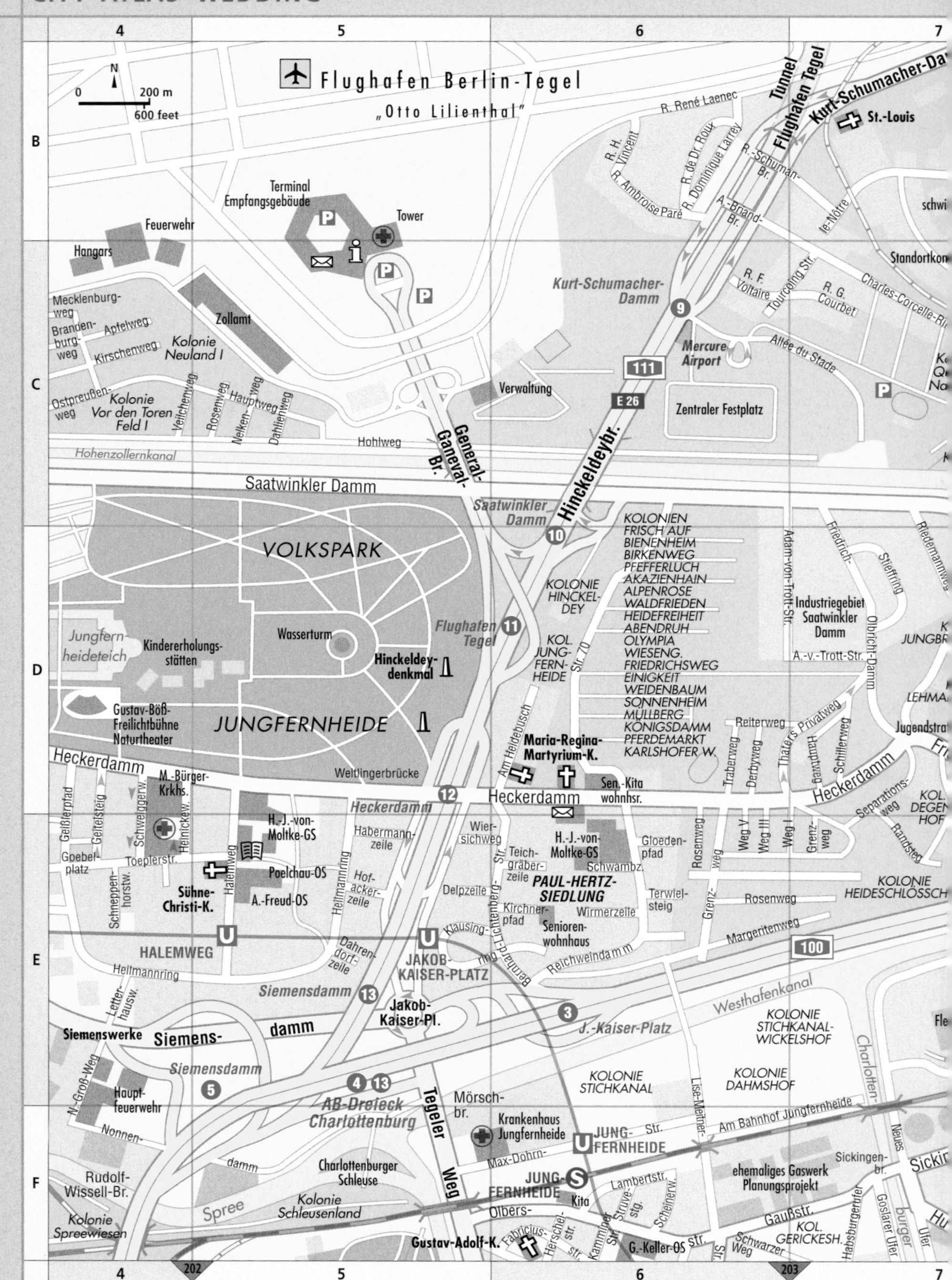
Flughafen Berlin-Tegel
„Otto Lilienthal"
Terminal
Empfangsgebäude
Tower
Feuerwehr
Hangars
Zollamt
Kolonie Neuland I
Kolonie Vor den Toren Feld I
Hohlweg
Hohenzollernkanal
General-Ganeval-Br.
Saatwinkler Damm
Hinckeldeybr.
Kurt-Schumacher-Damm
Mercure Airport
Verwaltung
Zentraler Festplatz
Tunnel Flughafen Tegel
Kurt-Schumacher-Damm
St.-Louis
VOLKSPARK
JUNGFERNHEIDE
Wasserturm
Hinckeldey-denkmal
Jungfernheideteich
Kindererholungsstätten
Gustav-Böß-Freilichtbühne Naturtheater
Heckerdamm
M.-Bürger-Krkhs.
H.-J.-von-Moltke-GS
Poelchau-OS
A.-Freud-OS
Sühne-Christi-K.
Maria-Regina-Martyrium-K.
Sen.-Kita wohnhsr.
PAUL-HERTZ-SIEDLUNG
Senioren-wohnhaus
HALEMWEG
JAKOB-KAISER-PLATZ
Siemensdamm
Siemenswerke
Haupt-feuerwehr
AB-Dreieck Charlottenburg
Tegeler Weg
Charlottenburger Schleuse
Kolonie Schleusenland
Spree
Rudolf-Wissell-Br.
Kolonie Spreewiesen
Krankenhaus Jungfernheide
JUNGFERNHEIDE
Gustav-Adolf-K.
G.-Keller-OS
Westhafenkanal
KOLONIE STICHKANAL
KOLONIE DAHMSHOF
KOLONIE STICHKANAL-WICKELSHOF
ehemaliges Gaswerk Planungsprojekt
Industriegebiet Saatwinkler Damm
KOLONIEN FRISCH AUF BIENENHEIM BIRKENWEG PFEFFERLUCH AKAZIENHAIN ALPENROSE WALDFRIEDEN HEIDEFREIHEIT ABENDRUH OLYMPIA WIESENG. FRIEDRICHSWEG EINIGKEIT WEIDENBAUM SONNENHEIM MÜLLBERG KÖNIGSDAMM PFERDEMARKT KARLSHOFER W.
KOLONIE HINCKELDEY
KOL. JUNGFERNHEIDE
KOLONIE HEIDESCHLÖSSCHEN
KOL. GERICKESH.
0 200 m
600 feet
202
203

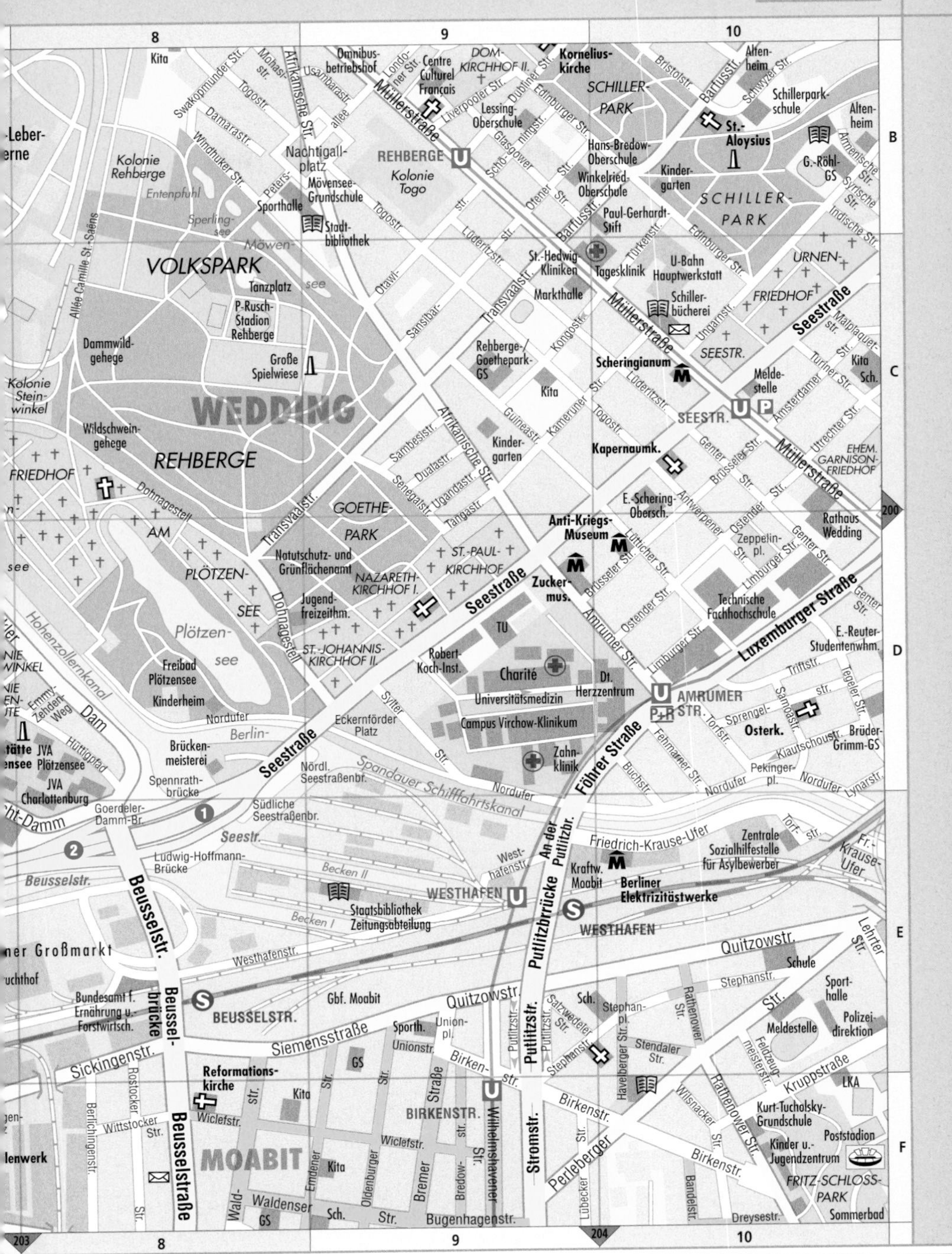

VOLKSPARK
WEDDING
REHBERGE
GOETHE-PARK
PLÖTZENSEE
Plötzensee
SCHILLER-PARK
MOABIT
Müllerstraße
Seestraße
Luxemburger Straße
Föhrer Straße
Putlitzbrücke
Putlitzstr.
Beusselstraße
Beusselstr.
Quitzowstr.
Siemensstraße
Berlin-Spandauer Schifffahrtskanal
WESTHAFEN
Charité
Universitätsmedizin
Campus Virchow-Klinikum
Anti-Kriegs-Museum
Scheringianum
Technische Fachhochschule
Rathaus Wedding
Staatsbibliothek Zeitungsabteilung
Berliner Elektrizitätswerke
Reformationskirche
Robert-Koch-Inst.
AMRUMER STR.
REHBERGE
SEESTR.
BEUSSELSTR.
BIRKENSTR.
FRITZ-SCHLOSS-PARK

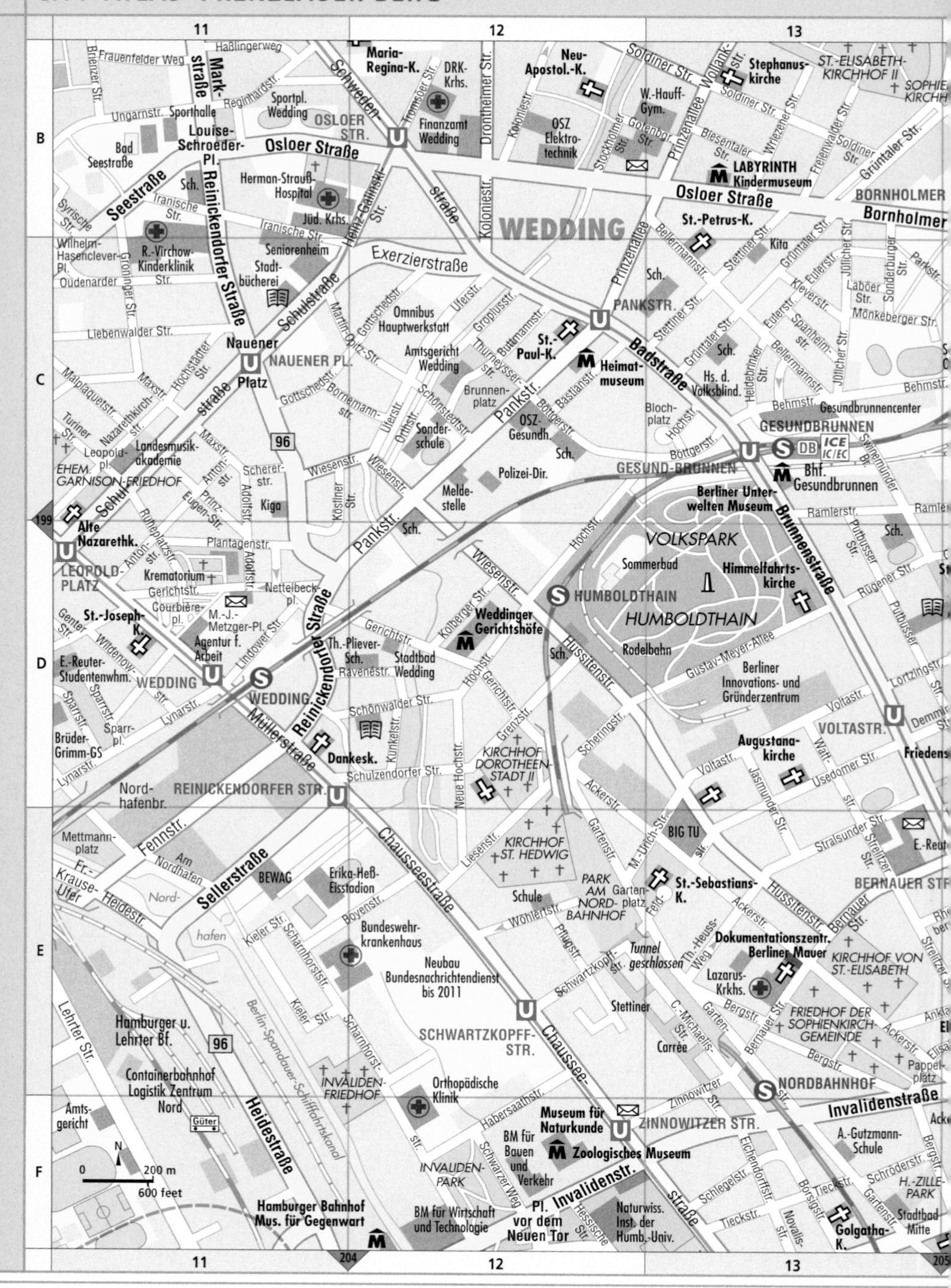
WEDDING
VOLKSPARK
HUMBOLDTHAIN
Osloer Straße
Seestraße
Reinickendorfer Straße
Schulstraße
Exerzierstraße
Pankstr.
Badstraße
Brunnenstraße
Müllerstraße
Chausseestraße
Sellerstraße
Heidestraße
Invalidenstraße
Invalidenstr.
Bornholmer
Hussitenstr.
Gustav-Meyer-Allee
Wiesenstr.
Prinzenallee
LABYRINTH Kindermuseum
Heimatmuseum
Berliner Unterwelten Museum
Bhf. Gesundbrunnen
GESUNDBRUNNEN
Gesundbrunnencenter
Dokumentationszentr. Berliner Mauer
Museum für Naturkunde
Zoologisches Museum
Hamburger Bahnhof Mus. für Gegenwart
Hamburger u. Lehrter Bf.
Containerbahnhof Logistik Zentrum Nord
Neubau Bundesnachrichtendienst bis 2011
Bundeswehrkrankenhaus
Erika-Heß-Eisstadion
Weddinger Gerichtshöfe
Berliner Innovations- und Gründerzentrum
Himmelfahrtskirche
Augustanakirche
St.-Sebastians-K.
Dankesk.
Alte Nazarethk.
St.-Joseph-K.
Stephanuskirche
St.-Petrus-K.
St.-Paul-K.
Maria-Regina-K.
Neu-Apostol.-K.
KIRCHHOF DOROTHEENSTADT II
KIRCHHOF ST. HEDWIG
PARK AM NORDBAHNHOF
INVALIDENFRIEDHOF
INVALIDENPARK
KIRCHHOF VON ST.-ELISABETH
FRIEDHOF DER SOPHIENKIRCHGEMEINDE
ST.-ELISABETH-KIRCHHOF II
EHEM. GARNISON-FRIEDHOF
H.-ZILLE-PARK
NORDBAHNHOF
ZINNOWITZER STR.
SCHWARTZKOPFF-STR.
REINICKENDORFER STR.
VOLTASTR.
NAUENER PL.
PANKSTR.
OSLOER STR.
LEOPOLDPLATZ
HUMBOLDTHAIN
BERNAUER STR.
Tunnel geschlossen
0
200 m
600 feet
11
12
13
B
C
D
E
F
199
204
205

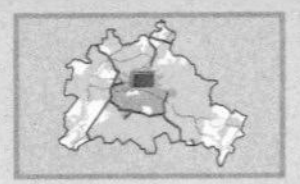

14
15
16
17
B
C
D
E
F
Tiroler Str.
Trienter Str.
Brennerstr.
Andreas-Hofer-Pl.
Brixener Str.
Toblacher Str.
Brenner-str.
Mühlen-straße
Berliner Str.
Vinetastr.
Westerlandstr.
VINETA-STR.
Esplanade
Hallandstr.
Neumannstr.
Gym.
Eschengraben
Prenzlauer Promenade
Berufssch.
Kita
Am Steinberg
Bühringstr.
Kolonie Bornholm 2
Sch.
Stavangerstr.
Berliner Straße
Trelleborger Str.
Eschengraben
GS
Talstr.
Thulestr.
Prenzlauer Promenade
Brauhaus-str.
Heinersdorfer Str.
Pistoriusstr.
Jacobsohn-str.
Ibsenstr.
Nordkapstr.
Gotlandstr.
Thulestr.
Baumbachstr.
Jacobsohnstr.
Charlottenburger Str.
Schönensche Str.
Kurze Str.
Spiekermannstr.
Langhansstr.
Bornholmer Straße
Czarnikauer Str.
Malmöer Str.
Paul-Gerhardt-Kirche
Wisbyer Straße
Max-Koska-Str.
Gustav-Adolf-Str.
Streustr.
Paul-Robeson-Str.
Kuglerstr.
Ärztehaus
Lehderstr.
Goethestr.
Driesener Str.
Arnim-pl.
Stadt-bibl.
Erich-Weinert-Str.
Schönfließer Str.
Seelower Str.
Rodenberg-str.
Greifenhagener Str.
Scherenbergstr.
Stahlheimer Str.
Varnhagenstr.
Gudvanger Str.
Schivelbeiner Str.
Wichertstr.
Kuglerstr.
Ostseestraße
St.-Augustin
Dänenstr.
Krüger-str.
Dunckerstr.
E.-Weinert-Platz
Paul-Grasse-Str.
Vitra Design Museum
SCHÖNHAUSER ALLEE
Humann-pl.
Ystader Str.
Kopenhagener Str.
Gethsemanestr.
Erich-Weinert-Str.
Meyerheimstr.
Allee
Altenhm.
Sültstr.
G.-Blank-Str.
Friesickestr.
Sonnenburger Str.
Rhinower Str.
Pantomimen Theater
Gethsemanek.
Pfarrk. z. Hl. Fam.
Holiday Inn
Linden-hoekweg
Korsörer Str.
Gleimstr.
96a
Stargarder Str.
Pappelallee
Musiksch.
Gym.
Wichertstr.
Zelterstr.
Erich-Weinert-Str.
Schlieritzstr.
Falkplatz
Am Falkplatz
Gaudy-str.
Cantianstr.
Kirche z. gut. Hirten
Lychener Str.
Kanzowstr.
Neuap. K.
Prenzlauer
Poliklinik
Küselstr.
Sodtkestr.
Gubitzstr.
Staatliche Ballettschule und Schule für Artistik
Milastr.
Friedrich-Ludwig-Jahn-Sportpark
Ev. Freik.
Schönhauser Allee
PRENZLAUER BERG
Ahlbecker Str.
PRENZLAUER ALLEE
Grellstr.
Preußstr.
Hosemannstr.
Naugarder Str.
Max-Schmeling-Halle
Gneiststr.
Raumerstr.
Lettestr.
Schliemannstr.
Helmholtz-pl.
Stargarder Str.
109
Hidden-seer Str.
Planetarium
Rietzestr.
Grellstr.
MAUER-PARK
Topsstr.
Stubben-kammerstr.
EBERS-WALDERSTR.
Friedrich-Ludwig-Jahn-Stadion
Eberswalder Straße
Raumer-str.
Senefelder Str.
Bezirksamt
Städtisches Krankenhaus
Zoll
St.-Elisabeth-Stift
Prater
Danziger Straße
Russisches Theater
ehem. Eliask.
Stadtbibl.
Schule
Raths.
Diesterwegstr.
Ella-Kay-Str.
Lilli-Henoch-Str.
Oderberger Str.
Kastanienallee
Kremmener Str.
Kulturbrauerei
Knaackstr.
Hagenauer Str.
Husemannstr.
Kollwitzstr.
Rykestr.
Fröbel-platz
ERNST-THÄLMANN-PARK
Rheinsberger Str.
Schwedter Str.
Sredzkistr.
Städtisches Krankenhaus
Danziger Straße
Theater Unterm Dach
Anton-Saefkow-Str.
Hallenbad
Schule
Friseur-museum
Chodowiecki-str.
Wins-str.
Kultur-haus
John-Schehr-Str.
O.-B.-Prestes-Str.
Arkona-platz
Fürsten-berger Str.
Wolliner Str.
Granseer Str.
Schule
Choriner Str.
Reha.-zentr.
Prenzlauer Allee
Jablonskistr.
96a
B.-Lichtenberg-Str.
E.-Schönhaar-Str.
Zionskirchstr.
Griebenow-str.
Segensk.
Wörther Str.
Handw.-kammer
Kollwitz-platz
Wörther Str.
Christburger Str.
Danziger Straße
JÜDISCHER FRIEDHOF
Zionskirche
Zionskirch-platz
Schule
Allee
Diedenhofer Str.
Wasser-turm
Kolmarer Str.
Knaackstr.
Winsstr.
Marienburger Str.
Schule
2
Gym.
VHS
Pasteurstr.
D.-Bon-hoeffer-Str.
Bötzowstr.
Schwedter Str.
Belforter Str.
Sch.
Immanuelkirche
Immanuelkirchstr.
Arnswalder Platz
Teutoburger Platz
Senefelder-platz
SENEFELDER-PLATZ
Esmarchstr.
Greifswalder Straße
Käthe-Niederkirchner-Str.
Hufelandstr.
Liselotte-Herrmann-Str.
Herz-Jesu-Kirche
Fehrbelliner Str.
Zehdenicker Str.
Weinbergsweg
Metzer Str.
Studenten-haus
Raabestr.
Heinrich-Roller-Str.
Gym.
Katharinen-stift
Hans-Otto-Str.
Hufeland-str.
Christinen-str.
Lottum-str.
Saarbrücker Str.
Prenzlauer
St.-Gertrud-Kirche
Rosenthaler Platz
ROSENTHALER PLATZ
Linienstr.
Torstraße
PRENZLAUER BERG
Prenzlauer Berg
Platz am Königstor
Am Friedrichshain
VOLKSPARK FRIEDRICHSHAIN
205
206

3
4
5
198
208
F
G
H
J
K
N
0
200 m
600 feet
Kolonie Tiefer Grund
Kolonie Eisenb.-Landw.
Kolonie Westend
Fürstenbrunner Weg
Sportplätze Westend
KAISER-WILHELM-GED.-KIRCHHOF
Spreetal-allee
Heinrich-Zille-Weg
Kolonie Golfplatz Westend Braunsfelde Sonntagsfrieden Wasserturm Gesundheitspflege Bismarksruh Rosstrappe Birkenwäldchen
Kol. Ruhwald
LUISEN-KIRCHHOF III
Kol. Fürstenbrunner Weg
Güterbahnhof Charlottenburg
Güter
Belvedere/ KPM-Porzellansamml.
SCHLOSS-GARTEN
Tegeler
Kinderklinik Kaiserin-Auguste-Viktoria
Karpfenteich
Pulsstr.
Max-Bürger-Krankenhaus
Heubnerw.
ESCP/EAP
Mausoleum
Mollwitzstr.
Schlosspark-klinik KG Gesundheitshaus
Schloss Charlottenburg
Spandauer Damm
Sophie-Charlotten-Str.
Senioren-heim
Ernst-Bumm-Weg
Senioren-wohnhaus
Museum für vor- und Frühgeschichte
Sammlung Berggruen
Birkenwäldchen
Institut für Tropenmedizin
Fürstenbrunner Weg
D.-Bonhoeffer-GS
Wasserwerk Charlottenburg
DRK-Kliniken Westend
Kinder-klinik
Spandauer-Damm-Br.
Gotha-allee
Akazienallee
Nußbaumallee
Wasserturm
St.-Elisabeth-Stift
Klinik d. FU
Bolivarallee
Ulmenallee
Eichenallee
Jugend-werkhm.
Lerschpfad
Grüstus-str.
Am Bf. Westend
Gardes-du-Corps-Str.
Klausener-pl.
Bröhan-museum
Stallst
Neufert-str.
St.-Kamillus
Neue Christ-str.
Christ-str.
WESTEND
Soorstr.
Königin-Elisabeth-Str.
Linden-pl.
Klinik Eibenhof
Zoll
DRK-Krkhs.
Ebereschenallee
Branitzer Platz
Strahlen-messstelle THU
Agentur f. Arbeit
LUISEN-KIRCHHOF II
CHARLOTTENBURG
Schloßstraße
Dankelmann-str.
Seeling-str.
Nehringstr.
Nehring-Grundschule
Kirschen-allee
NEU-WESTEND
Paulinen-Kinderklinik
Rüstern-allee
Tunesien
Ahornallee
WESTEND
Kaiserdamm West
Marathon-allee
Platanen-allee
Epiphanienw.
LVA
Epiphanien-K.
P.-Jordan-Sonderschule
Stadtbibliothek
Kloster St. Gabriel
Hessen-allee
Eschen-allee
Leistikow-str.
Gymn.
Evang. Krkhs.
Haeselerstr.
Knobelsdorffstr.
Knobelsdorff-str.
Knobelsdorff-brücke
Reichsstraße
Kastanienallee
Halmstr.
Stormstr.
K.-Groth-Str.
Soor-str.
Horst-str.
Vereinsw.-weg
Wundtstr.
Sophie-Charl.-Pl.
Kita
Fürsten-platz
Württembergallee
Bayernallee
E.-Hoepner-OS
Villa Kastania
Ärzte-kammer
Kath. Schule Liebfrauen
BVG
Meerscheidtstr.
Fredericia-str.
Hölderlinstr.
Stülpnagelstr.
Rognitzstr.
Kaiser-dammbr.
Saldernstr.
OSZ
SOPHIE-CHARLOTTE-PLATZ
Kaiser-
Kammergericht / Bundesgerichtshof
Länder-allee
THEODOR-HEUSS-PLATZ
Theodor-Heuss-Pl.
Kaiserdamm
Kaiserdamm Süd
KAISERDAMM
Witz-leben-platz
Steifensandstr.
Lietzensee-Grundschule
Heerstraße
Turkmenistan
RBB
Bredtschneiderstr.
Dresselstr.
Riehlstr.
Senioren-wohnhaus
LIETZENSEE-PARK
Slingen-weg
Alemannen-allee
Karolinger-platz
Pommern-allee
Haus d. Rundfunks
ZOB
Messe-damm
Spiegel-weg
Wundtstr.
Lietzen-see
Lietzenseeufer
St. Canisius
Pestalozzi
JVA
Jaffféstr.
Skirenweg
Warnenw.
Franken-allee
Ubierstr.
Thüringer Allee
St.-Hildegard-Krkhs.
Masurenallee
MESSE NORD/ICC WITZLEBEN
Neue Kantstraße
Soldauer Allee
Wandalenallee
Rundfunk-museum
Ostpreußen-brücke
Direktion Dt. Telekom
Witzleben-str.
Trendelen-burgstr.
Amts-gericht
Leonha
HEERSTR.
Palais
Funkturm
Dernburgstr.
Herbartstr.
Kuno-Fischer-Str.
Suarezstr.
Holtzendorff-Str.
Frauenburger Pfad
Allee
SOMMER-GARTEN
ICC
Messedamm
Senioren-zentrum
K. am Lietzensee
Friedberg-str.
Willenberger Pfad
Messegelände
JAPANISCHER GARTEN
Rönne-str.
Marien-burger Allee
Int. Stud.-heim
Messegelände
Messedamm
Brücke am Heiligenthalhügel
Harbigstr.
KOLONIE RÖNNESTR.
KOLONIE AUSSTELLUNG
Holtzen-dorff-platz
TU Sporthalle
Jaffé-str.
Eissport-halle
AB-Dreieck Funkturm
Heilbronner Str.
Harbigstr.
Nord-kurve
Avus
Mommsen-stadion
Deutschland-halle
WESTKREUZ
KOLONIE LÜTZENSTR.
HdK
Joachim-Friedrich-Str.
Kol. Waldschul-allee
Waldschulallee
Messedamm
Messedamm Süd
Lützenstr.
Katharinenstr.
Karlsruher Str.
E.-A.-Eschke-Sch. f. Gehörlose
MESSE SÜD
KOLONIE WASSER-TURM
Georg-Wilhelm-Str.
Ringbahnstr.
Kolonie Buchen-weg
H.-Keller-Sch.
Zikadenweg
Am Vogelherd
A. Fliederbusch
Eichkampstr.
Messe-dammbr.
Halenseestr.
FRIEDHOF GRUNEWALD
Bornstedter Str.
Kronprinzen-damm
Kurfürstend
A.-Magnus

6
7
8
9
198
199
F
G
H
J
K
204
208
209
Keller-OS
KOLONIE
PRETORIA
Schwarzer Weg
Neues Ufer
Klarenbach-
str.
Wiebestr.
Turbinenhalle
Huttenstr.
Reuchlinstr.
Beusselstraße
Wald-
str.
Turm-
Emdener
Str.
Oldenburger
Str.
Rathaus
Moabit
Armi-
nius-
str.
Jonasstr.
Keplerstr.
Lise-
Meitner-Str.
Ilsenburger
Str.
Mierendorff-
platz
Kaiserin-Augusta-Allee
Kaiserin-
Augusta-
Br.
Erasmusstr.
Gotzkowskystr.
Musiksch.
Str.
OTTO-
PARK
Otto-
platz
Ottostr.
er Str.
Maria-
Himmelfahrt-K.
MIEREN-
DORFFPL.
Nordhauser
Büch.
Goslarer
Pl.
Str.
Turnhalle
Kaiserin-Augusta-Allee
Zwinglistr.
Sondersch.
Alt-Moabit
Frauenh.-
institut
Spree
Kuchar-
skistr.
Schle-
singer-
str.
Alt-
Moabit
Tresе-
burger
Str.
Wernigeroder Str.
Klaustaler Str.
Sporth.
Quedlinburger
Str.
Goslarer Ufer
Neues Ufer
Str. 244
Pascal-
TU
Hallerstr.
Heisen-
bergstr.
Treidelw.
Gotz-
kowsky-
str.
Zinzen-
dorfstr.
Jagowstr.
Elberfelder Str.
Essener
Str.
Techn.
Sch.
Bochumer
Krefelder Str.
Mierendorff-
GS
Sömmeringstr.
Kraftwerk Charlottenburg
Darwinstr.
Wasserschutz-
polizei
Carnotstr.
Levetzow-
Feuerwehr
Ballettsch.
Dort-
munder
Str.
Bundesratsufer
Am Spreebord
Helmholtzstraße
GSG
Obersch.
Agricola-
Wikingerufer
Malteser
Hilfsdienst
Kita
Röntgen-
brücke
Bangladesh
Dovestraße
Stadt-
entwicklung
Franklinstraße
Tile-
Jagowstr.
Solinger Str.
Hansa-
br.
Herz-Jesu-
Kirche
Arcostr.
Lutgeweg
Röntgenstr.
Galvanistr.
Dove-
brücke
Teatr Studio
DEKRA
Wardenberg-
Str.
Hansaufer
Str.
Brauhofstr.
Wintersteinstr.
Alt-Lietzow
Alt-Lietzow
Rathaus
Charlotten-
burg
Gerickestr.
straße
Einsteinufer
Salzufer
TU
Wullenweberstr.
Sporthalle
TSV
Gutsmuths
Konsis-
torium
Spree
Schleswiger
Ufer
Flotow-
str.
Bachstraße
Otto-Suhr-Allee
Richard-
Wagner-
Pl.
Lietzowk.
Sch.
ALTER
LUISEN-
FRIEDH.
Gericke-
Eichamt
Abbestr.
FH Optik
March-
brücke
Landwehrkanal
Gutenberg-
str.
Stegmunds
Hof
Klopstockstr.
Luisen-
Kirche
Keramikmuseum
Behaimstr.
he-Obersch.
Haubachstr.
Warburg-
zeile
Sch.
Loschmidt-
str.
Sch.
Cauer-
Fraunhoferstr.
Phys.-
Techn.
Bundes-
anstalt
Marchstraße
Technische
Universität
Einsteinufer
Hannah-
Karminski-
Str.
Englische Str.
TU
TIERGARTEN
RICHARD-WAGNER-PL.
Wagner-
Str.
Krumme Str.
Otto-Suhr-
Allee
Entstehungs-
Thrasoltstr.
Stadt-
bad
AOK
Zillestr.
Fach-
schule
Hochsch.
Tribüne
Salzufer
Königliche
Porzellan-
manufaktur
J.-Haydn-
Str.
Berlin
Pavillon
Wilmersdorfer Str.
Friedens-
kapelle
Deutsche
Oper
LZB
M.-E.-
Lüders-
Str.
Ernst-
Reuter-
Platz
Straße des 17. Juni
Finanzamt
Senats-
bibliothek
Charlotten-
burger Br.
Bremer
Weg
Neuap.
Kirche
DEUTSCHE
OPER
straße
Bismarckstraße
Technische
Universität
Müller-Breslau-Str.
Versuchsanstalt
Bismarck-
BISMARCK-
STR.
Am
Schiller-
theater
Schiller-
theater
Schillerstr.
ERNST-REUTER-PL.
TU
Neuer
See
Gartenufer
Sesenheimer
Str.
Schiller-
Str.
St.-Thomas
Herder-
str.
Jugend-
freizeitheim
Renaissance-
theater
Hochschule
d. Künste
Universitäts-
bibliothek
Vogelhaus
Pestalozzi-
Hertzallee
Nilpferd-
haus
Wilmersdorfer Str.
Goethestr.
Trinitatis-
k.
Sch.
Goethe-Inst.
Goethe-
Grolmanstr.
Knesebeckstr.
Stein-
platz
Hardenberg-
Fasanen-
EKU
Bundes-
verwaltungs-
gericht
Bhf. Zoologischer
Garten
ZOOLOGISCHER
ZOOLOGISCHER GARTEN
GARTEN
Pestalozzistr.
Karl-
August-
Platz
Weimarer
Leibniz-
Pestalozzi-
str.
Schlüter-
str.
Carmerstr.
Fasanenstr.
ZOOLOGISCHER
GARTEN
Börse
ntstraße
WILMERSDORFER STR.
Inst. f.
Wirtsch.
Amerika-
haus
Staatliche
Kunsthalle
Aquarium
Stuttgarter
Pl.
Krumme Str.
SAVIGNYPL.
Savigny-
platz
Kant-
Savoy
Theater des
Westens
straße
Elefantentor
CHARLOTTEN-BURG
BEWAG
Umspannwerk
Breitscheid-
pl.
Palace
Gervinus-
str.
Niebuhrstr.
Otto-
Ludwig-
Str.
Jüd.
Gem.-Hs.
Kaiser-Wilhelm-
Gedächtnisk.
Europa-
Center
Tauentzienstraße
Mommsen-
Jugend-
freizeitheim
Niebuhr-
str.
Bleibtreu-
GS
Grol-
manstr.
Uhland-
Kempinski
Hotel Bristol
KURFÜRSTENDAMM
Lewishamstr.
Giesebrechtstr.
S.-
Charlotte-
Gymn.
Leibnizstraße
Mommsenstr.
Kurfürsten-
damm
Joachims-
taler Pl.
Swissôtel
Steigenberger
Ges.
Amt
Sybel-
str.
Wieland-
Schlüterstr.
Mondial
The Story
of Berlin
UHLAND-
STR.
Los-
Angeles-
Platz
Marburger
Walter-
Benjamin-
Pl.
damm
Th. am
Kurfürstend.
Meinekestr.
Joachimstaler
Augsburger
Nürnberger Str.
Senat
f.Fin.
Dahlmann-
Waitz-
Sen.
freiz.
Clausewitz-
str.
Kurfürsten-
Bundes-
rechnungshof
Finanzamt
Knese-
beckstr.
Ku'damm-
Karree
Käthe-Kollwitz-
Museum
Ranke-
Eislebener Str.
Passauer
Branden-
burger Hof
ADENAUER-
PLATZ
Olivaer
Platz
Lietzenburger Straße
Lietzenburger Straße
AUGSBURGER-
STR.
Neue
Schaubühne
Eisenzahn-str.
Branden-
burgische Str.
Xantener Str.
Konstanzer
Straße
Pariser
Str.
Bundesaufsichtsamt
Versicherungswesen
Pfalzburger
Str.
Uhland-
Fasanen-
str.
Schaper-
Ranke-
pl.
HdK
Lietzenburger Straße
Fasanen-
pl.
'Bar jeder
Vernunft'
Bundes-
allee
Spichernstr.
Fürther
Str.
Kelheimer
Str.
Eltaler Str.
Ansbacher
Str.
Albrecht-
Achilles-Str.
Paulsborner
Str.
Duisburger
Str.
Bregenzer
Str.
Bayerische
Str.
Württem-
bergische
Str.
Darmstädter
Str.
Ludwigkirchstr.
Emser
St.-Ludwig-K.
Nürnberger
Pl.
Geisbergstr.

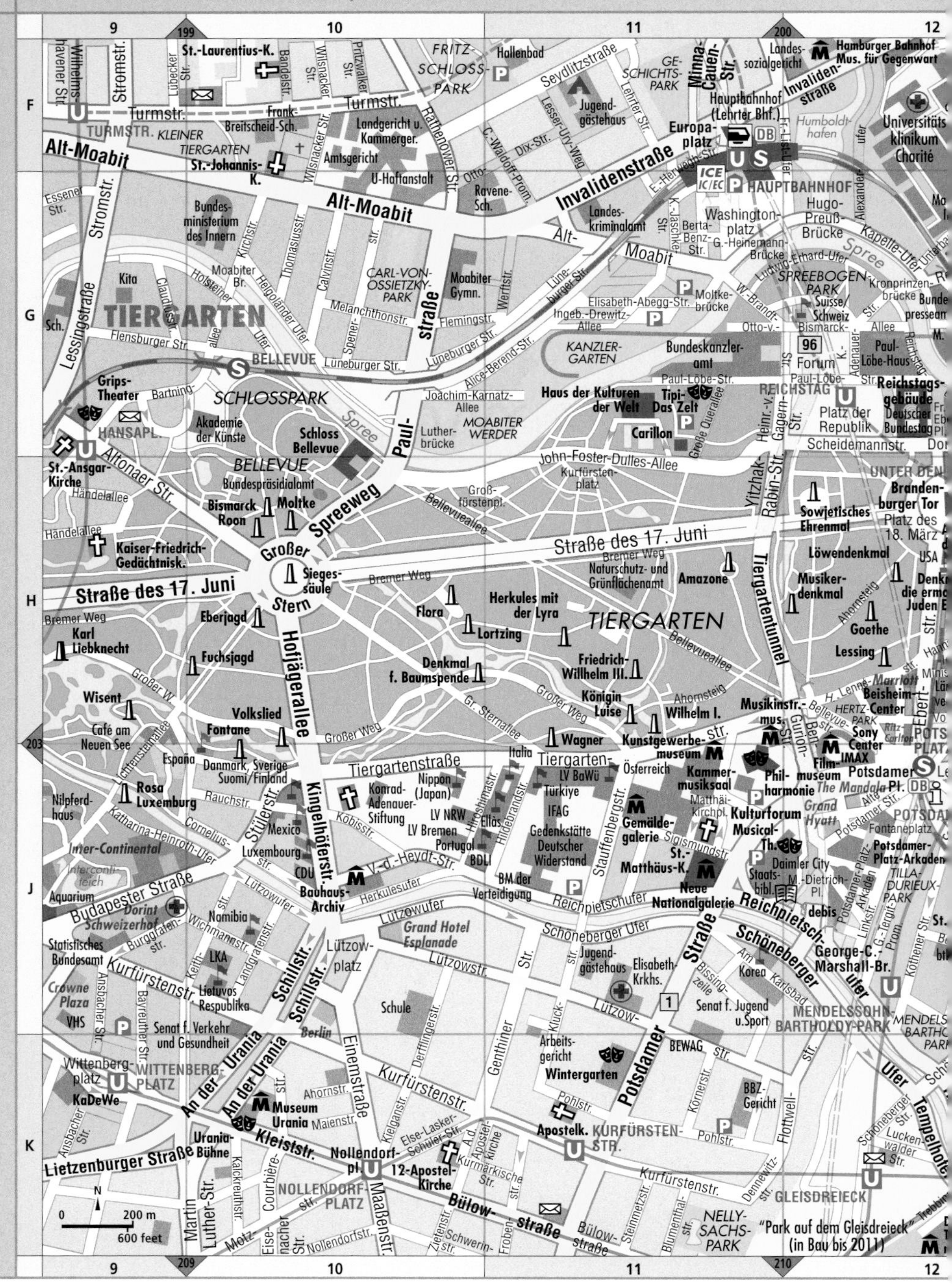
Alt-Moabit
Invalidenstraße
Hauptbahnhof (Lehrter Bhf.)
Europaplatz
HAUPTBAHNHOF
Universitätsklinikum Charité
Turmstr.
TIERGARTEN
BELLEVUE
SCHLOSSPARK
Schloss Bellevue
Akademie der Künste
Grips-Theater
HANSAPL.
Bundeskanzleramt
KANZLERGARTEN
Haus der Kulturen der Welt
Carillon
Reichstagsgebäude
Platz der Republik
John-Foster-Dulles-Allee
Spreeweg
Großer Stern
Siegessäule
Straße des 17. Juni
Sowjetisches Ehrenmal
Brandenburger Tor
Hofjägerallee
Tiergartentunnel
Löwendenkmal
Goethe
Lessing
Amazone
Flora
Lortzing
Friedrich-Wilhelm III.
Königin Luise
Wilhelm I.
Karl Liebknecht
Fuchsjagd
Eberjagd
Wisent
Rosa Luxemburg
Volkslied
Fontane
Wagner
Tiergartenstraße
Kunstgewerbemuseum
Philharmonie
Kammermusiksaal
Gemäldegalerie
Kulturforum
Neue Nationalgalerie
Sony Center
Potsdamer Pl.
Daimler City
Budapester Straße
Inter-Continental
Aquarium
Kurfürstenstr.
Lützowplatz
Grand Hotel Esplanade
Reichpietschufer
Schöneberger Ufer
Potsdamer Straße
Wintergarten
KaDeWe
Wittenbergplatz
An der Urania
Museum Urania
Kleiststr.
Nollendorfplatz
Bülowstraße
Lietzenburger Straße
GLEISDREIECK
MENDELSSOHN-BARTHOLDY-PARK
"Park auf dem Gleisdreieck" (in Bau bis 2011)
200 m
600 feet

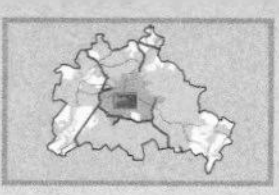

13
14
15
200
201
207
210
211
F
G
H
J
K
DOROTHEENSTADT. & FRANZ. FRIEDHOF
Torstraße
Hannoversche Str.
Institute der BM f. Bildung u. Forschung
Humboldt Universität
Schule
Deutsches Th.
ORANIENBURGER TOR
Stilles Museum
Tucholskystr.
Linienstr.
St.-Joh.-K.
Oranienburger Str.
Auguststr.
Fuhramt
Tacheles
ORANIENBURGER STR.
Johannisstr.
Friedrichstadtpalast
Ziegelstr.
Albrechtstr.
B.-Brecht-Platz
Zirkus
Am Zirkus
Uniklinik
Synagoge
Neue Synagoge
Heckmann-Höfe
St.-Hedwigs-Krankenhaus
Kleine Hamburger Str.
Große Hamburger Str.
Monbijoustr.
Sophie-Gips-Höfe
Gipsstr.
Sophienstr.
Krausnickstr.
Sophienkirche
Hackesche Höfe
Jugendhm.
Varieté Chamäleon
Kunstinst.
MONBIJOU-PARK
Monbijou-pl.
Hackescher Markt
HACKESCHER MARKT
Weidendamm
Schiffbauerdamm
Ensemble
Admirals-palast
Museums-höfe (i.Pl.)
Bode-Museum
Museumsinsel
Pergamon-museum
Alte National-galerie
Neues Museum
Planckstr.
FRIEDRICHSTR.
Friedrichstraße
Georgenstr.
Canada
Nederland
Univ.-Bibl.
Dorotheenstr.
Bundes-presseamt
Neustädt. Kirchstr.
Maritim proArte
Mittelstr.
Int. Handels-zentr.
Charlottenstr.
Universitätsstr.
Humboldt-Univ.
Gorki-Th.
Staatsbibl.
Dt. Guggenheim
Unter den Linden
Schadowstr.
ZDF
Komische Oper
Rossija
The Westin Grand
Rocco Forte
Dt. Staatsoper
Alte Bibliothek
St.-Hedwig-Kath.
Behrenstr.
Glinkastr.
Französische Str.
FRANZÖSISCHE STR.
Franz. Dom
Dorint
Belgie
Bauhofstr.
Jakob-Kaiser-Haus
Kupfergraben
Berliner Dom
Altes Museum
Lustgarten
Pei-Bau
Deutsches Historisches Museum
Zeughaus
Kron-prinzen-palais
Schinkel-pl.
Oberwallstr.
Friedrichs-werdersche K. (Schinkelmuseum)
Werderscher Markt
Auswärtiges Amt
Hausvogteiplatz
Jägerstr.
SAT 1
Gendarmenmarkt
Konzerthaus
Deutscher Dom
Taubenstr.
Mohrenstr.
MOHRENSTR.
BM f. Ern., Landw. u. Forsten
BM f. Arbeit
BM f. Familie
BM f. Gesundheit
LV Thüringen
Mauerstr.
Hilton
STADTMITTE
Kronenstr.
New Zealand
BM der Justiz
Tschech. Kulturzentr.
Leipziger Straße
Slovenija
MITTE
HAUSVOGTEIPLATZ
Niederwallstr.
Jerusalemer Str.
Kurstr.
Unterwasserstr.
Sea Life Center
Radisson SAS
Aquadom
DDR Museum
Karl-Liebknecht-Str.
Burgstr.
Alexander Plaza
Univ.
ehem. Palast der Rep.
Schloßpl.
Rathausstr.
Spandauer Str.
St.-Marien-K.
Neptunbrunnen
Berliner Rathaus (Rotes Rath.)
Nikolaik.
Nikolaikirch-pl.
Poststr.
Marstall
Spreeufer
Ephraim Palais
Breite Str.
ehem. Staatsratsgebäude
Mühlendamm
Gertraudenstraße
Fischerinsel
Scharrenstr.
Sperlingsgasse
Neumannsgasse
Gertrauden-brücke
Kita
Spittelmarkt
SPITTELMARKT
Wallstr.
Rosenthaler Str.
Joachimstr.
Gormannstr.
Mulackstr.
Rückerstr.
Alte Schönhauser Str.
Rosa-Luxemburg-Str.
ROSA-LUXEMBURG-PLATZ
Linienstr.
Luxemb.-Pl.
Volksbühne
WEINMEISTERSTR.
Weinmeisterstr.
Münzstr.
Neue Schönhauser Str.
Steinstr.
Max-Beer-Str.
Almstadtstr.
Kleine Alexanderstr.
Hirtenstr.
Memhardstr.
Karl-Liebknecht-Str.
Dircksenstr.
Rochstr.
Schule
Rosenstr.
Markth.
Fernsehturm
Panoramastr.
Galeria Kaufhof
Park Inn
Berolinahaus
Alexanderstr.
"die Mitte" (2009)
ALEXANDERPLATZ
Alexa (VII/07)
Jüdenstr.
Grunerstraße
Klosterkirche
Podewils'sches Palais
Parochialstr.
Molkenmarkt
KLOSTERSTR.
Klosterstr.
Waisenstr.
Littenstr.
Stralauer Str.
Nederland
Rolandufer
Spree
Mühlendammbrücke
Märkischer Pl.
Märkisches Mus.
Inselbrücke
Märkisches Ufer
Wallstr.
Brasil
Australia
Am Köllnischen Park
Zhongguo (China)
Türkiye
Rungestr.
Inselstr.
AOK
MÄRKISCHES MUSEUM
Schultze-Delitzsch-Pl.
Neue Jakobstr.
Köpenicker Str.
PRENZLAUER BERG
Prenzlauer Allee
Mollstr.
Mendelssohnstr.
Wadzeckstr.
Keibelstr.
Polizei-Präs.
Kfz-Zul.
BM f. Umwelt, Natursch. und Reaktorsicherh.
Otto-Braun-Str.
Haus der Gesundheit
Karl-Marx-Allee
Jacobystr.
BCC Kongresshalle
Magazinstr.
Voltairestr.
JANNOWITZBRÜCKE
Jannowitzbrücke
Ufer
Brückenstr.
Ohmstr.
Heizkraftwerk
Rungestr.
HEINRICH-HEINE-STR.
Krausenstr.
Markgrafenstr.
Schützenstr.
Zimmerstr.
Axel-Springer-Str.
Beuthstr.
Kommandantenstr.
Seydelstr.
Neue Grünstr.
Alte Jakobstr.
Sebastianstr.
Annenstr.
Neue Roßstr.
Schmidstr.
Michaelkirchpl.
Dresdener Str.
Museum für Kommunikation
Wilhelmstraße
Haus am Checkpoint Charlie
Mauermuseum
Topographie des Terrors
Martin-Gropius-Bau
Kochstraße
KOCHSTR. (Kochstr.)
Rudi-Dutschke-Str.
Berufssch.
VHS
Landesarbeitsamt
Charlottenstr.
Jerusalem u. Neue Kirche
Lindenstr.
Feilnerstr.
Alte Jakobstr.
Oranienstraße
Bundesdruckerei
Jakobstr.
WALDECK PARK
Stallschreiberstr.
Alexandrinenstr.
Stadtbibliothek
Schule
Kita
MORITZPLATZ
Moritzplatz
Heinrich-Heine-Straße
Michaelk.
Alte Luther-Kirche
Heinr.-Heine-Pl.
Luisenstädtischer Kanal
Engelbecken
Alfred-Döblin-Platz
Sebastianstr.
Legiendamm
Leuschnerdamm
Waldemarstr.
Anhalter Str.
St.-Clemens Kirche
Puttkamerstr.
Besselstr.
Enckestr.
Friedrichstr.
Senat für Stadtentw. und Umw.
Ritterstr.
Jacobi-Kirche
Jugendgästehaus
Am Berlin Museum
Blumengroßmarkt
E.-T.-A.-Hoffmann-Promenade
Rahel-Varnhagen-Promenade
Jüdisches Museum Berlin
Franz-Künstler-Str.
Lobeckstr.
Sporthalle
Prinzenstraße
Oranienstr.
Oranienplatz
Prinzessinnenstr.
Naunynstr.
Stresemannstr.
Willy-Brandt-Haus
Hallesche Str.
Schule
Franz-Klühs-Str.
Wilhelmstraße
Lindenstr.
St.-Agnes-Kirche
St.-Simeon
Wassertorstr.
Ritterstr.
Bergfriedstr.
Segitzdamm
Erkelenzdamm
Reichenberger Str.
Kreuzberg-museum
Adalbertstr.
Postbank
Großbeerenstr.
Hebbeltheater
Mehringplatz
Friedenssäule
Fr.-Stampfer-Str.
Brandesstr.
Neuenburger Str.
Alexandrinenstr.
Otto-Wels-Grundsch.
Moritzstr.
Wassertorstr.
Patentamt
PRINZENSTR.
KOTTBUSSER TOR
Hallesches Ufer
HALLESCHES TOR
Hall. Torbrücke
Ufer
HAU Drei
Mehringbrücke
Zossener Brücke
Gitschiner Straße
BÖCKLERPARK
Böcklerstr.
Skalitzer Straße
Wassertorplatz
Kohlfurter Str.
Admiralstr.
Kottbusser Str.

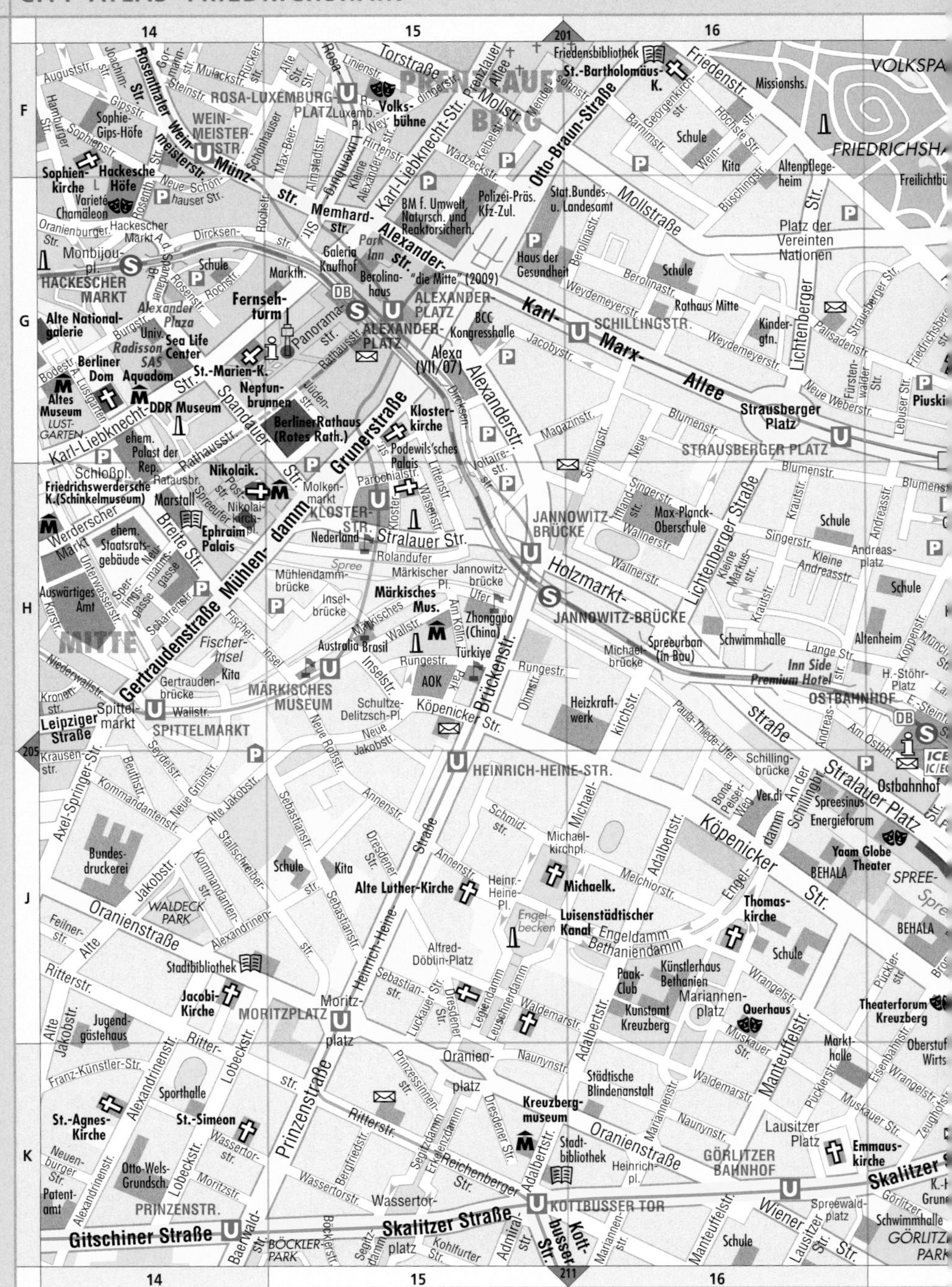
14
15
16
201
205
211
F
G
H
J
K
Auguststr.
Joachimstr.
Rosenthaler Str.
Gormannstr.
Mulackstr.
Steinstr.
Rückerstr.
Alte Schönhauser Str.
Rosa-Luxemburg-Str.
Linienstr.
Torstraße
Prenzlauer Allee
Friedensbibliothek
St.-Bartholomäus-K.
Friedenstr.
Missionshs.
VOLKSPA
ROSA-LUXEMBURG-PLATZ
Volksbühne
Luxemb.-Pl.
Wey-dingerstr.
PRENZLAUER BERG
Mollstr.
Mendelssohnstr.
Otto-Braun-Straße
Georgenkirchstr.
Barnimstr.
Schule
Höchste Str.
Hamburger Str.
Gipsstr.
Sophie-Gips-Höfe
Sophienstr.
WEINMEISTERSTR.
Weinmeisterstr.
Münzstr.
Max-Beer-Str.
Almstadtstr.
Kleine Alexanderstr.
Hirtenstr.
Karl-Liebknecht-Str.
Wadzeckstr.
Keibelstr.
Wein-
Kita
Büschingstr.
Altenpflegeheim
FRIEDRICHSHA
Freilichtbü
Sophienkirche
Hackesche Höfe
Varieté Chamäleon
Neue Schönhauser Str.
Rosenthaler Str.
Rochstr.
Memhardstr.
BM f. Umwelt, Naturschutz und Reaktorsicherh.
Polizei-Präs. Kfz-Zul.
Stat. Bundes- u. Landesamt
Mollstraße
Platz der Vereinten Nationen
Oranienburger Str.
Hackescher Markt
Dircksenstr.
Alexanderstr.
Park Inn
Galeria Kaufhof
Haus der Gesundheit
Berolinastr.
Monbijoupl.
HACKESCHER MARKT
Schule
Markth.
Berolinahaus
"die Mitte" (2009)
ALEXANDERPLATZ
Weydemeyerstr.
Rathaus Mitte
Strausberger Str.
Alte Nationalgalerie
Alexander Plaza
Fernsehturm
Panoramastr.
BCC Kongresshalle
Karl-Marx-Allee
SCHILLINGSTR.
Kindergtn.
Lichtenberger Str.
Palisadenstr.
Friedrichsberger
Burgstr.
Univ.
Radisson SAS
Sea Life Center
Rathausstr.
Alexa (VII/07)
Jacobystr.
Fürstenwalder Str.
Bodestr.
Berliner Dom
Aquadom
St.-Marien-K.
Neptunbrunnen
Jüdenstr.
Dircksenstr.
Neue Weberstr.
Lebuser Str.
Piuski
Altes Museum
Am Lustgarten
LUSTGARTEN
Karl-Liebknecht-Str.
DDR Museum
Spandauer Str.
Berliner Rathaus (Rotes Rath.)
Grunerstraße
Klosterkirche
Magazinstr.
Blumenstr.
Strausberger Platz
ehem. Palast der Rep.
Podewils'sches Palais
Littenstr.
Voltairestr.
Schillingstr.
Neue
STRAUSBERGER PLATZ
Schloßpl.
Rathausbr.
Nikolaik.
Poststr.
Parochialstr.
Friedrichswerdersche K. (Schinkelmuseum)
Marstall
Spreeufer
Nikolaikirchpl.
Molkenmarkt
Waisenstr.
Singerstr.
Max-Planck-Oberschule
Krautstr.
Andreasstr.
Blumenstr.
Werderscher Markt
ehem. Staatsratsgebäude
Breite Str.
Ephraim Palais
KLOSTERSTR.
Klosterstr.
JANNOWITZBRÜCKE
Wallnerstr.
Schule
Singerstr.
Kleine Andreasstr.
Andreasplatz
Unterwasserstr.
Neumannsgasse
Mühlendamm
Nederland
Stralauer Str.
Rolandufer
Spree
Holzmarktstraße
Kleine Markusstr.
Auswärtiges Amt
Sperlingsgasse
Mühlendammbrücke
Märkischer Pl.
Jannowitzbrücke
Ufer
Schule
Kurstr.
MITTE
Scharrenstr.
Gertraudenstraße
Fischerinsel
Inselbrücke
Märkisches Mus.
Märkisches Ufer
Am Köllnischen Park
Zhongguo (China)
JANNOWITZ-BRÜCKE
Wallstr.
Australia
Brasil
Türkiye
Michaelbrücke
Spreeurban (In Bau)
Schwimmhalle
Altenheim
Koppenstr.
Lange Str.
Niederwallstr.
Inselstr.
Rungestr.
Inn Side Premium Hotel
H.-Stöhr-Platz
Gertraudenbrücke
Kita
MÄRKISCHES MUSEUM
AOK
Ohmstr.
Heizkraftwerk
Kirchstr.
OSTBAHNHOF
Kronenstr.
Spittelmarkt
Wallstr.
Schultze-Delitzsch-Pl.
Köpenicker Str.
Brückenstr.
Paula-Thiede-Ufer
Straße
Am Ostbhf.
Leipziger Straße
SPITTELMARKT
Neue Jakobstr.
Neue Roßstr.
Krausenstr.
Seydelstr.
HEINRICH-HEINE-STR.
Schillingbrücke
Stralauer Platz
Ostbahnhof
Axel-Springer-Str.
Beuthstr.
Kommandantenstr.
Neue Grünstr.
Alte Jakobstr.
Annenstr.
Schmidstr.
Michaelkirchstr.
Bona-Peiser-Weg
Ver.di
An der Schillingbrücke
Spreesinus
Energieforum
Köpenicker Straße
Bundesdruckerei
Stallschreiberstr.
Sebastianstr.
Dresdener Str.
Straße
Michaelkirchpl.
Adalbertstr.
Yaam
Globe Theater
BEHALA
SPREE-
Jakobstr.
Kommandantenstr.
Schule
Kita
Alte Luther-Kirche
Heinr.-Heine-Pl.
Michaelk.
Melchiorstr.
Engeldamm
Thomaskirche
WALDECK PARK
Alexandrinenstr.
Luisenstädtischer Kanal
Engelbecken
Engeldamm
Bethaniendamm
BEHALA
Oranienstraße
Feilnerstr.
Alte
Heinrich-Heine-Straße
Alfred-Döblin-Platz
Schule
Stadtbibliothek
Ritterstr.
Sebastianstr.
Paak-Club
Künstlerhaus Bethanien
Wrangelstr.
Pücklerstr.
Jacobi-Kirche
Moritzplatz
MORITZPLATZ
Luckauer Str.
Dresdener Str.
Legiendamm
Leuschnerdamm
Waldemarstr.
Kunstamt Kreuzberg
Mariannenplatz
Querhaus
Theaterforum Kreuzberg
Alte Jakobstr.
Jugendgästehaus
Ritterstr.
Lobeckstr.
Muskauer Str.
Manteuffelstr.
Markthalle
Oberstuf Wirts
Franz-Künstler-Str.
Alexandrinenstr.
Sporthalle
Prinzenstraße
Prinzessinnenstr.
Oranienplatz
Naunynstr.
Städtische Blindenanstalt
Waldemarstr.
Eisenbahnstr.
Wrangelstr.
Zeughofstr.
St.-Agnes-Kirche
St.-Simeon
Wassertorstr.
Ritterstr.
Kreuzbergmuseum
Oranienstraße
Mariannenstr.
Naunynstr.
Lausitzer Platz
Emmauskirche
Muskauer Str.
Neuenburger Str.
Otto-Wels-Grundsch.
Moritzstr.
Bergfriedstr.
Segitzdamm
Erkelenzdamm
Reichenberger Str.
Stadtbibliothek
Heinrichpl.
GÖRLITZER BAHNHOF
Skalitzer Str.
Patentamt
Wassertorstr.
Wassertorplatz
Adalbertstr.
KOTTBUSSER TOR
Spreewaldplatz
Görlitzer
Schwimmhalle
PRINZENSTR.
Gitschiner Straße
Baerwaldstr.
BÖCKLERPARK
Böcklerstr.
Skalitzer Straße
Kohlfurter Str.
Admiralstr.
Kottbusser Str.
Mariannenstr.
Manteuffelstr.
Schule
Wiener Str.
Lausitzer Str.
GÖRLITZ PARK

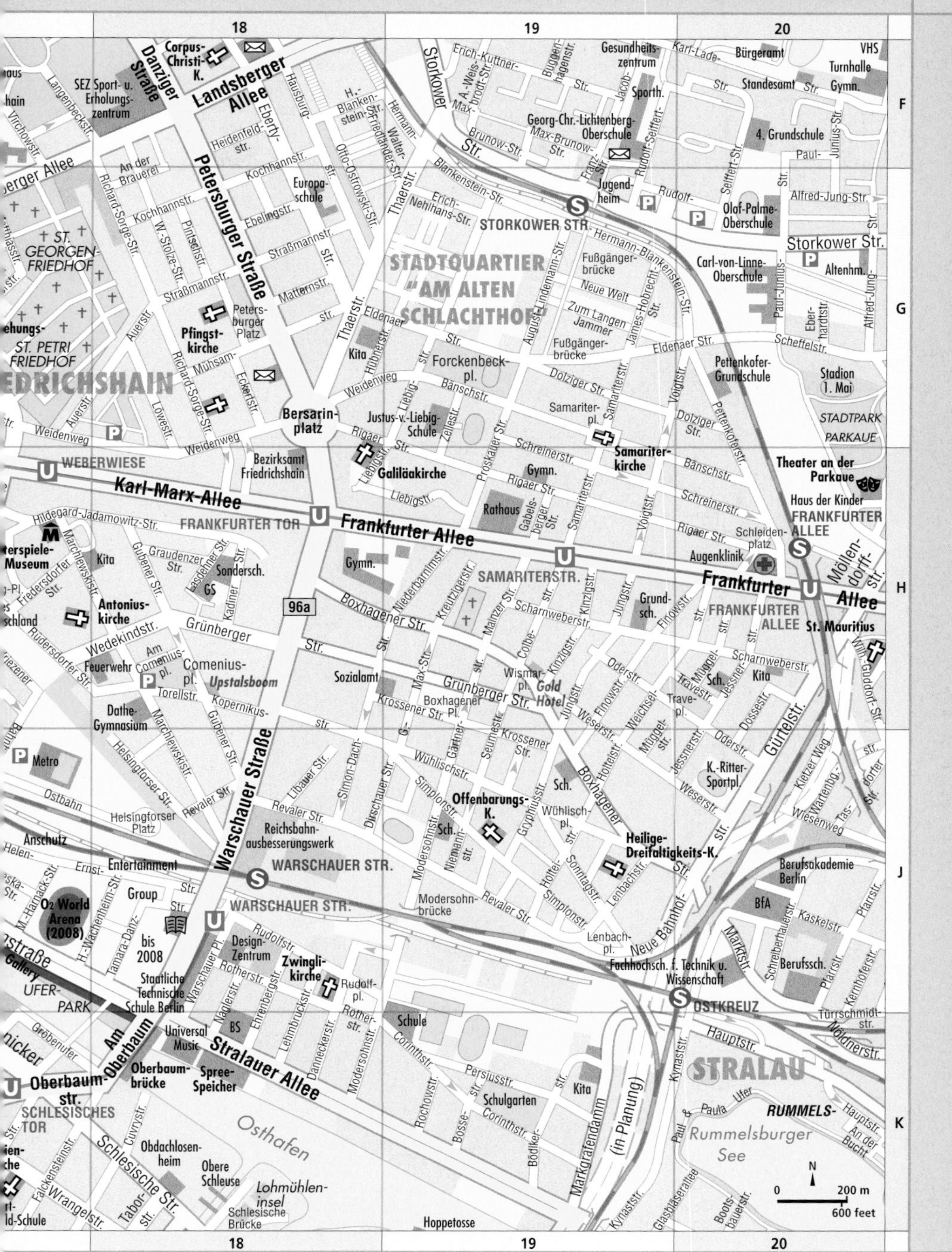

18
19
20
F
G
H
J
K
Corpus-Christi-K.
Danziger Straße
Landsberger Allee
SEZ Sport- u. Erholungs-zentrum
Langenbeckstr.
Virchowstr.
Hausburg.
Heidenfeld-str.
Eberty-
An der Brauerei
Richard-Sorge-Str.
Petersburger Straße
Kochhannstr.
Europa-schule
Ebelingstr.
W.-Stolze-Str.
Pintschstr.
Straßmannstr.
Matternstr.
ST. GEORGEN-FRIEDHOF
ST. PETRI FRIEDHOF
Peters-burger Platz
Pfingst-kirche
Auerstr.
Mühsam-
Eckertstr.
Löwestr.
Bersarin-platz
Weidenweg
Bezirksamt Friedrichshain
WEBERWIESE
Karl-Marx-Allee
Hildegard-Jadamowitz-Str.
FRANKFURTER TOR
Frankfurter Allee
Marchlewskistr.
Kita
Graudenzer Str.
Gubener Str.
Sondersch.
GS
Kadiner
Antonius-kirche
Wedekindstr.
Grünberger Str.
Feuerwehr
Am Comenius-pl.
Comenius-pl.
Upstalsboom
Torellstr.
Kopernikus-
Dathe-Gymnasium
Metro
Ostbahn
Helsingforser Str.
Helsingforser Platz
Revaler Str.
Warschauer Straße
96a
Anschutz Entertainment Group
O2 World Arena (2008)
bis 2008
WARSCHAUER STR.
Reichsbahn-ausbesserungswerk
Design-Zentrum
Zwingli-kirche
Rudolfstr.
Rotherstr.
Rudolf-pl.
Staatliche Technische Schule Berlin
Universal Music
Stralauer Allee
Am Oberbaum
Oberbaum-brücke
Spree-Speicher
SCHLESISCHES TOR
Schlesische Str.
Wrangelstr.
Falckensteinstr.
Cuvrystr.
Obdachlosen-heim
Obere Schleuse
Osthafen
Lohmühlen-insel
Schlesische Brücke
Taborstr.
UFER-PARK
Storkower
Erich-Kuttner-
A.-Weis-brodt-Str.
Max-
Buggenhagenstr.
Gesundheits-zentrum
Karl-Lade-
Bürgeramt
VHS
Turnhalle
Standesamt
Gymn.
Sporth.
Jacobi-
Georg-Chr.-Lichtenberg-Oberschule
Max-Brunow-Str.
Brunow-Str.
Rudolf-Seiffert-
4. Grundschule
Junius-Str.
Paul-
Seiffert-Str.
Alfred-Jung-Str.
Jugend-heim
Rudolf-
Olof-Palme-Oberschule
H.-Blanken-stein-Str.
Otto-Ostrowski-Str.
Walter-Friedländer-Str.
Hermann-
Thaerstr.
Blankenstein-Str.
Erich-Nehlhans-Str.
STORKOWER STR.
Storkower Str.
STADTQUARTIER „AM ALTEN SCHLACHTHOF"
Fußgänger-brücke
Neue Welt
Zum Langen Jammer
Hermann-Blankenstein-Str.
August-Lindemann-Str.
James-Hobrecht-Str.
Carl-von-Linné-Oberschule
Altenhm.
Paul-Junius-
Eberhardtstr.
Alfred-Jung-
Eldenaer Str.
Scheffelstr.
Kita
Hübnerstr.
Forckenbeck-pl.
Pettenkofer-Grundschule
Stadion 1. Mai
Weidenweg
Bänschstr.
Dolziger Str.
Samariter-pl.
Samariterstr.
Voigtstr.
Justus-v.-Liebig-Schule
Liebigstr.
Zellestr.
Rigaer Str.
Proskauer Str.
Schreinerstr.
Samariter-kirche
STADTPARK PARKAUE
Galiläakirche
Gymn.
Theater an der Parkaue
Haus der Kinder
Rathaus
Gabelsberger Str.
Schleiden-platz
Augenklinik
FRANKFURTER ALLEE
Möllendorffstr.
Gymn.
Niederbarnimstr.
Kreutzigerstr.
SAMARITERSTR.
Mainzer Str.
Scharnweberstr.
Kinzigstr.
Jungstr.
Grund-sch.
Finowstr.
St. Mauritius
Boxhagener Str.
Sozialamt
Max-Str.
Colbe-
Wismar-pl.
Gold Hotel
Grünberger Str.
Boxhagener Pl.
Krossener Str.
Odersstr.
Mügglestr.
Travestr.
Sch.
Jessnerstr.
Kita
Trave-pl.
Dossestr.
Weserstr.
Weichsel-
Gürtelstr.
Simon-Dach-
Libauer Str.
Gärtner-
Seumestr.
Wühlischstr.
Krossener Str.
Holteistr.
K.-Ritter-Sportpl.
Kietzer Weg
Wartenbg.
Wiesenweg
Dirschauer Str.
Simplonstr.
Offenbarungs-K.
Wühlisch-pl.
Grphiusstr.
Heilige-Dreifaltigkeits-K.
Lenbachstr.
Sonntagstr.
Modersohnstr.
Niemannstr.
Sch.
Modersohn-brücke
Revaler Str.
Neue Bahnhof-str.
Lenbach-pl.
Berufsakademie Berlin
BfA
Kaskelstr.
Markstr.
Schreiberhauer Str.
Berufssch.
Pfarrstr.
Kernhoferstr.
Fachhochsch. f. Technik u. Wissenschaft
OSTKREUZ
Türrschmidt-str.
Nöldnerstr.
Hauptstr.
Schule
Corinthstr.
Persiusstr.
Schulgarten
Rochowstr.
Bossestr.
Bödikerstr.
Kita
Markgrafendamm
(in Planung)
Kynaststr.
STRALAU
Paul & Paula Ufer
RUMMELS-
An der Bucht
Rummelsburger See
Glasbläserallee
Bootsbauerstr.
Hoppetosse
0
200 m
600 feet
N

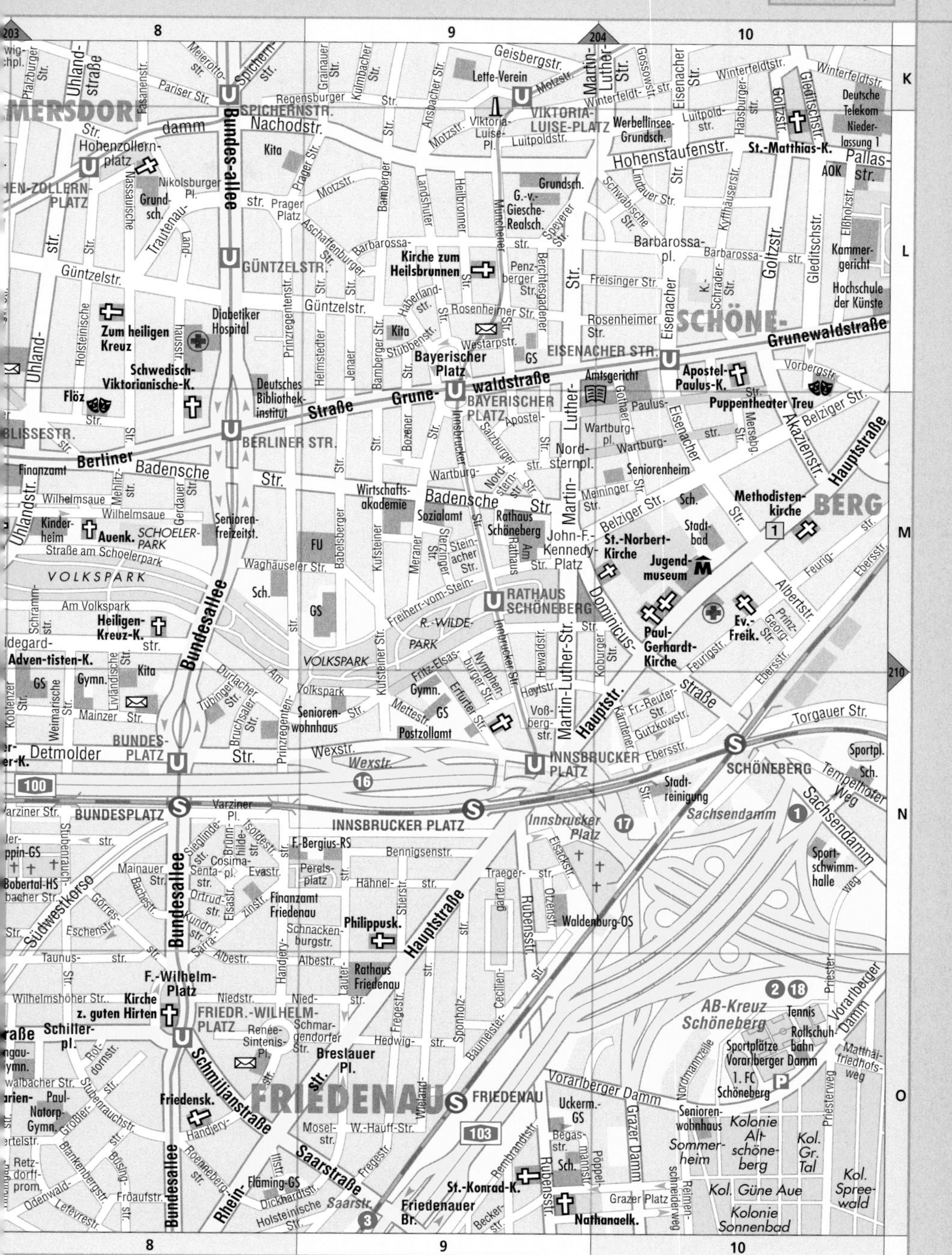

203
8
9
204
10
K
L
M
N
O
210
MERSDORF
SCHÖNE-
BERG
FRIEDENAU
SPICHERNSTR.
VIKTORIA-LUISE-PLATZ
HOHENZOLLERNPLATZ
GÜNTZELSTR.
BAYERISCHER PLATZ
EISENACHER STR.
BERLINER STR.
BLISSESTR.
RATHAUS SCHÖNEBERG
INNSBRUCKER PLATZ
BUNDESPLATZ
FRIEDR.-WILHELM-PLATZ
SCHÖNEBERG
FRIEDENAU
Uhlandstraße
Pariser Str.
Meierottostr.
Spichernstr.
Regensburger Str.
Grainauer Str.
Kulmbacher Str.
Ansbacher Str.
Geisbergstr.
Motzstr.
Martin-Luther-Str.
Gossowstr.
Eisenacher Str.
Winterfeldtstr.
Winterfeldt-str.
Habsburgerstr.
Goltzstr.
Gleditschstr.
Pallasstr.
Lette-Verein
Deutsche Telekom Niederlassung 1
Nachodstr.
Hohenzollerndamm
Nikolsburger Pl.
Grundsch.
Kita
Prager Str.
Prager Platz
Trautenaustr.
Landhausstr.
Nassauische Str.
Bundesallee
Viktoria-Luise-Pl.
Luitpoldstr.
Werbellinsee-Grundsch.
Hohenstaufenstr.
St.-Matthias-K.
AOK
G.-v.-Giesche-Realsch.
Lindauer Str.
Schwäbische Str.
Speyerer Str.
Münchener Str.
Heilbronner Str.
Landshuter Str.
Bamberger Str.
Aschaffenburger Str.
Barbarossastr.
Barbarossapl.
Kyffhäuserstr.
Elßholzstr.
Kammergericht
Hochschule der Künste
Kirche zum Heilsbrunnen
Penzberger Str.
Berchtesgadener Str.
Freisinger Str.
Schraderstr.
Güntzelstr.
Haberlandstr.
Rosenheimer Str.
Diabetiker Hospital
Zum heiligen Kreuz
Holsteinische Str.
Prinzregentenstr.
Helmstedter Str.
Jenaer Str.
Stübbenstr.
Westarpstr.
Kita
GS
Grunewaldstraße
Apostel-Paulus-K.
Vorbergstr.
Schwedisch-Viktorianische-K.
Flöz
Deutsches Bibliothek-institut
Amtsgericht
Gothaer Str.
Paulusstr.
Puppentheater Treu
Belziger Str.
Akazienstr.
Hauptstraße
Mersbg. Str.
Finanzamt
Berliner Str.
Badensche Str.
Bozener Str.
Innsbrucker Str.
Salzburger Str.
Apostel-Paulus-Str.
Nordsternpl.
Wartburgpl.
Wartburgstr.
Seniorenheim
Methodistenkirche
Wilhelmsaue
Mehlitzstr.
Gerdauer Str.
Wirtschaftsakademie
Sozialamt
Rathaus Schöneberg
Meininger Str.
Sch.
Stadtbad
Kinderheim
Auenk.
SCHOELERPARK
Seniorenfreizeitst.
FU
Kufsteiner Str.
Meraner Str.
Sterzinger Str.
Steinacher Str.
John-F.-Kennedy-Platz
St.-Norbert-Kirche
Jugendmuseum
Feurigstr.
Eberstr.
Straße am Schoelerpark
VOLKSPARK
Waghäuseler Str.
Babelsberger Str.
Freiherr-vom-Stein-Str.
Dominicusstr.
Albertstr.
Am Volkspark
Heiligen-Kreuz-K.
Schrammstr.
R.-WILDE-PARK
Paul-Gerhardt-Kirche
Ev.-Freik.
Prinz-Georg-Str.
Hildegard-str.
Adventisten-K.
Gymn.
Livländische Str.
VOLKSPARK
Fritz-Elsas-Str.
Nymphenburger Str.
Hewaldstr.
Koburger Str.
Weimarische Str.
Durlacher Str.
Tübinger Str.
Am Volkspark
Senioren-wohnhaus
Gymn.
GS
Erfurter Str.
Heylstr.
Voßbergstr.
Fr.-Reuter-Str.
Gutzkowstr.
Torgauer Str.
Koblenzer Str.
Mainzer Str.
Bruchsaler Str.
Mettestr.
Postzollamt
Kärntener Str.
Sportpl.
Detmolder Str.
Wexstr.
Eberstr.
Tempelhofer Weg
100
16
Varziner Pl.
Stadtreinigung
Sachsendamm
1
Varziner Str.
INNSBRUCKER PLATZ
Innsbrucker Platz
17
Sieglindestr.
Brünnhildestr.
Isoldestr.
F.-Bergius-RS
Bennigsenstr.
Cosimapl.
Elsackstr.
Sportschwimmhalle
Südwestkorso
Mainauer Str.
Bachestr.
Ortrudstr.
Elsastr.
Perelsplatz
Hähnelstr.
Traegerstr.
Görresstr.
Finanzamt Friedenau
Stierstr.
Rubensstr.
Ozenstr.
Eschenstr.
Kundrystr.
Sarrazinstr.
Schnackenburgstr.
Philippusk.
Hauptstraße
Waldenburg-OS
Taunusstr.
Albestr.
Handjerystr.
Lauterstr.
Rathaus Friedenau
Cecilien-gärten
Priesterweg
Vorarlberger Damm
F.-Wilhelm-Platz
Niedstr.
2
18
Wilhelmshöher Str.
Kirche z. guten Hirten
AB-Kreuz Schöneberg
Tennis
Rollschuhbahn
Schillerpl.
Renée-Sintenis-Pl.
Schmargendorfer Str.
Hedwigstr.
Fregestr.
Sponholzstr.
Baumeisterstr.
Sportplätze Vorarlberger Damm
Matthäifriedhofsweg
Rotdornstr.
Breslauer Pl.
1. FC Schöneberg
Stubenrauchstr.
Schmiljanstraße
Friedensk.
Wielandstr.
Uckerm.-GS
Grazer Damm
Nordmannzeile
Senioren-wohnhaus
Kolonie Altschöneberg
Kol. Gr. Tal
Handjerystr.
Moselstr.
W.-Hauff-Str.
103
Begasstr.
Sommerheim
Blankenbergstr.
Büsingstr.
Roennebergstr.
Saarstraße
Fregestr.
Ilsstr.
Rembrandtstr.
Sch.
Poppelmannstr.
Reimerschneiderweg
Kol. Spreewald
Fläming-GS
Dickhardtstr.
St.-Konrad-K.
Kol. Güne Aue
Odenwaldstr.
Fröaufstr.
Lefèvrestr.
Rheinstr.
Holsteinische Str.
Saarstr.
3
Friedenauer Br.
Beckerstr.
Nathanaelk.
Grazer Platz
Kolonie Sonnenbad

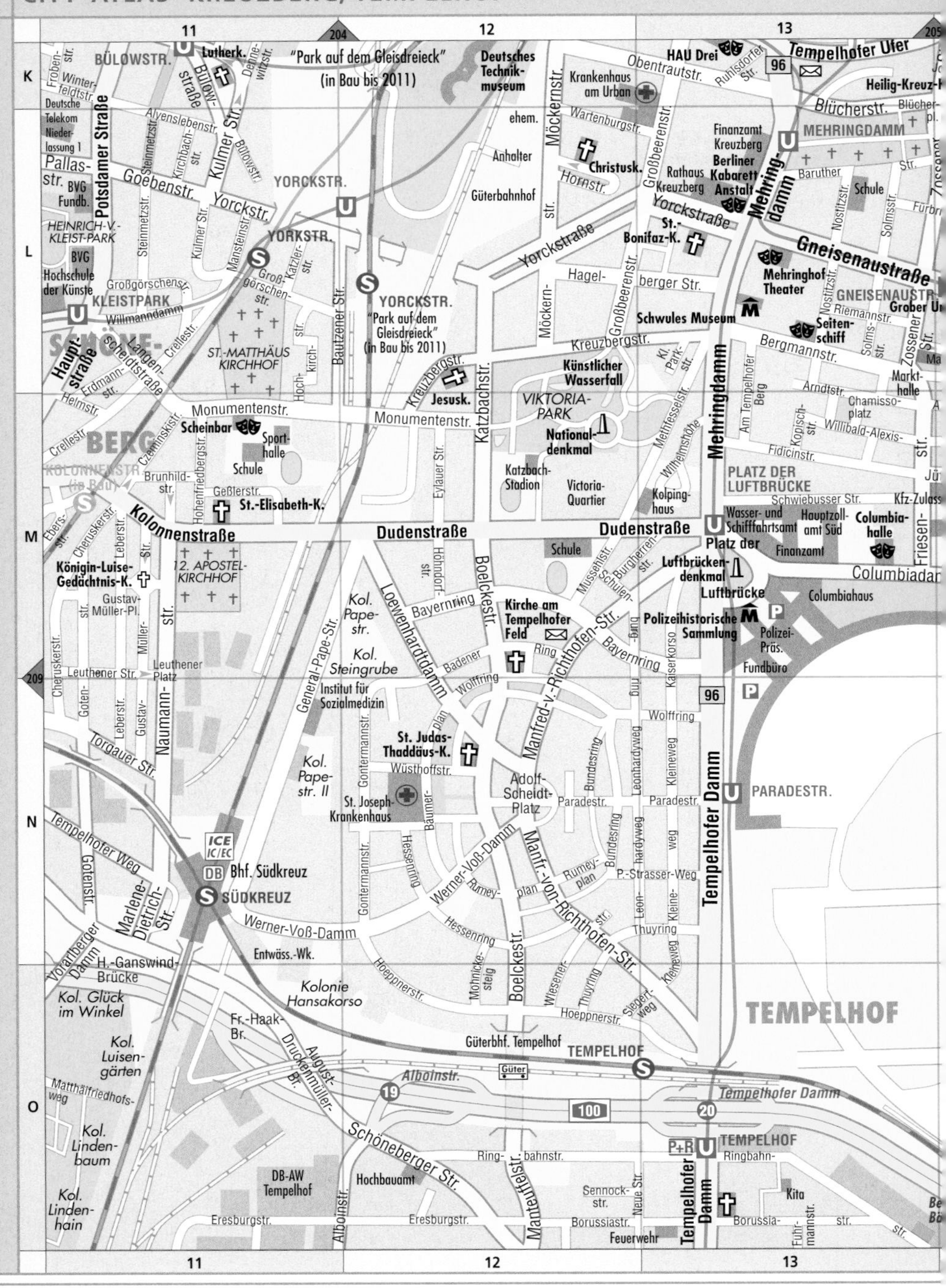
11
12
13
204
205
209
K
L
M
N
O
Bülowstr.
Lutherk.
Bülow-straße
Dennewitzstr.
"Park auf dem Gleisdreieck" (in Bau bis 2011)
Deutsches Technik-museum
Krankenhaus am Urban
Obentrautstr.
HAU Drei
Ruhlsdorfer Str.
96
Tempelhofer Ufer
Heilig-Kreuz-
Blücherstr.
Wartenburgstr.
Mehringdamm
Finanzamt Kreuzberg
Berliner Kabarett Anstalt
Rathaus Kreuzberg
Christusk.
Hornstr.
Großbeerenstr.
Möckernstr.
ehem. Anhalter Güterbahnhof
Deutsche Telekom Niederlassung 1
Potsdamer Straße
Alvenslebenstr.
Steinmetzstr.
Kirchbachstr.
Kulmer Str.
Bülowstr.
Pallasstr.
BVG Fundb.
Goebenstr.
Yorckstr.
YORCKSTR.
Heinrich-v.-Kleist-Park
BVG
Hochschule der Künste
Großgörschenstr.
Kleistpark
Willmanndamm
Mansteinstr.
Katzlerstr.
Bautzener Str.
St.-Matthäus Kirchhof
Hauptstraße
Langenscheidtstraße
Crellestr.
Erdmannstr.
Helmstr.
Hochkirchstr.
Yorckstraße
St.-Bonifaz-K.
Baruther Str.
Schule
Nostitzstr.
Solmsstr.
Gneisenaustraße
Mehringhof Theater
Gneisenaustr.
Hagelberger Str.
Schwules Museum
Riemannstr.
Seitenschiff
Kreuzbergstr.
Bergmannstr.
Zossener Str.
Marktballe
Kreuzbergstr.
Jesusk.
Katzbachstr.
Künstlicher Wasserfall
Viktoria-Park
Nationaldenkmal
Kl. Parkstr.
Methfesselstr.
Am Tempelhofer Berg
Arndtstr.
Chamissoplatz
Kopischstr.
Willibald-Alexis-Str.
Fidicinstr.
Monumentenstr.
Scheinbar
Sporthalle
Schule
Czeminskistr.
Kolonnenstr. (in Bau)
Brunhildstr.
Hohenfriedbergstr.
Geßlerstr.
St.-Elisabeth-K.
Eylauer Str.
Katzbach-Stadion
Victoria-Quartier
Wilhelmshöhe
Kolpinghaus
Platz der Luftbrücke
Schwiebusser Str.
Kfz-Zulass.
Wasser- und Schifffahrtsamt
Hauptzollamt Süd
Columbiahalle
Friesenstr.
Kolonnenstraße
Dudenstraße
Schule
Finanzamt
Columbiadamm
Ebersstr.
Cheruskerstr.
Leberstr.
Königin-Luise-Gedächtnis-K.
12. Apostel-Kirchhof
Gustav-Müller-Pl.
Höhndorfstr.
Boelckestr.
Mussehlstr.
Burgherrenstr.
Schulenburgring
Luftbrückendenkmal
Luftbrücke
Columbiahaus
Kol. Papestr.
Loewenhardtdamm
Bayernring
Kirche am Tempelhofer Feld
Manfred-v.-Richthofen-Str.
Polizeihistorische Sammlung
Polizei-Präs.
Fundbüro
Kaiserkorso
Kol. Steingrube
General-Pape-Str.
Badener Ring
Wolffring
Leuthener Str.
Leuthener Platz
Naumannstr.
Goten-
Gustav-
Müllerstr.
Institut für Sozialmedizin
Gontermannstr.
St. Judas-Thaddäus-K.
Wüsthoffstr.
Adolf-Scheidt-Platz
Paradestr.
Bundesring
Leonhardyweg
Kleineweg
Tempelhofer Damm
Paradestr.
Torgauer Str.
Kol. Pape-str. II
St. Joseph-Krankenhaus
Bäumerplan
Tempelhofer Weg
Gotenstr.
ICE IC/EC
DB Bhf. Südkreuz
Südkreuz
Hessenring
Werner-Voß-Damm
Rumeyplan
P.-Strasser-Weg
Marlene-Dietrich-Str.
Thuyring
Werner-Voß-Damm
Entwäss.-Wk.
Vorarlberger Damm
H.-Ganswind-Brücke
Hoeppnerstr.
Mohnickesteig
Wiesenerstr.
Siegertweg
Kol. Glück im Winkel
Kolonie Hansakorso
Tempelhof
Kol. Luisengärten
Fr.-Haak-Br.
August-Druckenmüller-Br.
Güterbhf. Tempelhof
Tempelhof
Alboinstr.
Güter
Matthäifriedhofsweg
19
100
20
Tempelhofer Damm
Kol. Lindenbaum
Schöneberger Str.
P+R
Tempelhof
Ringbahnstr.
Kol. Lindenhain
DB-AW Tempelhof
Hochbauamt
Sennockstr.
Neue Str.
Kita
Eresburgstr.
Alboinstr.
Manteuffelstr.
Borussiastr.
Feuerwehr
Fuhrmannstr.

14
15
16
17
205
206
K
L
M
N
O
Sommerbad Kreuzberg
Carl-Herz-Ufer
Baerwaldstr.
Baer-wald-brücke
BÖCKLER-PARK
Stadthaus Böcklerpark
Urbanhafen
J.-Nygahl-Grundsch.
Admiralstr.
Kohlfurter Str.
Kottbusser Str.
Mariannenstr.
Kottbusser Brücke
Manteuffelstr.
Reichen-
Schule
Lausitzer Str.
St.-Marien-Krkhs.
Ohlauer Str.
Wiener Str.
GÖRLITZER PARK
Wilmsstr.
Tau
Fraenkelufer
Planufer
Admiral-brücke
Melanchtonkirche
Apostelk.
Geibelstr.
Krankenhaus Am Urban
Dieffenbachstr.
Sch.
Böckhstr.
Graefestr.
Schule
179
Schinkestr.
Maybachufer
Paul-Lincke-Ufer
Ölberg-kirche
Hobrecht-brücke
Ohlauer Str.
berger Str.
Reichenberger Str.
Forsterstr.
Glogauer Str.
KREUZBERG
Urbanstr.
Grimmstr.
R.-Koch-Gymn.
Bethesda-Krkhs.
SCHÖNLEINSTR.
Bürknerstr.
Paul-
Landwehrkanal
Maybachufer
Liegnitzer Str.
Martha-kirche
Sport-halle
Schule
Gesundheitsamt
Müllenhoffstr.
Christus-kirche
Hohen-staufen-pl.
Kottbusser Damm
Sander-
Hobrechtstr.
Friedelstr.
Liberdastr.
Lincke-
Thielen-brücke
Ufer
Blücherstr.
Fontane-promenade
Freiligrathstr.
Körtestr.
Fichtestr.
Graefestr.
Schönleinstr.
Boppstr.
Islamische Grundschule
Pflügerstr.
Altenheim
Manitiusstr.
Maybachufer
Kirche am Südstern
Freiligrath-Hauptsch.
SÜDSTERN
Werner-Düttmann-Pl.
Urbanstr.
Lenaustr.
Reuterstr.
Nansenstr.
Framstr.
Nicodemus-kirche
Pflügerstr.
Bergmannstr.
KIRCHHOF JERUSALEM U. NEUE KIRCHE
LUISENSTÄDTISCHER GEM.-FRIEDHOF
Hasenheide
St.-Johannes-Basilika
Lilienthalstr.
STANDORT-FRIEDHOF LILIENTHALSTR.
Jahnstr.
Weserstr.
Reuter-platz
St.-Christopherus-Kirche
Rütlistr.
Schule
Weichselstr.
Herrmann-platz
Sonnenallee
Sch.
Pannierstr.
Weserstr.
Zülichauer Str.
VOLKSPARK
HASENHEIDE
HERMANNPLATZ
Wissmannstr.
Hermannstraße
ST.-JAKOBI-KIRCHHOF
Karl-Marx-Straße
Rixdorfer Grundsch.
Donaustr.
Tellstr.
Jansastr.
M.-Luther-Kirche
E.-Abbe-Gymn.
Lilienthalstr.
Tennishalle
Karlsgarten-Grundschule
Mainzer Str.
Reuterstr.
Weichselstr.
Fuldastr.
Rixdorfer Teich
K.-Löwenstein-Oberschule
Karlsgartenstr.
Biebricher Str.
Erlanger Str.
Amtsger.
Schönstedtstr.
Rathaus Neukölln
Rosinenbomber
Columbiadamm
Naturdenkmal Jahneiche
Fontanestr.
Neuapostolische Kirche
Flughafenstraße
RATHAUS NEUKÖLLN
Erkstr.
ISLAMISCHER FRIEDHOF
GARNISON-FRIEDHOF
Sommerbad Neukölln
Jahn-Sporthalle
Schwarzer Weg
Flughafenstraße
Mahlower Str.
Weisestr.
Boddinstr.
BODDIN-STR.
Boddin-pl.
Isarstr.
H.-Boddin-Grundsch.
Neckarstr.
Rollbergstr.
Selchower Str.
Schiller-prom.
Mercure Berlin Neukölln
Rollberg-str.
Werbellinstr.
St-Clara-Kirche
Genezarethkirche
Herrfurth-platz
K.-Weise-Grundsch.
Briesestr.
Falkstr.
Morusstr.
Kienitzer Str.
Bornsdorfer Str.
Oderstr.
Lichtenrader Str.
Kienitzer Str.
Kopfstr.
Oberschule
LESSING-HÖHE
Flughafen Berlin-Tempelhof
(closed)
Allerstr.
Schillerpromenade
Weisestr.
Leykestr.
Mittelweg
Okerstr.
ST.-MICHAEL-KIRCHHOF
THOMAS-HÖHE
LEINESTR.
Thomasstr.
ST.-THOMAS-KIRCHHOF
Leinestr.
Carl-Legien-Oberschule
NEUKÖLLN
Sch.
Selkestr.
ST.-THOMAS-KIRCHHOF
Kap.
Ilsestr.
KÖRNER-PARK
KIRCHHOF JERUSALEM U. NEUE KIRCHE V
Jonasstr.
Galerie
Altenbraker
Netzestr.
Jugend-freizeitheim
Hockeypl.
Warthestr.
Warthe-platz
Schierker
Kita
Nogatstr.
ST.-JACOBI-KIRCHHOF II
Kap.
Stadion Neukölln
N
0
200 m
600 feet
Eis-stadion
Emser Str.
Kita
Siegfriedstr.
HERMANNSTR.
HERMANNSTR.
E.-Müller-Platz
Oderstraßen-brücke
Silberstein-str.
Hertastr.
Bendastr.

PAGES 198–211

INDEX OF KEY PEOPLE AND PLACES, WITH WEBSITES

INDEX OF KEY PEOPLE AND PLACES, WITH WEBSITES

INDEX OF KEY PEOPLE AND PLACES, WITH WEBSITES

Note: In the German language "ss" can also be written as "ß" – you will find examples of both in this book.

Picture credits

Abbreviations
AKG = AKG-images
B = Bieker
C = Corbis
Hub = Bildagentur Huber
IFA = IFA Bilderteam
L = Laif
Mau = Mauritius
P = Premium
Sch = Schapowalow
W = Wandmacher
Z = Zielske

Picture credits are given per page, from top left to below right.

Cover front: getty/The Image Bank
Cover back above: L/Boening/Zenit | L/Westrich | travelstock/J. Held

1 and 2/3: Zielske; 4/5: L/Hemisphères; 6/7: Arco/Kiedrowski; 8: TV-yesterday; 8/9: L/Boening; 10-15: AKG; 16-17: AKG up to 17 right column 1st image: Voller, Ernst; 18-19: AKG up to 19 right column 2nd image: C/Bettmann; 3rd image: C/Stapleton Collection; 20-21: AKG; 22 above: 4 x AKG; 22 right: C/Yevgeny Khaldai; 23 left above and below: AKG; 23 right above and below: C/Yevgeny Khaldai; 24 above and left Spalte: AKG; 24 left above: Ostkreuz/Seidel; 24 left below and right above: Schapowalow; 24 right below: Helga Lade; 25 left: Arco/Hildebrandt; 25 right: C; 26 above: AKG; 26 right: Schilke; 27 above: 2 x AKG; 27 left 1 + 2.: AKG; 27 3: H. P. Stiebing; 27 right 1st: C/Hulton-Deutsch; 27 right 2nd: AKG; 27 right 3rd: C/Bettmann; 28 above: alimdi/Lehmann; 28 left: visum; 29 left: visum/Göttlicher; 29 right above: artur/Huthmacher; 29 right below: vario; 30/31: Schapowalow/Menges; 34 above: L/Langrock; 34 left above: C/Ullstein; 34 left middle: C/Hulton-Deutsch; 34 left below: C/Bettman; 34/35: L/Boening; 36 above: travelstock44; 36/37: L/Langrock; 37 above left: L/Adenis; 37 above middle: L/Shiley; 37 above right: L/Galli; 38 above: Mauermuseum; 38/39: L/Chavakis; 40 above: L/Adenis; 40/41: travelstock44; 42 above: L/Boening; 42 left: L/Kirchner; 43: L/Maeckl; 44 above: L/Buessmeier; 44/45: L/Fürth; 45: L/Fechner; 46 above: L/Galli; 46/47: Monheim; 48 above: L/Galli; 48/49: L/Galli; 49 right (all): Aris; 50 above: L/Galli; 50/51: L/Galli; 51: L/Hoffmann; 52 above: Böttcher; 52/53: L/Boening; 52 below (all): L/Adenis; 54 above and 54/55: L/Adenis; 54 below (all) and 55 (both): L/Boening; 56 above: L/Boening; 56/57: L/Galli; 58 above: L/Westrich; 58/59: L/Adenis; 59: Ostkreuz; 60 above: Zielske; 60 and 61: L/Adenis; 62 above: L/Wieland; 62/63: L/Wieland; 63: L/Galli; 64 above left: Keystone; 64 above right: Schapowalow; 64 below: Schapowalow; 64/65: L/Langrock; 66: L/Westrich; 66/67: L/Adenis; 67: Bilderbox; 68 above: L/Johaentges; 68/69: L/Galli; 69 right above: Visum; 69 right below: travelstock44; 70 above: Arco/Larsson; 70/71: L/Langrock; 71: DFA/Schickert; 72/73: L/Langrock; 76 above: L/Hahn; 76 left 1st: C/Bettmann; 76 left 2nd: C/Bettmann; 76 left 3rd: C/Hoppé; 76 left 4th: C/Khaldei; 76/77: L/Langrock; 78 above: travelstock44; 78/79: L/Boening; 80 above: L/Palmbeck; 80 below: L/Baltzer; 80/81: L/Galli; 81 below 1, 2, 3 and 5: images.de; 81 and 4: vario; 81 6 and 7: Boness/Ipon; 82 Hansephoto.de; 84 above: L/Galli; 88 left above: 84 left below: L/Butzmann; 86 above: L/Adenis; 86 below: L; 86/87: L/Plambeck; 88 above: L/Langrock; 88/89: L/Butzmann; 89 right above: archivberlin/Henckelmann; 87 right middle: travelstock44; 88/89: L/Butzmann; 89 right above: archivberlin/ Henckelmann, 89 right middle: travelstock44; 89 right below: L/Galli; 90 above: L/Palmbeck; 90 left and 90/91: L/Boening: Weinhaus Hut; 92 above and 92/93: L/Langrock; 94 above: Billy Wilder's; 94/95: L/Palmbeck; 96 above: L/Plambeck; 96 left above: L/Adenis; 96 left 2nd: L/Adenis; 96 left 3rd: L/Boening; 96/97: L/Boening; 98 above: L/Langrock; 98 left: L/Adenis; 98/99: Zielske; 100 above: Ostkreuz/Hiss; 100 left (all): L/Adenis; 100/101: artur; 102/103: Getty/The Image Bank; 106 above: Hansephoto.de; 106 l.: Michalke; 106/107: Böttcher; 108 above: Zielske; 108/109: Schapowalow; 110 above left: buchcover; 110 above middle: Okapia; 110 above right: vision photos; 110/111: Ostkreuz/Meyer; 112 above: Caro; 112 below: Getty/Stone; 112/113: L/Galli; 114 above: L/Westrich; 114/115: DFA/Scheibner; 115 right above: Visum; 115 right middle: Henckelmann; 115 right above: L/Maeckl; 116 above: L/Boening; 116/117: C;118 above: L/Steussloff; 118 left: Images/Scherhaufer; 118/119: C; 120/121: L/Galli; 124 above: L/Langrock; 124/125: L/Langrock; 125 and left: images/Rother; 125 below right: M. Luedecke; 126 above: L/Kohlbecker; 126 below 1st: L/Kohlbecher; 126 below 2nd: L/Jörgensen, 126 below 3rd: Bolesch; 126 below 4th: L/Jörgensen; 126: Images/Zöllner; 127 left: Ostkreuz/Akhtar; 127 right: Intro/Ausserhofer; 128 above: Ehrenburg Espresso Bar; 128: Visum/Reents; 129 right: Ipon/Boness; 130 above: Caro/Teich; 130 below: Caro/Teich; 130/131: L/Hoffmann; 132 above: archivberlin/Henckelmann; 142 below: Focus/Zimmermann; 142/143: Zielske; 134 above: L/Galli; 134 left: L/Henglein-Klover; 134/135 and 135: L/Plambeck; 136 above: L/Adenis; 136 left above: L/Boening; 136 left below: L/Adenis; 136/137: L/Langrock; 137 right above: L/ Langrock; 137 right below: L/Langrock; 138 above: L/Geilert; 138 left: L/Biskup; 138/139: L/Geilert; 140 above: Monheim; 140 left (all): L/Chavakis; 140/141: L/Adenis; 142/143: blumebild/Waldkirch; 146 above: L/Adenis; 146 left: L/Adenis; 146/ 147: alimdi/Steiner; 148: L/Futh; 148/149 (all): Monheim; 150 above: Wirtshaus Schildhorn; 150 left 1st: L/Adenis; 150 left 2nd: L/Neumann; 150 left 3rd: Luedecke; 150 left 4th: Kolvenbach; 150/151: L/Modrow; 152 above: L/Riehle; 162/163: L/Kürschner; 154/155: travelstock44/ Held; 156 1 and 2: L/Langrock; 156 3rd: L/Adenis; 156 4th: L/Kirchner; 156 5th: Sudek; 157: L/Galli; 158 1st: l/Wieland; 158 2nd: l/Boening/Zenit; 158 3rd: l/Galli; 158 4th: L/Boening; 158 6th: L/Adenis; 159 1st: F; 159 2nd: Joker/Eckenroth; 160 1st: L/Boening; 162 2nd: L/Chavakis; 162 3rd: L/Boening; 162 4th: travelstock44; 161 1st: L/Galli; 161 2nd: Newton Bar; 162 1st: L/Hahn; 162 2nd: L/Plambeck; 162 3rd: travelstock44; 162 4th. Sage Club; 163 1st: L/Galli; 164 1st: Zielske; 164 2nd: Michalke; 164 3rd: L/Galli; 164 4th: Schapowalow; 164 5th: DFA/Scheibner; 165 1st: Caro/ Jahndke; 165 2nd: L/Westrich; 165 3rd: L/Chavakis; 166 1st: L/Langrock; 166 2nd: L/Westrich; 166 3rd: ?; 166 4th: Schlosshotel Grunewald; 167 1st: C/Svenya-Foto; 167 2nd: Michalke; 168 1st: L/Hemispheres, 168 2nd: Luedecke; 168 3rd: Caro/Teich; 169 1st: Orient Lounge; 170 1st: L/Adenis; 170 2nd: alimdi/Steiner; 170 3rd: L/Adenis; 170 4th: Club 90 Grad; 171: L/Riehle; 172/173: L/Boening; 174 above: L/Boening; 174 left: AKG; 174 below: von Brauchitsch; 175 above: Ostkreuz/Akhtar; 175 right: AKG; 176 above: artur/Goerner; 176 l. and below: AKG; 177 above: Visum/Koall; 177 below: Bildarchiv Preussischer Kulturbesitz; 177 right: Bilder-berg/Kunz; 178 above: Visum/Fragasso; 178 left: A1PIX; 178 below: AKG; 179 above: L/Boening; 179 below: Otto; 179 right: Otto; 180 above: Otto; 180 left: AKG; 180 below: artur/Fedonu; 181 above: Schapowalow/Atlantide; 181 below and right (both): AKG; 182 above: Bildmaschine; 182 left: L/Adenis; 182 below: Weisflog; 183 above: Caro/ Ullrich; 183 below: L/Plambeck; 184/185: L/Plambeck; 186 1st: Henckelmann, 186 2nd: Getty/The Image Bank; 186 3rd: Hansephoto.de; 186 4: Restaurant Nueatdrinkwomaqn; 186 below Böttcher; 188 1st: L/Langrock; 188 2nd: L/Boening; 188 3rd: Galeries Lafayette; 188 4th: Café Einstein; 188 5th: Monheim; 190 1st: artur; 190 2nd: L/Langrock; 190 3rd: L/Hoffmann; 191 1st: Alice Schauhoff Fotografie; 192 1st: L/Langrock; 192 2nd: Arkaden; 192 3rd: Caro/ Jandke; 193: Facil; 194 1st: L/Adenis; 194 2nd: Exil Wohnmagazin/ Brains Werkstatt GmbH; 194 4th: DFA/ Arslan; 195 1st: Restaurant Liebermanns.
Image p. 177, below left: bpk/Gemäldegalerie Kaiser-Friedrich-Museum SMB/Jörg Anders; image p. 180, left: Hans Geissler; Gaienhofen; image p. 181, above right: VG Bild-Kunst, Bonn; image p. 181, below right: Alexander © Pechstein, Hamburg/Tökendorf.

MONACO BOOKS is an imprint of Verlag Wolfgang Kunth

Concept: Wolfgang Kunth
Editing and design: Verlag Wolfgang Kunth GmbH&Co.KG
English translation: JMS Books LLP (translation Nicola Coates, editor Maggie Ramsay, design cbdesign)

For distribution please contact:

Monaco Books
c/o Verlag Wolfgang Kunth, Königinstr.11
80539 München, Germany
Tel: +49 / 89/45 80 20 23
Fax: +49 / 89/ 45 80 20 21
info@kunth-verlag.de

www.monacobooks.com
www.kunth-verlag.de

ISBN 978-3-89944-483-4

Printed in Germany

S U Netz B

Tarifbereich Berlin A B C

A B Haltestellen in Berlin

S

- S1 Wannsee ↔ Oranienburg
- S2 Blankenfelde ↔ Bernau
- S25 Teltow Stadt ↔ Hennigsdorf
- S3 Erkner ↔ Ostbahnhof
- S3 Erkner ↔ Ostkreuz
- S41 Ring im Uhrzeigersinn
- S42 Ring gegen Uhrzeigersinn
- S45 Flughafen Berlin-Schönefeld ↔ Hermannstraße (nur Mo-Fr)
- S46 Königs Wusterhausen ↔ Westend
- S46 Königs Wusterhausen ↔ Südkreuz
- S47 Spindlersfeld ↔ Südkreuz
- S47 Spindlersfeld ↔ Bundesplatz (nur Mo-Fr)
- S47 Spindlersfeld ↔ Schöneweide
- S5 Strausberg Nord ↔ Westkreuz
- S5 Strausberg Nord ↔ Potsdam Hbf
- S7 Ahrensfelde ↔ Potsdam Hbf
- S7 Ahrensfelde ↔ Lichtenberg
- S75 Wartenberg ↔ Spandau
- S8 (Zeuthen ↔) Grünau ↔ Hohen Neuendorf
- S8 Grünau ↔ Pankow (↔ Hohen Neuendorf)
- S85 (Grünau ↔) Schöneweide ↔ Waidmannslust
- S9 Flughafen Berlin-Schönefeld ↔ Spandau
- S9 Flughafen Berlin-Schönefeld ↔ Warschauer Straße

S2 **S-Bahn-Nachtverkehr**
nur Fr/Sa ca. 0.30-5.00 Uhr
Sa/So und vor Feiertagen ca. 0.30-6.30 Uhr

U

- U1 Warschauer Straße ↔ Uhlandstraße
- U2 Pankow ↔ Ruhleben
- U3 Nollendorfplatz ↔ Krumme Lanke
- U4 Nollendorfplatz ↔ Innsbrucker Platz
- U5 Hönow ↔ Alexanderplatz
- U6 Alt-Tegel ↔ Alt-Mariendorf
- U7 Rathaus Spandau ↔ Rudow
- U8 Wittenau ↔ Hermannstraße
- U9 Osloer Straße ↔ Rathaus Steglitz

U7 **U-Bahn-Nachtverkehr**
nur Fr/Sa ca. 0.30-5.00 Uhr
Sa/So und vor Feiertagen ca. 0.30-6.30 Uhr

Kremmen RB55 RE6 Wittenberge
Stralsund/Rostock RE5 RB12 Templin Stadt
Sachsenhausen (Nordb)
Oranienburg S1 RB20 · Lehnitz · Borgsdorf · Birkenwerder
Vehlefanz · Bärenklau · Velten (Mark) · Hohen Neuendorf West
Hennigsdorf S25 RB55 · Heiligensee · Schulzendorf
Hohen Neuendorf S8 · Bergfelde · Frohnau · Hermsdorf · Waidmannslust S85 · Wittenau U8 · Wilhelmsruh
Rathaus Reinickendorf · Karl-Bonhoeffer-Nervenklinik · Alt-Reinickendorf · Lindauer Allee · Paracelsus-Bad · Residenzstr. · Franz-Neumann-Pl. Am Schäfersee · Osloer Str. U9
Alt-Tegel U6 · Tegel · Borsigwerke · Holzhauser Str. · Eichborndamm · Otisstr. · Scharnweberstr. · Kurt-Schumacher-Platz 128 · Afrikanische Str. · Rehberge · Seestr. · Nauener Platz · Leopoldplatz · Amrumer Str.
Tegel TXL · TXL X9 109 128
Wismar RE4 · Brieselang · RB10 RB14 Nauen · Finkenkrug · Falkensee · Seegefeld · Albrechtshof · Dallgow-Döberitz · Elstal · Rathenow RE2 · Wustermark RB13 RB21 · Staaken · Priort · Marquardt · Golm
Paulsternstr. · Rohrdamm · Siemensdamm · Halemweg · Jakob-Kaiser-Platz X9 109 · Haselhorst · Zitadelle · Altstadt Spandau
Spandau S75 S9 RE6 RB13 · Rathaus Spandau U7
Beusselstr. TXL · Westhafen · Wedding · Gesundbrunnen · Humboldthain · Nordbahnhof · Oranienburger Tor · Jungfernheide X9 109 · Birkenstr. · Reinickendorfer Str. · Schwartzkopffstr. · Zinnowitzer Str. · Mierendorffplatz · Turmstr. · Hauptbahnhof U55 · Bundestag · U55 im Bau
Westend S46 · Richard-Wagner-Platz · Bellevue · Tiergarten · Hansaplatz · Unter den Linden U55
Stresow · Pichelsberg · Olympiastadion · Heerstr. · Messe Süd
Ruhleben U2 · Olympia-Stadion · Neu-Westend · Th.-Heuss-Pl. · Kaiserdamm · Messe ZOB ICC · Messe Nord/ICC · Sophie-Charlotte-Platz · Deutsche Oper · Bismarckstr. · Ernst-Reuter-Platz · Wilmersdorfer Str. · Savignyplatz · Zoologischer Garten · Mendelssohn-Bartholdy-Park · Potsdamer Platz · Anhalter Bf
Westkreuz S5 · Charlottenburg RB10 · Halensee · Uhlandstr. U1 · Kurfürstendamm · Wittenbergplatz · Kurfürstenstr. · Gleisdreieck · Adenauerplatz · Augsburger Str. · Nollendorfplatz U3 U4 · Bülowstr. · Yorckstr. Großgörschenstr. · Yorckstr.
Grunewald · Spichernstr. · Hohenzollernplatz · Viktoria-Luise-Platz · Güntzelstr. · Konstanzer Str. · Fehrbelliner Platz · Blissestr. · Berliner Str. · Bayerischer Platz · Rathaus Schöneberg · Eisenacher Str. · Kleistpark · Julius-Leber-Brücke · Platz der Luftbrücke
Hohenzollerndamm · Heidelberger Platz · Bundesplatz S47 · Innsbrucker Platz U4 · Schöneberg · Südkreuz S47 S46
Rüdesheimer Platz · Breitenbachplatz · Podbielskiallee · Dahlem-Dorf · Thielplatz · Oskar-Helene-Heim · Onkel Toms Hütte · Krumme Lanke U3
Friedrich-Wilhelm-Platz · Walther-Schreiber-Platz · Schloßstr. · Rathaus Steglitz U9 · Friedenau · Feuerbachstr. · Priesterweg · Attilastr. · Südende · Lankwitz
Schlachtensee · Mexikoplatz · Botanischer Garten · Lichterfelde West · Zehlendorf · Sundgauer Str. · Lichterfelde Ost · Osdorfer Str. · Lichterfelde Süd
nur S1 Nikolassee · Wannsee S1 RB33 P+R · Griebnitzsee RB21 P+R · Babelsberg · Charlottenhof · Park Sanssouci
Potsdam Hbf S7 S5 RB22 RB20
Brandenburg RE1 · Magdeburg RE1 · Werder (Havel) · Pirschheide · Caputh-Geltow · Caputh Schwielowsee · Ferch-Lienewitz · Seddin · Michendorf · Wilhelmshorst · Rehbrücke · Medienstadt Babelsberg · Saarmund · Genshagener Heide
Teltow Stadt S25 · Teltow Großbeeren · Birkengrund · Ludwigsfelde · Thyrow
Blankenfelde (Kr. Teltow-Fläming) S2 P+R
Dessau RE7 · RB33 Jüterbog · Jüterbog RE4 RE5 Lutherstadt Wittenberg/Falkenberg (Elster) · Elsterwerda